Leisure services
preparation

LEISURE SERVICES PREPARATION

A competency based approach

Edith L. Ball

Robert E. Cipriano

Prentice-Hall, Inc., Englewood Cliffs, New Jersey 07632

Library of Congress Cataloging in Publication Data

BALL, EDITH L
    Leisure services preparation.

    Includes bibliographies and index.
    1. Recreation leadership.   2. Leisure.
I. Cipriano, Robert E. (date) joint author.
II. Title.
GV181.4.B34   790   77–13017
ISBN 0–13–528273–X

Printed in the United States of America

10   9   8   7   6   5   4   3   2   1

PRENTICE-HALL INTERNATIONAL, INC., *London*
PRENTICE-HALL OF AUSTRALIA PTY. LIMITED, *Sydney*
PRENTICE-HALL OF CANADA, LTD., *Toronto*
PRENTICE-HALL OF INDIA PRIVATE LIMITED, *New Delhi*
PRENTICE-HALL OF JAPAN, INC., *Tokyo*
PRENTICE-HALL OF SOUTHEAST ASIA PTE. LTD., *Singapore*
WHITEHALL BOOKS LIMITED, *Wellington, New Zealand*

Contents

Preface

Many books have been written about the individual areas of leisure services program leadership. *Leisure Services Preparation* combines the fundamental materials and competencies that are needed for successful leadership in all areas of the leisure services program. The book provides substantive materials and evidence of specific competencies for the students. It also presents resource materials for both supplementary study for instructors and independent study by students. Each of the ten modules is divided into three parts: substantive content, student assignments, and resource materials. Although each module is arranged in sequential order, the sections within the module are complete units; instructors can take units from a number of modules to build a single course to fit particular student needs. Thus they can develop a course for the pre-service training of volunteers or one for the inservice education of specialists who, although expert in one area of leisure services, lack an overview of the entire field.

The module approach allows the instructor to limit or expand student learning experiences to relate to needs of specific individuals or groups. The basic competencies indicated in each module represent the minimum required for leadership of leisure services programs. Individual instructors can build into each module a greater depth of content if the experience and maturity of the students warrants it. In groups with diverse backgrounds, all students should complete the basic general competency. The more experienced students can extend their learning experiences to their level of competency. Students who achieve the basic competency more quickly than others can explore areas of the module in greater depth in accordance with their particular interests.

The "extended" module approach requires interpersonal relationships between instructors and students while permitting students to learn at their individual levels of capacity. The student assignments in each module furnish the means to assess the competency of each student in relation to each objective. After achieving the minimum competency, the student then can pursue his interests independently. In some modules assessment materials for pre-testing the student's knowledge of the topic are provided. From this pre-testing the instructor can determine the major weaknesses of the students and put more emphasis on the weak areas.

We have tried to provide, in one book, the materials needed in introductory courses for the professional preparation of personnel for leadership in leisure services programs. We have not, however, tried to present an exhaustive investigation of the field. Instead we focus on the basic information that a student needs to develop skills, attitudes, and behaviors that are essential for program leadership in leisure services. Because we have found that beginning students seldom are ready for the in-depth references required for intensive study of a topic and need only basic information to help them understand the scope of the field, we have limited our chapter-end references to those selections we think will best establish a ground-level knowledge.

An instructor's manual has been developed to give guidelines for conducting each individual module as a course. The manual includes the general purpose of each module, behavioral objectives, daily course sequence, checklist of tasks completed, teaching strategies, and techniques for evaluating student performance.

We wish to thank the many friends and colleagues whose support and stimulation have made this book possible. Particularly, we wish to acknowledge the class participation of many students, as a result of which we were inspired to try to reach higher levels of competency in teaching.

Special acknowledgment and heartfelt thanks are also extended to Rae Cipriano for the typing and proofreading of the manuscript. Without her persistent attention to detail, half of this text might never have been completed.

Leisure services preparation

MODULE 1

An overview of concepts of leisure and recreation

Interpretations

Many concepts of leisure and recreation have been held by people from primitive times to the present. As societies grew more complex, the interpretations of work, leisure, and recreation changed as a result of changing values and beliefs. In all societies up to the present time, man has been obligated to perform certain subsistence tasks. However, when the necessary tasks were completed, man sought release from the stresses they created. The type of release depended on the particular culture and the individual's own desires. In the twenty-first century very little time may be devoted to subsistence work, and man will have many hours of free time. This module gives insights into the patterns of leisure and recreation that are found in different societies and shows their relationship to work patterns. We will also consider some possible directions that leisure, recreation, and work will take in the future. As we examine previous patterns of leisure, recreation, and work, we will evaluate how they influence leisure and recreation today and what may be patterns in the future.

1

DEFINITIONS

The interpretations of leisure and recreation depend on how a person defines such terms as *work, play, leisure,* and *recreation.* There is no general concensus on their meanings as they apply to leisure and recreation.

The American College Dictionary definitions of these words are:

- *Work:* exertion directed to produce or accomplish something.
- *Drudgery:* tedious, hard, or uninteresting work.
- *Play:* exercise or action by way of amusement or recreation . . . fun, jest, or trifling as opposed to earnest . . . to perform on an instrument . . . to act a part.
- *Leisure:* free or unoccupied time . . . ease.
- *Leisurely:* done without haste, deliberate.
- *Recreation:* a pastime, diversion, exercise, or other resource affording relaxation and enjoyment.[1]

These are the common interpretations of the words. However, there are a variety of definitions that have been expressed by scholars through the years that are related to beliefs, values, and psychological, sociological, economic, or political interpretation. In the *Journal of Leisure Research*, an article by James F. O'Leary discusses Plato's interpretations of work and leisure. Part of this essay follows:

> The "work-leisure" distinction reportedly began with the Greek philosophers. . . . It is argued that the Greeks regarded work as instrumental in procuring the necessities of life, while leisure was valued by them as those moments of life in which one contemplated the eternal truths of reality or participated in the music and drama of private banquets or public festivals. . . . Accordingly, work was supposed to have been associated with the toil and difficulty involved in manual labor, and leisure was presumed to have been regarded by the Greeks as the sweet moments of life which were made possible by work.
>
> In this article, it will be shown that Plato did not share this understanding of the relationship between work and leisure. Our objective is simply to indicate how Plato described leisure as instrumental and subordinate to the necessity and pleasure of work. To illustrate this, we will review Plato's use of the term *skole* (leisure).
>
> The following schema [Table 1] summarizes the characteristics of three types of *skole* which can be distinguished in Plato's dialogues as well as in his attitude towards each type. Included in the table is an additional concept, *agria,* which must be given some attention so that Plato's concept of leisure can be seen more clearly.
>
> The *Republic* is the main source of information about Plato's concept of

---

[1]C. L. Barnhart, ed., *American College Dictionary* (New York: Random House, 1963).

TABLE 1. A paradigm of Plato's leisure types

Types of skole	Characteristics of the type	Plato's attitude toward the type
I. As spare time	The subject engages in an activity which is not made possible by work nor work related.	Negative
II. As freedom	The subject's activity is not distracted by other activities.	Positive
III. As self-expression	The attention of the subject is not distracted by unrelated emotions or sentiments.	Positive
IV. Idleness	The subject is preoccupied in unproductive activities, such as daydreaming, musing, etc.	Negative

leisure. In that dialogue, Plato employs *skole* with three distinct meanings.

- *skole* as spare time;
- *skole* as freedom from other activities;
- *skole* as self-possession or freedom from impending states of soul[2]

There is another concept in Plato's *Dialogues* which is translated as leisure but which really means *idleness*. When Plato refered to that concept, he employed a totally different word, *agria*. *Agria* is relevant to the third distinction because Plato did not consider idleness as leisure (*skole*) but as a degenerate condition of the soul.

Two principles directed Plato in his examination of social organization—justice and equality. Both had a direct bearing on Plato's concept of leisure. On the one hand, Plato observed that "every man should practice that activity for which his nature is best adapted" (*Republic* 433A); on the other hand, he followed the principle that "no class or individual of society is to be necessarily more happy than another (*Republic* 520A). Strict observance of both of these rules, Plato argued, would allow a society to work effectively and efficiently (*Republic* 520C). These principles and the end which they promote actually determined Plato's concept of leisure.

Leisure can be defined as a quality of activity. The criteria Plato established to determine this quality are listed in Table 1 under the characteristics of each leisure type. Although the types refer to various leisure possibilities, Plato did not designate any specific type as leisure time. Nor did he argue that certain activities, such as contemplation and the making of

[2]James F. O'Leary, "Skole and Plato's Work Ethic," *Journal of Leisure Research*, vol. 5, no. 2 (Spring 1973): 49–51. © Copyright National Recreation and Park Association 1973.

music, are *true* leisure and as such should be prompted at the expense of other activities such as making shoes or politicking.

In *Recreation: Pertinent Readings*, edited by J.B. Nash, an article by Allen Sapora and Elmer Mitchell is quoted and shows the many interpretations of leisure:

Play

- *Schiller:* The aimless expenditure of exuberant energy.
- *Guts Muths:* The natural exercise and recreation of body and mind.
- *Froebel:* The natural unfolding of the germinal leaves of childhood.
- *Lazarus:* Play is activity which is in itself free, aimless, amusing, or diverting.
- *Hall:* The motor habits and spirit of the past persisting in the present.
- *Groos:* Instinctive practice, without serious intent, of activities that will later be essential to life.
- *Lee:* Instinctive activity, looking toward an idea.
- *Dewey:* Activities not consciously performed for the sake of any result beyond themselves.
- *Gulick:* What we do because we want to do it.
- *Stern:* Play is voluntary, self-sufficient activity.
- *Patrick:* Those human activities which are free and spontaneous and which are pursued for their own sake alone. Interest in them is self-sustaining, and they are not continued under any internal or external compulsion.
- *Rainwater:* Play is a mode of behavior, either individual or collective, involving pleasurable activity of any kind, not undertaken for the sake of a reward beyond itself and performed during any age period of the individual.
- *Curtis:* Highly motivated activity which, as free from conflicts, is usually, though not always, pleasurable.
- *Pangburn:* Activity carried on for its own sake.
- *Dulles:* An instinctive form of self-expression and emotional escape value . . .
- *Slavson:* Play and recreation . . . are leisure-time activities . . . motivated by pleasure and serve as diversions from the more pressing and serious occupations of daily living.
- *Nash:* Any act other than such survival activities as eating and sleeping which carries its own drive, or any act in which an individual enters of his own volition, without feeling, in any way, outer compulsion.
- *Dictionary of Education:* Any pleasurable activity carried on for its own sake, without reference to ulterior purpose or future satisfactions.
- *Mitchell:* Play is self-expression for its own sake.
- *Huizinga:* Play is more than a mere physiological phenomenon or a psychological reflex. . . . It is a significant function—that is to say there is some sense to it. In play there is something "at play" which transcends the immediate needs of life and imparts meaning to the action.

• *Piaget:* Play is a symbolical manifestation . . . it is a sensory-motor exercise, regulated and essentially social, and symbolic—especially with infants after the second year.

Recreation

• *Butler:* Recreation may be considered as any form of leisure-time experience or activity in which an individual engages from choice because of the enjoyment and satisfaction which it brings directly to him.

• *Neumeyer:* Recreation is . . . any activity, either individual or collective, pursued during one's leisure time. Being relatively free and pleasurable it has its own appeal.

• *Meyer and Brightbill:* Recreation is activity voluntarily engaged in during leisure time and primarily motivated by the satisfaction or pleasure derived from it.

• *Fitzgerald:* Recreation is the natural expression during leisure of human interests seeking satisfaction. . . . [3]

Some more recent interpretative definitions are:

• *Ellis:* Play is that behavior that is motivated by the need to elevate the level of arousal towards the optional. . . . Its corollary, work is the behavior emitted to reduce the level of stimulation, fits nicely the concept of drive-reduction theories of behavior.[4]

• *Gray and Greben:* Recreation is an emotional condition within an individual human being that flows from a feeling of well-being and self-satisfaction. It is characterized by feelings of mastery, achievement, exhilaration, acceptance, success, personal worth, and pleasure. It reinforces a positive self-image. Recreation is a response to aesthetic experience, achievement of personal goals, or positive feedback from others. It is independent of activity, leisure (time), or social acceptance.[5]

OBJECTIVES

1. To become aware of the variety of definitions of leisure and recreation that exists.

2. To understand basic human needs and how they affect choices of leisure and recreation experiences.

3. To know the history of leisure from primitive times to the present and to consider leisure in the future.

[3] Allen V. Sapora and Elmer D. Mitchell, *The Theory of Play and Recreation,* 3rd ed., Copyright © 1961, The Ronald Press Company, New York, pp. 114–15. Also quoted in Jay B. Nash, ed., *Recreation: Pertinent Readings* (Dubuque, Iowa: W. C. Brown, 1964), pp. 41–42.

[4] M.J. Ellis, *Why People Play* (Englewood Cliffs, N.J.: Prentice-Hall, 1973), p. 110.

[5] David Gray and S. Greben, "Future Perspectives," 1973 Work Program, Building Professionalism (Arlington, Va.: National Recreation and Park Association, 1973), p. 42.

4. To know the factors that condition leisure experiences.

5. To be able to define the elements in a leisure experience.

6. To identify factors that condition choices of experiences in free time.

7. To be aware of methods for developing habits of participation.

8. To know experiences that people identify as leisure/recreation activities.

9. To be able to define the role of the schools and community in educating people for leisure.

10. To be aware of the need to provide leisure services for special populations.

11. To be able to interpret leisure and recreation and their meaning for you as an individual.

FOUNDATIONS FOR INTERPRETATIONS OF LEISURE AND RECREATION

Human needs

Human needs form the foundation for the development of leisure and recreation experiences. A need is defined as the difference between what an individual desires and what he has. A need may also be defined as the difference, perceived by others, between what the individual or group has and what each should have. Satisfaction of a need does not always result in behavior that continues to be satisfying. When one is hungry, a good meal is satisfying; but when the hunger is gone, to continue to eat may not only be unsatisfying—it may be repugnant. An individual who has reached a satiation level in relation to a given need must seek another experience requiring greater effort if constantly higher levels of fulfillment are to be achieved. If one aspires to achieve a golf score of 90 and consistently does so, the motivation to continue to improve will be lost unless a new goal of a lower score is set. Nash defines this continuous resetting of goals as "to travel hopefully." [6]

Today the hierarchy of needs as stated by Maslow is commonly used as a definition of how human beings behave in relation to needs:

> *Physiological needs.* These include such needs as food but could include almost any physiological function.
> *Safety needs.* Man needs to feel secure in his environment to be able to function in that environment without fear of bodily harm.
> *Belongingness and love needs.* Man is a gregarious animal and needs love, affection, and a sense of being part of a group if he is to function effectively.

[6]J. B. Nash, *Philosophy of Recreation and Leisure* (Dubuque, Iowa: W. C. Brown, 1953), p. 210.

Esteem needs. Each person needs a sense of self-worth and a recognition of that worth by others.

Self-actualization needs. This may be defined in terms of achieving that for which the individual feels he is fitted. It is related to the physical, intellectual, emotional, and social growth and development of the individual.[7]

Maslow describes these needs as a hierarchy—as lower needs are satisfied, particularly physiological and safety needs, the other levels become important. In leisure services this hierarchy has real significance for we must recognize that the higher levels will be difficult to achieve if the lower levels have not been satisfied.

Albert Tillman examined needs and identified ten which are important in determining leisure needs of people:

1. New experiences—Adventure, exploration, discovery, challenge and seeking the unknown.

2. Relaxation/Escape—Blank mind, forgetting, running away, fantasy, removing stress.

3. Recognition—To be verbally or materially rewarded for achievement. Involves identity.

4. Security—To avoid pain, physical injury, illness, emotional hurt and death. To be free of concern about thirst, food or warmth. To feel needed, necessary, and safe in the environment, comfort.

5. Dominance—To take charge and control one's environment. To direct the behavior of others by manipulation, orders, suggestion, or persuasion.

6. Response/Social Interaction—To relate and re-act to individuals and to have individuals re-act to you. Often one finds his essence or identity reflected by others. It, therefore, follows that everyone will have some operative need for social interaction. An extreme in this would be the individual who cannot stand to be alone.

7. Mental Activity—The rational ability to perceive, interpret, and understand various alternatives. Mental concentration as opposed to sense perception and emotion.

8. Creativity—Creation of a new image, construction, idea, or product in contrast to a copy or imitation of an original. The ability to see and express concepts never consciously encountered. Internal drive to express oneself in a form that does not already exist in the participant.

9. Service to Others—Altruism, humanitarisms, contributing, helping, assisting and concern for the well-being of others. No *pure* altruism— frequently the do-gooder is *getting* more from helping than those whom he is helping. This relates to the need to be needed.

[7]Adapted from pp. 35–46 in *Motivation and Personality* by Abraham H. Maslow. Copyright © 1970 by Abraham H. Maslow. By permission of Harper & Row, Publishers.

10. Physical Activity—Provides release from muscular tension, fitness, physiological health, the response to the internal flexings of any living organism is a specific need.[8]

HISTORICAL BACKGROUND OF LEISURE

Leisure in primitive cultures

Not too much is known of primitive man in prehistoric times. However, archeological finds in areas where early man is known to have lived indicate the kind of culture that he had. From what is known and through the study of primitive tribes that exist today, it is possible to determine certain cultural patterns. Primitive tribes lived in accordance with nature. They measured time by the sun, the moon, and the seasons. Time as it is known today—measured by the clock—was unknown. Vestiges of early man's time concept can be observed today in some of the remaining primitive tribes who get up with sun and work when there is need for work in order to subsist. It is also seen among American Indians who cannot understand the white man's subservience to the clock. As a result, Indians are frequently accused of not being willing to work when they *are willing* to work. However, they will do so when it seems necessary to them.

Many of the leisure activities of primitive tribes were related to work. Men hunted and they had a festival when there was a kill. These festivals were frequently dedicated to the spirit who had brought success, and they became religious rites as well as celebrations of material success.

When primitive man first made utensils, they were strictly utilitarian. Then, he began to decorate them, frequently in the image of a god or spirit whose blessing he was seeking. Thus, another activity that was work-related became recreational.

Children's play and games were imitations of adult activities. These included types of war games, activities related to hunting, and others. An example of a game used to develop the stamina, strength, and agility of young boys is lacrosse. The modified version played today is very different from the roving game played by early Indian tribes. The game in primitive times ranged across the plains and frequently resulted in severe injuries and death. In addition, play for both adults and children included celebrations of tribal events, or religious rites. Play also was used for:

1. education
2. maintaining tribal morale

[8]Reprinted from *The Program Book for Recreation Professionals* by Albert Tillman, by permission of Mayfield Publishing Company (formerly National Press Books). Copyright © 1973 by Albert Tillman.

3. communication

4. relaxation after labor, as a means for replenishing one's capacity for work

Leisure in early civilizations

Oriental. Not very much is known about these early civilizations' play. There are some remnants today of certain ceremonies that date back to early civilizations in Asian countries. As in certain primitive tribal customs, the early Asian civilizations related their play and games to certain survival activities and to religious rites.

Egyptian. Much more is known about play of Egyptians for they left records of it in their pyramids and in paintings and carvings. The Egyptian civilization is considered to have been prominent from about 5000 B.C. until well into the Roman era. Their artifacts show that they engaged in many kinds of activities. Because there was a definite class structure, it is probable that most play activities were primarily activities of the nobles and upper strata of military and religious groups. The activities included a wide variety of sports, dance, entertainment, music, and drama as well as activities related to the hunt and to warfare.

Early Greek. The early Greek civilization, particularly that of Athens, has probably influenced current leisure interpretations more than many others. This is due primarily to the writings of Plato and Aristotle, which expressed philosophical concepts that had a profound influence on all later cultures. In the Athenian culture the work was done by slaves. Concepts of leisure related only to those who might be considered a leisure class. For those people the ideal was a balance in living that included nurture of the mind, body, and spirit. Consequently, there were great achievements in the arts, in sports, and in philosophy.

Other early cultures. A marked contribution was made by the Babylonian civilization, where a leisure class was supported by slaves. A major contribution that still affects leisure today is the development of parks and gardens.

Leisure in the Roman civilization

The Roman civilization which was dominant until about the sixth century A.D. was a different kind of civilization than the other early civilizations. The Romans were builders, organizers, and warriors. As warriors they were also frequently conquerers. As a result, many of the patterns of Roman life were spread to other cultures.

There was a variety of leisure living in the Roman civilization. Baths, amphitheaters, and sports arenas were constructed for the benefit of the mass of the population. Great emphasis was placed on sports, a means of maintaining physical fitness which kept men fit for war. As the Roman civilization advanced, conquered people were made slaves, and the Romans used them for entertainment. At first, the entertainment included theater, music, and sports contests. But as the civilization deteriorated, the contests became exhibitions of violence. Gladiators fought each other to the death, or they were pitted against wild beasts. As Christianity began to develop, Christians were frequently thrown into the arenas to fight against the animals. Gradually the civilization became more decadent. The phrase, "bread and circus," originated in this era, when food and entertainment were given free to prevent the populace from revolting. Historians have indicated that the inability to cope with leisure was a major cause of the fall of the Roman Empire.

Leisure in the Middle Ages
Early Middle Ages. The early part of the Middle Ages, usually called the Dark Ages, covers the period from about 400 A.D. to 1000 A.D. In this period the Roman civilization declined and the Christian Church developed. In reaction to the atrocities and extremes of Rome, the Church prohibited all kinds of activities except those related to religious observance.

Life in the Dark Ages was harsh. Work was glorified as a means of finding a way to heaven in the hereafter. Idleness was evil. In this era religious music developed and morality plays depicting the ideal of Christian life flourished.

Late Middle Ages. This period from about 1000 A.D. to 1500 A.D. saw certain relaxations from the strictures of the Dark Ages. Life was still bleak for the masses whose only surcease from labor was found in religious activities, festivals, cock fighting, and other robust activity. However, for the feudal nobility, leisure activities included hunting and hawking, music and dance. Sports and jousting in tournaments were favored as a means of entertainment but primarily because they prepared men for war which was always imminent among feuding noblemen.

Leisure in the Renaissance
The Renaissance. The fifteenth century marks the beginning of the period and might be considered the transition between the medieval world and modern Western civilization. In this period there was a rebirth of the arts and secular literature. Most leisure pursuits were enjoyed by the nobility, but the peasants had both secular and religious festivals as well as many sporting activities. The arts flourished, sponsored by the nobility who served as patrons, and many of the greatest artists of all times produced works that are cherished today. Leonardo Da Vinci and Michelangelo produced some of the world's greatest art works. In Florence,

frescoes were painted that are one of the marvels of today's world. It was during this period that printing was developed, and literature that had been available only in monasteries or universities for the use of scholars could be printed and disseminated more widely. Music, dance, and drama became professionalized and were performed in theaters open to a variety of people. Education of the nobility during this period included such leisure skills as dance, riding, and athletics. Later, educators such as Rousseau and Locke espoused the benefits of play in the education of children.

In the seventeenth and eighteenth centuries great parks and gardens were developed by nobles for hunting, fishing, and for the aesthetic enjoyment of the beauty of cultivated gardens. In addition, commons and plazas were developed by kings for the use of the masses. They were the forerunners of today's parks and outdoor recreation areas.

During the Renaissance most people had considerable free time. For the upper classes, leisure time was made possible by the labor of others. For the masses there were many holidays, including the Church holy days and holidays declared by kings and feudal lords to celebrate important events, such as birthdays and weddings.

The Reformation. In the latter part of the Renaissance period, the Protestant Reformation began. Martin Luther started a movement against the practices of the Church in the sixteenth century. The Reformation was marked by austerity in all things. As a result, there was a reemphasis on religion and a curtailing of all other activity.

Leisure in colonial America

Since America was colonized during the late Renaissance, many of the cultural patterns seen in Europe were brought to the new colonies.

Northern colonies. Settlers in the northern colonies fled Europe to escape religious persecution. The various sects developed during the Reformation were completely arbitrary in their beliefs. Anyone disagreeing with those beliefs usually paid for it with his life. In America different sects settled in different locales, but each promoted its own beliefs. As a result, the work ethic and the idea that play was sinful became prominent in the northern colonies. This ethic served the purpose of the developing country because work was necessary to subsist and to expand the frontiers of the new land. The only activities that were condoned were those related to work—a feast at a barn raising or activities related to religious participation. Harsh laws prohibited many kinds of recreation.

Southern colonies. In the southern colonies a different type of development took place. Large land holdings worked by slaves were developed. This left the land owners with greater free time. Soon they were indulging in the activities pursued in Europe by the nobility and upper classes. The restrictions on recreation broke down. Participation in music, dance, and many forms of athletics resulted. Horse breeding was a part of plantation life. Soon horse racing became popular and, with it, gambling. Social activities involving great parties and feasts included music, dancing, and drinking as part of the festivities.

Leisure during the Industrial Revolution

By the middle of the eighteenth and continuing into the nineteenth century, the industrial revolution brought about changes in life both in Europe and in America. The invention of machines, such as the cotton gin, the spinning and weaving machines, and the steam engine, affected work by mechanizing industry.

Home industries were no longer the mode of work; mechanization centralized work. Factories brought about the growth of cities and the uprooting of people from small towns and villages. This pattern was seen in all of western Europe and in America. It gave rise to overcrowding in urban areas and the concomitant evils of poor housing, inadequate food, increased crime and desire to produce as much as possible with the least capital outlay. Further, people were forced to work long hours for mere subsistence because of meager pay. Some classic examples of the poor conditions are descriptions of the mine workers in Wales and the weavers in the English and Scottish cities.

As working conditions became intolerable in the cities of Europe people emigrated to America. Many of the same conditions existed in America, but because the country was new and growing, the opportunity seemed greater for better living.

However, the people who came to America, particularly to the northern states, brought with them basic beliefs about leisure and recreation. Work was the most important element of their lives, and the Protestant ethic that play was sinful conditioned the early leisure and recreation patterns in the United States.

In the cities recreation had the same forms as in Europe. There was theater, music, drama and other forms of spectator activities such as vaudeville and burlesque, gambling, all forms of racing, boxing, wrestling, and others.

But as urbanization and slums developed in Europe and the United States, the social reform movement also developed to counteract these conditions. The result was the beginning of the agencies known today as the Y's and the settlement houses. Other similar agencies developed. They were committed to the idea of helping people to help themselves find a better life. The Boston Sand Gardens, started in 1886 to care for children of industrial laborers, is considered the beginning of organized recreation in the United States.

As the American frontier expanded westward, work continued to be the most important part of living. However, there was some relaxation of the strict Puritan ethic, and greater permissiveness in regard to recreation resulted. In addition, people from many parts of the country settled in new areas, and the plurality of life style which is so predominant today had some of its beginnings.

Leisure and recreation in the twentieth century

Greater and greater industrialization in the United States and the continued expansion on the western frontier brought continuously changing patterns of leisure and recreation. One of the new developments that continues to exert a strong influence on leisure patterns was the invention of the automobile. People became more mobile and were able to enjoy many recreational pursuits that previously had not been available to them.

In 1906 the Playground Association of America was formed for the purpose of promoting better recreational opportunities for children. This organization has gone through several changes, and today it is called the National Recreation and Park Association. Although the focus of the organization has developed as society in the United States has changed, its purpose remains essentially the promotion and development of leisure services that will bring a better quality of life not only for children but for all people.

One of the first changes in focus of The Playground Association was the establishment of War Camp Services during World War I. Services were provided for military men both in the United States and in Europe. These services were heavily sports-oriented but also provided shows, music, crafts, and other activities. This exposure to a variety of recreational activities was the first for many men. Returning to their own communities, these men began to seek the same kinds of services at home. Thus, a real emphasis on the need for community recreation programs began.

In 1918 "The Seven Cardinal Principles of Education" was published by the Commission on Secondary Education. [9] One of these principles was "the worthy use of leisure time." This principle has not been implemented in the schools in general. However, with ever-increasing amounts of free time for all people, the schools now may recognize the need to educate for leisure as well as for work.

As the United States moved into the Great Depression, totally different patterns of living were found. The most profound change was the extent of unemployment and its attendant ills—idleness, poverty, and low

[9]Commission on Higher Education, "Seven Cardinal Principles of Education" (Washington, D.C.: National Education Association, 1918).

morale. Programs to alleviate unemployment influenced the development of leisure services.

One major program—WPA—included construction of outdoor and indoor facilities for recreation. In addition, program services were introduced into communities, including many leisure pursuits for all ages. Unemployed people worked in these programs, and extensive inservice training programs were conducted to give them the necessary skills to lead programs. Out of these activities grew many community programs and professional preparation programs in colleges. As communities began to enjoy their community recreation programs, they began to ask for trained leaders.

During World War II many advances were made in the delivery of leisure services. The armed forces provided extensive services for all personnel both at home and abroad. These services were extended to dependents at home during the war and overseas at war's end. The services demonstrated the advantages of giving people leisure programs. The armed forces also provided recreation services in hospitals. These services sparked the development of therapeutic recreation services for all handicapped people which have been and are continuing to be developed and refined.

Communities provided recreation services for all kinds of war workers. Some of these were inplant services, others were conducted by community departments. Many times these services were conducted around the clock in order to care for the recreational needs of shift workers. At the close of the war many leisure service programs were continued as people in communities demanded more of these kinds of programs.

Leisure Services in the 1960s and 1970s

After World War II society in the United States experienced profound changes in cultural patterns. As a result of war experiences and the development of the atomic bomb, people began to question the older values. A desire for immediate gratification developed, particularly among young people. They believed that they might not be alive in the future to enjoy the satisfaction of their desire because nuclear war would destroy the world. Many new lifestyles evolved and there was, and is, a relaxation in mores.

All of these developments had an influence on leisure services. Some have been fulfilling, others destructive. The following are examples of such developments.

1. Creation of the Land Water Conservation Fund in 1965 and the establishment of the Bureau of Outdoor Recreation will affect leisure services for many years.

2. Automation has brought increased free time to many people who have begun to try to find satisfying ways to fill that free time. Automation has alienated workers, for work no longer challenges them.

3. As outdoor facilities have been developed by local, state, and federal governments and by private enterprise, there has been increased interest in outdoor sports and camping. A great increase in use of all kinds of recreational vehicles has developed including all varieties from snowmobiles to luxurious homes on wheels.

4. Health care has improved, and people are living longer. Many live for years on retirement from work during which time they seek increased leisure services.

5. A youth culture has developed which challenges traditional values and no longer accepts traditional leisure pursuits.

6. The challenges given to the leisure services programs have caused professionals to continuously reexamine the programs that are being offered and to involve the users in the planning and organizing of those services.

7. Changes in sexual morals have affected leisure services programs.

8. The prevalence of drug addiction among many segments of society has caused many changes in societal patterns. Among them is the increase in crime and changed patterns of leisure participation because of crime.

9. With the increased use of television, people satisfy their leisure needs by watching programs rather than participating in them.

10. Family structure has changed from the extended family to the nuclear family bringing with it a failure in cross-generation understanding and a failure in transmission of cultural patterns from one generation to the next.

Trends for the future
As the United States looks toward the twenty-first century, certain developments seem inevitable:

1. Shorter hours of work will be required to gain satisfaction of subsistence needs.

2. There will be a greater emphasis on both paid and volunteer work in service types of work.

3. People will seek challenges in their free time; they will not be satisfied with busy work.

4. There will be gradual recognition that education for leisure is as important as education for work.

5. Education will become a life-long endeavor.

6. More than one career will become a pattern for many people.

7. New patterns of funding of leisure services will be introduced as economic pressures affect the delivery of services.

The challenge of the future is the need for leisure services personnel to be constantly alert to the changing needs of society.

FACTORS INFLUENCING LEISURE PURSUITS IN THE UNITED STATES TODAY

Philosophical factors

A number of philosophical concepts affect leisure pursuits. The influence of some have shaped values held through centuries, whereas others have more recently been embraced as a result of a discarding of the traditional values.

Idealism. Idealism is based on the concept that there are absolutes against which all things are measured. It represents an emphasis on ideas. This concept has greatly influenced values in America for it largely constitutes the foundation of the Judaic-Christian religions. Puritanism and the glorification of the work ethic are largely an outgrowth of idealism. Idealism, therefore, has been a major concept in the development of American democracy.

Realism. Realism emphasizes that only that which can be perceived through the senses exists. It, therefore, is the antithesis of idealism which deals with abstracts. The influence of realism can be seen in many areas of science. According to realistic concepts, all knowledge is gained from experiences and can be tested.

Pragmatism. The meaning of an idea is based on the consequences and values that it engenders. Very simply stated pragmatism means, "If it works it is right." It is seen frequently as short-term expediency that fails to take long-range consequences into consideration. It is also perceived as a concept in which value changes are made as often as the direction of a feather in the wind.

Existentialism. This is a fairly recent philosophical concept that is based on the idea that what is, is all that exists. It has grown out of a world without purpose or direction and negates ideals and ideas.

Hedonism. This is a concept that emphasizes the importance of immediate gratification of one's needs and desires. It is a prevalent philosophy particularly among youth. Circumstances of living today lead many to this concept. It is evident as a result of the mobility of people. People need many kinds of relationships but because they are so constantly mobile, these relationships must be achieved quickly and in as great a depth as is possible.

These concepts may have a profound effect on the delivery of leisure service.

Environmental factors

Geography. Climate and topography condition the participation in and delivery of leisure services, even though machines have made leisure experiences possible in areas that otherwise could not have them. However, even with machines, people living in mountainous areas are unable to pursue some activities because of difficult terrain. Similarly, people living in hot, dry areas cannot easily engage in winter sports.

Climate and productivity. There is some evidence that those living in areas that experience regular changes in climate tend to be more productive. An unanswerable question is, "Do changes in climate condition us and make it necessary for a person to be more flexible and thus more open to accept new ideas?"

Density of population. Density affects leisure services in many ways. It has been shown that the pressure of crowds and lack of privacy affects people deeply. They tend to become tense, overly agressive and combatative, and frequently rigid in the expression of the rightness of their personal beliefs. A balance between populated and open space will permit people to have a chance to breathe and stretch and thus relieve tension and the oppressiveness of crowds.

Noise and pollution. Noises of all kinds assail people on every side. People adjust to noise to the extent that they say that they do not hear it. However, it has been proven that high decibels of noise cause deafness and create tensions. Environmental pollution has become a major concern. Many leisure services contribute to this pollution. For example, motor boats contaminate the lakes and snowmobiles tear up fragile lands.

Working conditions. People's working conditions influence their leisure pursuits. Urbanization has made it necessary for people to travel many hours to their jobs. Frequently this means that there is little time for leisure pursuits. It also means that families have fewer opportunities to do things together. Part of a weekend or a once-a-year vacation are often the only available time. Travel to work also means that both individuals and groups have fewer occasions when easy communication is possible.

The great increase in the number of women working outside the home influences leisure pursuits not only of the women but also of the family. In addition, this factor has a decided effect on the delivery of leisure services. For example, if couples want to do things together provision must be made for the care of their children. Many experiments have been tried. Cooperatives have developed in which members agree to care for others' children and their own on a prearranged basis. Leisure services departments also serve as a training and placement center for baby sitters.

Still another approach provides programs for parents and for children at the same time.

Population migration due to job changes also affects leisure services. Consideration must be given to offering programs for short periods. Provisions must also be made to give regular leisure information. All kinds of media must be used to disseminate this information.

Population migration also tends to give people a certain rootlessness. Therefore, it is imperative that leisure services help people gain a sense of belonging and develop satisfying interpersonal relationships.

Ease of mobility brings with it many problems of intergroup pressures. Whereas like groups used to remain together for a life time, today, groups with totally different life styles are thrown into a close proximity which creates friction. Leisure services must be aware of this and strive to offer experiences that break down tensions and create friendliness.

Political organization. The political organization of nations influences leisure services because government defines policies and establishes priorities. The potential for the development of leisure services depends on the priorities. The development of the human, physical, and financial resources for public leisure services are completely dependent on the priorities established.

Influence of the church today. The traditional values that have been the foundation of religion for centuries have been much undermined. People are turning away from traditional beliefs. Many new religious groups have sprung up, and for youth in particular, the groups seem to provide a foundation of beliefs that are meaningful. In addition, such secular philosophies as yoga, transcendental meditation, and many others seem to be helping people to find values and, therefore, meaningful living.

Increase in hedonistic philosophy. Based on immediate gratification of needs or desires, this philosophy has brought with it many destructive types of behavior. These include an increase in violent crime, drug abuse, obsessive gambling, and alcoholism. The outcome has been the displacement of many traditional beliefs related to personal integrity, property rights, sexual mores, and family structure to name a few.

All of these factors indicate that society in the United States is involved in a social revolution that will ultimately end in life styles and cultural patterns different from any that have existed before in this country. A major question that must be faced is how leisure services can contribute constructively to these new patterns for the benefit of all people.

SIGNIFICANCE OF LEISURE EXPERIENCES FOR THE INDIVIDUAL

Through leisure experiences an individual can complement work experiences and thus live more fully. Leisure experiences can bring to the individual a sense of physical and emotional well-being and intellectual and social development.

Physical well-being

All individuals must be able to respond to physical demands and emergencies. Leisure activities (for example, sports and games, camping, outdoor recreation, and so forth) lend themselves to promoting healthy growth and development. They can also be developed in childhood and continue in adulthood.

Physical inactivity can lead to obesity and related health problems. Leisure activities which are of a physical nature can reduce emotional stress and overweight.

People recognize that exercise is vital to physical health, especially in middle and later life. An enjoyable experience (that is, a recreational activity) is a most attractive way in which to gain much-needed exercise.

Emotional well-being

Play is an essential aspect of an individual's life. Leisure is a vital force in maintaining or improving the emotional well-being of an individual. It is a means of providing for the emotional development of children and adults. Positive self-concepts may be established or reinforced through leisure experiences. A leisure activity can help individuals maintain a healthy emotional equilibrium.

Intellectual development

Leisure experiences contribute to learning, self-expression, and intellectual growth. Such activities as reading, art, music, drama, appreciation and discussion groups, and nature study all promote intellectual development.

Recreational activities have been used effectively with mentally retarded youngsters. Play, artistic, and cultural programs have helped disadvantaged children to improve in IQ scores.

Social values

Leisure experiences serve to alleviate isolation by providing people an opportunity to socialize. This helps to promote a feeling of belonging. Group participation affords people an occasion for cooperation and competition. Positive character traits, such as the ability to play by the rules, to accept a majority decision, win and lose gracefully, and others, may be developed and strengthened through leisure activities.

CHOOSING ACTIVITIES IN FREE TIME

When people have the opportunity to choose what they want to do, their choices depend upon a number of factors. They seek to satisfy certain needs and desires in an effort to make their lives more meaningful. They also seek a state of being called *happiness*.

Elements that contribute to happiness include the individual's aspirations, his self-concept and feelings of self-worth, his role expectancy (what he conceives as his place in life), and acceptance by his peers. The extent to which these elements are compatible with each other and the extent of the individual's physical, mental, and social health will determine the extent to which the individual is able to achieve that state of being called happiness.

Factors that condition choice

The specific factors that condition leisure choices are the needs, interests, and attitudes of the individual, his education, and the physical and human resources available in his environment. The individual chooses on the basis of certain personal and social elements current in his life. Personal elements include, but are not necessarily limited to, frustration, boredom, insecurity, tension, strain, hostility, adventure, restlessness, physical need for activity. Choices are also conditioned by certain social factors such as life style and standards of behavior, availability of resources, and the skills and knowledge of the individual.

Conflict and cooperation also condition the individual's choices. Conflict results from trying to balance struggle and ease. It has been stated that creative or innovative approaches occur only when the need to solve a problem exists. One problem is determining the extent to which people can be pushed into activity. Who does the pushing? Is the individual inner-directed or outer-directed, and if outer-directed, will activity cease when the outside force is removed? A second problem is determining the level at which the struggle is satisfying and at which it becomes frustrating.

Cooperation as a basis for activity choice in free time also presents certain problems. The principal problem is the extent to which it brings about a decrease in the potential for individual achievement. There may be a leveling off in achievement at a level of mediocrity.

Other factors influence individual choices. Urbanization makes the selection of activities difficult. Some of the problems of urban living are: unavailability of resources, population density, and conformity to dominant patterns of leisure choices.

DEVELOPING PATTERNS OF PARTICIPATION

Developing patterns of participation requires developing the individual's taste and ability to discriminate among possible choices. Exposure to a variety of experiences, determining the many experiences that may be satisfying, and defining one's personal responses are ways to achieve this development.

Participation in leisure experiences should start in the home. Every person needs to be able to live with himself, to be part of a group, and to experience anonymity of being one in a mass. Interpersonal relationships start with the intimate family unit and move gradually to groups outside the family unit. The modern nuclear family often makes this transition difficult because of the failure of cross-generation cultural understandings.

The leisure services delivery system must consider how it may provide services to families in the form of experiences for families as units and experiences that will develop appreciation for varying cultural patterns and life styles.

LEISURE EXPERIENCES AS RE-CREATIVE EXPERIENCES

The basic assumption is that any experience whether in free time or work time may be re-creative, revitalizing. It is the individual who defines what is re-creative for him. An unemployed person may find that his most re-creative experience is finding a satisfying job.

There are certain experiences which people think of as particularly suitable for free time.These include at least fourteen major categories each of which can be broken down into numerous subdivisions. They are:

Crafts	Language activities
Collecting	Music activities
Dance	Nature, camping, and
Drama	outing activities
Education activities	Religious activities
Fine arts	Service to others
Games, sports, and	Social activities
physical activities	Water activities

The individual should have exposure to all of these activities. He should learn the skills involved, how the activity developed, why people find it satisfying, and how one may participate, and should develop attitudes toward them, and habits of participation in them. People seek new experiences because they are curious, they desire achievement, they want adventure, and many other reasons. However, when the individual is ready to learn, he will have the greatest potential for success. In general, skill learning is easiest when an individual is young, but new skills, knowledge, and changes in attitude and habits can occur at any age. The older person frequently resists change but can learn if he is given adequate time.

THE ROLE OF THE SCHOOLS IN EDUCATING FOR LEISURE

Although leisure education has been a basic principal of education since 1918, it has not been implemented in the schools. Because of increased free time, there is an effort today to bring into reality leisure education. Leisure education is not conceived of as a special course but as a process through which the individual will learn to use the entire school curriculum to enhance his free time and to provide himself with satisfying re-creative experiences. The schools need to introduce leisure education into all parts of the curriculum and provide time and facilities for students to develop habits of participation.

THE ROLE OF THE COMMUNITY IN EDUCATING FOR LEISURE

The school has a major responsibility for educating children and youth for leisure, but other community agencies must take the responsibility for leisure education of others in the community. The public leisure services department can play a major role as a catalyst and coordinator of leisure education. Adult leisure education includes development of programs through a variety of mass media and a master calendar of events, information, counseling, and resources for participation. Working together, schools and the community can provide adequate leisure services for all people.

LEISURE PROBLEMS OF SPECIAL POPULATIONS

Retired persons

On retirement many people are lonely, physically handicapped, and economically insecure. Generally, they have worked much of their lives, have had little leisure, and have had no education for it. With this group it is necessary to help to accent their assets rather than their liabilities. Re-creators must help retired people:

1. recognize that through the years they have gained wisdom through experience and have a mature outlook which can be successfully balanced against the vitality of youth.

2. accept that aging starts at birth and continues until death and that every age level has certain problems.

3. make the most of their capacity without anxiety about their incapacity.

4. understand that contentment comes from living actively, not from reading about living.

Leisure services can help older people recognize that the American culture has put an accent on youth, that this accent is left over from pioneer days when strength and stamina were necessary to build a new country. Today that vitality is no longer necessary. Today mature judgement is a greater value if the complex problems of society are to be solved. A good recreation program can help the elderly to accept with serenity the attributes of aging.

Ill and disabled

The ill or disabled person may find that he has increased amounts of free time and little or no capacity to use it to his satisfaction. In addition, the individual is usually incapable of contributing to the solution of society's problems which makes him feel useless and gives him a poor self-image.

Leisure services help the ill or disabled person to use free time to his own satisfaction. It is necessary to understand the individual's physical and/or mental handicap and the resulting emotional problems, the economic insecurity, and the fears of rejection that he experiences because of his incapacity. Leisure programs may be secondary to treatment or part of treatment in institutional settings. In all settings leisure pursuits must be based on the needs and interests of the individual and adapted to his incapacities as well as his capacities.

Delinquents

Delinquency results from various elements, including the environment, parental and peer relationships, and individual development. Delinquent individuals are usually undisciplined and seek immediate gratification of their needs and desires. A structured program of leisure pursuits is often needed to overcome the individual's inability to structure his own involvement in leisure.

SUMMARY

There are many concepts of leisure. In the United States today most people equate leisure with the time in which they are free to choose experiences that bring them satisfaction. Leisure as a quality of living has not been fully defined and consequently is not a generally accepted concept. Recreational experiences may be part of work or obligated time or they may be pursued in time free from any obligations. Recreation is an individual necessity providing balance between stress and relaxation and can be an important social force. Recreational experiences can be either constructive for the individual or destructive; they are those activities the individual engages in for the satisfaction he derives from them.

Because leisure participation involves freedom of choice, it is closely related to the democratic structure of society. This indicates that there is a discipline but that there is freedom within the discipline and that the individual has helped to shape the structure of the society in which he functions.

Every leader in leisure services must be able to accept each person as an individual of worth and dignity. The individual has special leisure needs and interests, and leisure services must provide the experiences that will satisfy *his* needs and interests.

Student assignments

This part consists of 11 objectives. You will be called upon to demonstrate your mastery of each objective.

OBJECTIVE	ACHIEVEMENT OF COMPETENCY
1. To know the variety of leisure and recreation definitions	Identify three of the leisure and recreation definitions given in Module 1 which influence leisure and recreation concepts today. Discuss each and indicate the evidence of its influence on leisure services.
2. To understand basic human needs and how they affect choices of leisure and/or recreational experiences.	a. Define *need*. b. Discuss Maslow's hierarchy of needs. c. Discuss similarities and differences between Maslow's hierarchy of needs and Tillman's listing of needs.
3. To know the history of leisure and recreation from primitive times to the present and to show trends of leisure in the future.	a. Discuss five leisure pursuits or services and show their historical backgrounds. Indicate how these are seen in society today. b. Discuss current leisure and recreation pursuits and services and indicate how they show trends for the future.
4. To know factors that condition leisure experiences.	a. Show how the philosophical concepts of idealism, realism, pragmatism, existentialism, and hedonism influence leisure today.

b. Indicate the environmental factors which might be considered as having a major effect on leisure and recreation today.

5. To define elements of a leisure experience.

Discuss the importance of leisure experiences for the individual.

6. To identify factors that condition choices of experiences in free time.

a. Discuss the factors that will condition the state of being called "happiness."

b. Discuss the personal elements that affect a person's choices.

c. Discuss the influence of conflict and cooperation on choices.

d. Show how urbanization influences selection of experiences.

7. To become aware of methods for developing habits of participation.

a. Show the effect of the development of taste and discrimination on patterns of participation.

b. Indicate how patterns of participation may be developed from birth to old age.

8. To know the experiences that people define as leisure/recreation activities.

List the major categories of activities and how people may develop habits of participation in them.

9. To define the role of the school and the role of the community in leisure education.

a. Discuss the role of the school.

b. Discuss the role of the community.

10. To become aware of the need to provide leisure services for special populations.

Indicate how leisure services should be provided for the elderly, the ill or disabled, and the delinquent.

11. To interpret leisure and recreation and their meaning for you as an individual.

a. Write your own interpretation of leisure and recreation.

b. Learn a new leisure activity and indicate the concepts you learned: how you acquired knowledge about the activity, how you developed attitudes toward, and habits of, participation.

Resources

TEXTBOOK

MURPHY, JAMES F. *Concepts of Leisure*. Englewood Cliffs, N.J.: Prentice-Hall, 1974.

GENERAL REFERENCES RELATED TO LEISURE AND RECREATION

BRANTLEY, HERBERT, and SESSOMS, H. DOUGLAS. *Issues and Perspectives*. Columbia, S.C.: Wing Publications, 1969.

BRIGHTHILL, CHARLES. *Education for Leisure-Centered Living*. Harrisburg, Pa.: Stackpale, 1966.

CARSON, RACHEL. *Silent Spring*. Boston: Houghton Mifflin, 1962.

CORBIN, DAN, and TAIT, WILLIAM. *Education for Leisure*. Englewood Cliffs, N.J.: Prentice-Hall, 1973.

DE GRAZIA, SEBASTIAN. *Of Time, Work and Leisure*. Garden City, N.Y.: Doubleday, 1964.

DULLES, FOSTER R. *A History of Recreation: Americans Learn to Play*. New York: Appleton-Century-Crofts, 1965.

HAUN, PAUL. *Recreation, A Medical Viewpoint*. New York: Columbia University Press, 1965.

KRAUS, RICHARD. *Recreation and Leisure in Modern Society*. New York: Appleton-Century-Crofts, 1971.

LARRABEE, ERIC, and MEYERSOHN, ROLF, eds. *Mass Leisure*. Glencoe, Ill.: The Free Press, 1958.

MASLOW, ABRAHAM. *Toward a Psychology of Being*. New York: Van Nostrand Reinhold, 1968.

NASH, J. B. *Philosophy of Recreation and Leisure*. Dubuque, Iowa: W. C. Brown, 1953.

SAPORA, ALLEN V., and MITCHELL, ELMER D. *The Theory of Play and Recreation*, 3rd ed. New York: Ronald Press, 1961.

STALEY, EDWIN J., and MILLER, NORMAN, eds. *Leisure and the Quality of Life*. Washington, D.C.: American Association for Health, Physical Education, and Recreation, 1972.

TOFFLER, ALVIN. *Future Shock*. New York: Random House, 1970.

TOYNBEE, ARNOLD. *Change and Habit: The Challenge of Our Times*. New York: Oxford University Press, 1966.

OTHER READING MATERIALS

BENEDICT, RUTH. *Patterns of Culture*, 2nd ed. Boston: Houghton Mifflin, 1959.

BERNE, ERIC. *Games People Play*. New York: Grove Press, 1964.

CAMUS, ALBERT. *The Fall*. New York: Knopf, 1956.

DAHL, GORDON. *Work, Play and Worship*. Minneapolis: Augsburg Press, 1972.

DEWEY, JOHN. *Freedom and Culture*. New York: Capricorn Books, 1939.

DURANT, WILL. *Story of Philosophy*. New York: Simon & Schuster, 1926.

ELLIS, N. J. *Why People Play*. Englewood Cliffs, N.J.: Prentice-Hall, 1973.

ERNST, MORRIS. *The First Freedom*. New York: Macmillan, 1946.

FABUN, DON. *The Dynamics of Change*. Englewood Cliffs, N.J.: Prentice-Hall, 1967.

GIBRAN, KAHLIL. *The Prophet*. New York: Knopf, 1923.

GOODMAN, PAUL. *Growing Up Absurd*. New York: Random House, 1956.

HOFFER, ERIC. *The Temper of Our Times*. New York: Harper & Row, 1964.

———. *The Ordeal of Change*. New York: Harper & Row, 1952.

HUIZINGA, J. *Homo Ludens: A Study of the Play Element in Culture*. Boston: Beacon Press, 1955.

JACKS, L. P. *Education Through Recreation*. New York: Harper, 1932.

JENSON, CLAYNE. *Outdoor Recreation in America*. Minneapolis: Burgess, 1970.

KERR, WALTER. *The Decline of Pleasure*. New York: Simon & Schuster, 1962.

McKUEN, ROD. *Lonesome Cities*. New York: Random House, 1967.

McLUHAN, MARSHALL. *Understanding Media*. New York: McGraw-Hill, 1964.

MEAD, MARGARET. *Culture and Commitment*. Garden City, N.Y.: Doubleday, 1970.

NASH, J. B., ed. *Recreation: Pertinent Readings*. Dubuque, Iowa: W. C. Brown, 1960.

NEILL, A. S. *Summerhill*. New York: Hart, 1960.

PACKARD, VANCE. *A Nation of Strangers*. New York: David McKay, 1972.

PEIPER, JOSEPH. *Leisure: The Basis of Culture*, 2nd ed. New York: Mentor-Omega Books, 1963.

PIAGET, JEAN. *Play Dreams and Imitation in Childhood*. New York: W. W. Norton, 1962.

POOR, RIVA, and STEELE, JAMES L., eds. *Four Days, Forty Hours*. Cambridge, Mass.: Bursk & Poor, 1970.

REICH, CHARLES. *The Greening of America*. New York: Random House, 1970.

RUSSELL, BERTRAND. *Authority and the Individual*. New York: Simon & Schuster, 1949.

SMITH, ROBERT. *Where did you go? Out. What did you do? Nothing.* New York: W. W. Norton, 1957.

Thoreau on Man and Nature: A Compilation. Edited by Arthur G. Volkman from the writings of Henry D. Thoreau. New York: Peter Pauper Press, 1960.

FILMS

Of Time, Work and Leisure. Bloomington, Ind.: Audio-Visual Center, Indiana University.

When All the People Play. Ottawa, Canada: National Film Board of Canada.

MODULE 2
Program activities

Social recreation

       We live, work, and play in a rapidly changing and highly complex society. There is little stability in our fast-paced, competitive, twentieth-century civilization. Indeed, the highly technical and specialized nature of man's employment in an automated society has served to seriously hinder close social relationships found in the work of our ancestors. Consequently, the joys of companionship and interchange are not adequately provided for in today's work experience.

       People need people. An individual cut off from interactions with others loses a great deal of his concern for others. Social recreational activities serve to bring people together in a congenial, cooperative, and fun-filled environment. Cooperation rather than competition is the substance of social recreation. People engage in social recreational activities because of the satisfaction derived from fellowship and sociability. Social recreation can be a positive force to bridge the gap between people.

29

DEFINITIONS

• *Heaton:* "Those recreational activities which two or more people do together where the joy of being together is the primary motivating factor."[1]

• *Tillman:* "[Social recreation] yields invigorating vibrations."[2] He believes that the primary reason that people engage in social recreation is the opportunity to be with desirable companions. Therefore, the social recreational situation should, according to Tillman, be a relaxed one where the stress to excel is minimal.

• *Pomeroy:* "Those activities and experiences in which the primary purpose is sociability."[3] Thus, according to Pomeroy, social recreation activities appeal to individuals because of the satisfaction of fellowship and sociability inherently contained within the activities.

• *Weiskopf:* "Social recreation includes activities that help create a spirit of fun, fellowship, and sociability."[4]

FUNCTION OF SOCIAL RECREATION

Man is, for the most part, a gregarious, friendly individual. He has an urge to mingle freely and informally with his fellow man. Because of the competition, stress, and depersonalization in modern society, there is less opportunity for such interaction. Social recreational activities provide the chance to interact and respond freely in a group endeavor. An inherent value of social recreation is that it brings people together for laughter and companionship, for play and good fellowship. A social situation provides opportunity for growth, new ideas, and better understanding and appreciation of others. Community and family solidarity can be strengthened. Everyone can benefit from a social recreational experience. Social recreation functions through many different types of activities. Few social recreation activities require such physical skill or degree of proficiency that they cannot be readily adapted to meet the needs of all people.

CLASSIFICATION OF SOCIAL RECREATIONAL ACTIVITIES

The following are advantages of a standard system for classifying social recreational activities:

[1]Israel C. Heaton, *Planning for Social Recreation* (Provo, Utah: Brigham Young University Press, 1968), p. 2.

[2]Albert Tillman, *The Program Book for Recreation Professionals.* (Los Angeles: National Press Books, 1973), p. 132.

[3]Janet Pomeroy, *Recreation for the Physically Handicapped.* (New York: Macmillan, 1964), p. 326.

[4]Donald C. Weiskopf, *A Guide to Recreation and Leisure* (Boston: Allyn & Bacon, 1975),

1. A classification system enables the leader to locate quickly an activity selected (*type*).

2. It helps to clarify activities which the leader may possibly select for inclusion in a program (*purpose*).

3. It enables the leader to plan programs in a logical, sequential order (*formation*).

4. It saves the leader energy in searching for and selecting specific activities, in explaining why the activity is offered, and in determining how the activity is presented (*eclectic*).

The system for classifying social recreational activities will encompass the following three ingredients:

1. Type of activity
2. Purpose of the activity
3. Formation in which the activity is played [5]

TYPES OF SOCIAL RECREATIONAL ACTIVITIES

Type is one criterion for classifying social recreational activities. They may be grouped according to the following 14 types:

1. Brain teaser
2. Dance
3. Group contest
4. Group stunt
5. Guessing game
6. Individual activity
7. Leader's stunt
8. Musical mixer
9. Puzzle
10. Relay
11. Skill game
12. Song[6]
13. Table games
14. Paper-and-pencil games

---

p. 262.
[5]Heaton, *Planning for Social Recreation*, pp. 3-5.
[6]Ibid., pp. 3–4.

CHARACTERISTICS OF SPECIFIC TYPES

1. Brain teaser—An activity in which the problems are solvable; you can always check the answers.

2. Dance—Any activity that has musical accompaniment, either instrumental or vocal, and which has a definite pattern of steps.

3. Group contests—An activity in which one group as a unit competes against other groups, not a relay.

4. Group stunt—An activity requiring at least one practice session, by a small group for the entertainment of others.

5. Guessing game—Any activity involving questions to which the answer cannot be arrived at by using logic.

6. Individual activity—An activity that does not fit any other classification in which each participant is working by himself.

7. Leader's stunt—An activity led by one person for the entertainment of the group; there is a minimum of group organization.[7]

8. Musical mixer—An activity that is most enjoyable with musical accompaniment; not a dance.

9. Puzzle—The manipulation of objects to fit a pattern.

10. Relay—An activity in which each person on a team covers a portion of a prescribed course.

11. Skill game—An activity involving physical skill and/or coordination.

12. Song—Melody and words combined. [8]

13. Table games—Games that are played on a table by two or more people seated at it or standing about it. [9]

14. Pencil-and-paper games—Games that are played by two or more people using paper and a writing implement; the participants are usually seated.

MODEL FOR SELECTING AND LEADING SOCIAL RECREATIONAL ACTIVITIES: ONE, TWO, THREE, GO!

I. *Motivate.* Get the participants interested through your own enthusiasm.

II. *Activate.* Let them play the game as quickly as possible.

III. *Educate.* Answer and teach the more complicated rules and game strategies as they play.

[7] Ibid., p. 3.
[8] Ibid., p. 4.
[9] Pomeroy, *Recreation for the Physically Handicapped*, p. 331.

- *Formation:* Get the participants into the formation the activity requires.
- *Explanation:* "The object of this game is . . ."
- *Demonstration:* "This is the way you should do it."
- *Reexplain:* Show and tell at the same time.
- *Play*[10]

GROUP FORMATIONS IN SOCIAL RECREATION

The five group formations and example activities are:

1. Circle ("Patty Cake Polka")
2. Lines ("Bean Bag Relay")
3. Mass ("The More We Get Together")

[10]Formulated by Elaine Eliopolos, Northeastern University.

TABLE 2. Purpose, definition and types of social recreational activities

Purpose	Definition	Types of activities
1. Preopener	Activities used when people are assembling for an evening of social recreation.	Brain teasers, skill games, guessing games, individual activities, puzzles.
2. Starter (unifier)	Activities designed to bring the group closer together, to get them to respond as a unit to the leader's suggestions, and to get them to feel at ease.	Musical mixer, songs, individual activity, leader's stunt.
3. Get acquainted	Activities which use the names of participants.	Individual activities, musical mixers.
4. Partner pairing	Activities which organize participants by partners, threes or small groups.	Individual activities, musical mixers, table games, pencil-and-paper games.
5. Changing formations	Activities which begin in one formation and end in another.	Group contests, musical mixers individual activities.
6. Rester	Physically quiet games. The group is usually seated and the activities are entertaining in nature or involve a minimum of group activity and organization.	Paper-and-pencil games, table games, brain teasers, group stunts, leader's stunts, puzzles.
7. Finale	Activities especially suitable for closing an evening's program.	Songs, dances.
8. Just for fun	Activities not having any special purpose except fun.	All of the 14 types identified.

Source: Heaton, *Planning for Social Recreation,* p. 4.

4. Small Group ("Shouting Proverbs")

5. Special ("Bean Bag Toss")

Definition of activity for each formation

1. Circle—The groups are in one or more circles.

2. Lines—The participants are in one or more ranks or columns, such as a relay formation or two facing lines.

3. Mass—Participants are scattered informally around the area in any type of formation.

4. Small Groups—Participants are divided into two or more small groups; they may be seated or standing in circles, lines, mass, or special formations within the small groups.

5. Special—A formation, other than the above, which is characteristic of a specified activity.

Type of activity for each formation

1. Circle—dances, individual activities, musical mixers.

2. Lines—relays, paper-and-pencil games, table games.

3. Mass—brain teasers, group stunts, guessing games, leader's stunts, songs.

4. Small groups—group contests, table games, paper-and-pencil games.

5. Special—puzzles, skill games, table games, and paper-and-pencil games.[11]

PROGRAM PLANNING CONSIDERATIONS IN SOCIAL RECREATION

The following factors need to be considered in planning programs:

1. The age of the participants

2. The sex of the participants

3. The number of participants

4. Weather factors

5. Topography

6. Transportation

7. The timing of the program (for example, prevent duplication of programs)

8. The amount of money needed

[11]Ibid.

9. The supplies and equipment needed
10. Interests and desires of the people to be served
11. The amount of leadership available
12. Nationality, race, occupation, education, and standard of living
13. Amount of leisure time participants have available
14. Facilities and spacial requirements needed
15. The day and time the activity is offered

FORMAT FOR A PORTFOLIO OF SOCIAL RECREATIONAL ACTIVITIES

The following format will be adopted for use to aid leaders in selecting appropriate activities:

Name of game

Type of activity _____ Group formation _____
Purpose of activity _____ No. of participants _____
Age of participants _____ Sex of participants _____
Equipment and supplies _____ Facility _____
　　　　　　　　　　Space _____
Directions: _____

(include diagrams in the directions to better help you lead this game)

Student assignments

This part consists of 12 objectives. You will be called upon to demonstrate your mastery of each objective. Some answers will require written responses. You will also be required to construct 28 social recreation activities.

OBJECTIVE	ACHIEVEMENT OF COMPETENCY
1. To describe social recreation.	Write a definition of social recreation.
2. To describe functions of social recreation.	Write a minimum of 300 words discussing the functions of social recreation.
3. To identify types of social recreational activities.	Identify a minimum of 12 types of social recreation activities.

OBJECTIVE	ACHIEVEMENT OF COMPETENCY
4. To construct social recreational activities.	Construct a minimum of two social recreation activities for each of the fourteen types of social recreation activities identified.
5. To describe the types of social recreation.	Recall and match correctly at least 75% of the types of social recreation activities listed.
6. To describe the purpose of social recreational activities.	Recall and write the purpose of a minimum of six of the social recreational activities identified.
7. To list social recreational activities for specific purposes.	List and construct a minimum of two social recreation activities for each purpose identified.
8. To describe group formations in social recreation.	Recall and match correctly at least 60% of the group formations used in social recreation.
9. To list types of social recreational activities for group formations.	List and construct a minimum of two types of social recreational activities for each group formation.
10. To construct a social recreational program.	Construct a sample one-hour social recreational program in a specific setting.
11. To describe program planning considerations in social recreation.	Orally describe a minimum of ten program planning considerations in social recreation.
12. To write a model for social recreation.	Write a model for a systematic approach in selecting and conducting social recreational activities.

Resources

TEXTBOOKS

ALLEN, CATHERINE L. *Fun for Parties and Programs.* Englewood Cliffs, N.J.: Prentice-Hall, 1956.

BUTLER, GEORGE D. *Introduction to Community Recreation.* New York: McGraw-Hill, 1967.

EISENBERG, HELEN and EISENBERG, LARRY. *Omnibus of Fun.* New York: National Board of Young Men's Christian Associations, 1956.

HARRIS, JANE A. *File of Fun for Social Recreation.* Minneapolis: Burgess, 1962.

HEATON, ISRAEL C. *Planning for Social Recreation.* Provo, Utah: Brigham Young University Press, 1968.

KRAUS, RICHARD. *Recreation Today: Program Planning and Leadership.* New York: Appleton-Century-Crofts, 1966.

POMEROY, JANET. *Recreation for the Physically Handicapped.* New York: Macmillan, 1964.

The Recreation Program. Chicago, Illinois: The Athletic Institute, 1963.

TILLMAN, ALBERT. *The Program Book for Recreation Professionals.* Los Angeles: National Press Books, 1973.

WEISKOPF, DONALD C. *A Guide to Recreation and Leisure.* Boston: Allyn & Bacon, 1975.

Informal activities

Recreation is an extremely diverse field. What is recreation to one person is not necessarily recreation to another. Many people think that recreation is merely sports and games. Indeed, because recreation is a relatively young profession and because sports is one aspect of recreation, some people view recreation as synonymous with physical education. This misconception is most unfortunate for recreation. If sports and recreation were synonymous, many young, elderly, and handicapped people would not have an opportunity to engage in a re-creative experience. Many recreational programs are individually prescribed to meet the needs of people. These person-centered recreation programs offer a wide variety of activities. Informal activities is one example of the wide spectrum of recreational offerings.

Recreation personnel should acquire competencies that will enable them to serve more people. Informal activities appeal to all ages and socioeconomic groups; they can be used with preschoolers as well as with the elderly and the handicapped. Skills are required to lead such activities. The proficient recreation leader is a well-rounded professional who contributes to the field of recreation and ensures that all segments of the population are served. Informal activities offer the leader the opportunity to help people become more knowledgeable, articulate, and wider read and to keep abreast of societal changes.

DEFINITION

Informal activities are socializing, individualistic, and relatively inexpensive to conduct. Participants are afforded many opportunities to learn. Informal activities can be conducted almost anywhere and can serve as an impetus for the formation of special interest clubs.

Types of informal activities

The following recreational activities are considered informal by most recreators:

1. Discussion group
2. Appreciation group
3. Reading
4. Writing
5. Speaking

CHARACTERISTICS OF INFORMAL ACTIVITIES

1. Discussion group
   a. presents more than one view of a topic
   b. potential to grasp interest of all participants
   c. high in participatory and experiential elements
   d. geared to individual needs and interests of participants
   e. should be a learning experience
   f. can be conducted mostly anywhere
   g. has goals, a definite beginning, closing, and an evaluation
   h. supplies and equipment may not be needed
   i. relatively inexpensive to conduct
   j. socialization factor high
   k. highly individualistic
2. Appreciation group
   a. almost identical to discussion group
   b. presents values in a subject
   c. participants gain an appreciation of a topic

3. Reading, writing, and speaking
  a. relatively inexpensive to conduct
  b. can be conducted most anywhere
  c. learning should occur; supplement to educational offerings
  d. highly individualistic
  e. develop an interest to pursue during leisure
  f. personally satisfying
  g. clubs could easily develop
  h. socialization factor high
  i. excellent outlet for creative expression
  j. should be streamlined and informal in recreation settings

SIGNIFICANCE OF INFORMAL ACTIVITIES

A high degree of proficiency is not needed to enjoy informal activities. These activities afford participants an opportunity to meet, learn, and enjoy themselves. All people can benefit from participating in informal activities. In addition, many of these activities have high carryover values. This factor makes the activities valuable to people with a great deal of time with little or nothing to do. Numerous informal activities are fine outlets for creative expression. Because they are highly individual, most informal activities are satisfying to all who participate.

The social aspect of informal activities is important. Many informal activities lend themselves ideally to the formation of clubs. A mutual bond is shared among club members because they have a common interest.

Another significant factor is that informal activities can be a learning experience. A person with a slight speech impediment can practice diction in order to narrate a play. Senior citizens can learn about new benefits of social security through discussion groups. They can learn to respect and enjoy a diversity of things through an appreciation group.

Recreation personnel should be aware that informal activities are beneficial to their programs. Such activities are relatively inexpensive to conduct, supplies and equipment are limited, and most can be administered without elaborate preplanning. Informal activities can also help fill the void often seen between a traditional recreation sports program for the athletic and very little offerings for the not-so-athletic.

FORMAT FOR INFORMAL ACTIVITIES

1. Advantages of a format
  a. lists all elements

    b. saves time and energy in preparation

    c. is a diagnostic tool to measure the activity's effectiveness

    d. clarifies the purpose of an activity

    e. clarifies the group and location

2. Ingredients of a format

    a. goals of activity

    b. recreational activity and/or topic

    c. location

    d. age of participants

    e. equipment and/or supplies needed

    f. number of participants

    g. sex of participants

    h. amount of time

    i. organizational pattern

    j. lead in to activity

    k. summary

    l. evaluation

READING, WRITING, AND SPEAKING ACTIVITIES

1. Reading activities

    a. Great Books program

    b. reading for others

    c. Book Review Club

    d. Expressive Reading Club

    e. New Books Club

    f. Classics Club

    g. talking books

2. Writing activities

    a. business and social letter writing

    b. writing for fun

    c. writing for magazines

    d. technical writing (e.g., how to do it materials)

    e. writing of greeting card verse and poetry

    f. writing short stories

    g. writing plays

    h. newspaper writing

3. Speaking activities
   a. debate
   b. voice and diction clubs
   c. Toastmasters Club
   d. public speaking
   e. play reading
   f. TV and radio speaking
   g. foreign language clubs
   h. story telling techniques

Student assignments

This part consists of nine objectives. You will be called upon to demonstrate your mastery of each objective. Some answers will require written responses. You will be conducting and participating in a variety of informal activities throughout this part of the module.

OBJECTIVE	ACHIEVEMENT OF COMPETENCY
1. To describe importance of informal activities in recreation.	Without the aid of references, write a minimum of 200 words in 30 minutes describing the significance of informal activities in recreation.
2. To describe advantages of leading informal activities.	Orally describe a minimum of three reasons why recreation personnel should acquire skills in leading informal activities.
3. To be able to adapt an informal activity.	Lead an informal activity and adapt that activity for a specific group.
4. To conduct informal activities.	Without the aid of references, conduct a minimum of two informal activities.
5. To construct a format in informal activities.	Without the aid of references, construct a format used to lead informal activities.
6. To identify types of informal activities.	Given a list of ten recreation activities, recall and identify a minimum of eight of the types of informal activities.

OBJECTIVE	ACHIEVEMENT OF COMPETENCY
7. To describe reading, writing, and speaking activities.	Describe a minimum of three recreation experiences for reading, writing, and speaking activities.
8. To construct a portfolio of informal activities.	Construct a portfolio of a minimum of ten informal activities.
9. To describe characteristics of informal activities.	Describe a minimum of two characteristics for each type of informal activity.

Resources

This part is divided into two sections: (1) a list of text-books and (2) specific informal activities.

TEXTBOOKS

BUTLER, GEORGE D. *Introduction to Community Recreation.* New York: McGraw-Hill, 1967.

HJELTE, GEORGE and SHIVERS, JAY S. *Public Administration of Recreational Services.* Philadelphia: Lea and Febiger, 1972.

KRAUS, RICHARD. *Therapeutic Recreation Service Principles and Practices.* Philadelphia: W. B. Saunders, 1973.

POMEROY, JANET. *Recreation for the Physically Handicapped.* New York: Macmillan, 1964.

The Recreation Program. Chicago: The Athletic Institute, 1963.

SHIVERS, JAY S. *Camping Administration, Counseling, Programming.* New York: Appleton-Century-Crofts, 1971.

WEISKOPF, DONALD C. *A Guide to Recreation and Leisure.* Boston: Allyn & Bacon, 1975.

SPECIFIC INFORMAL ACTIVITIES

The informal activities that follow are representative of many that could have been included. Note that the format is identical for all three of the activities.

Form 1. Discussion group.

1. Goals of activity
   a. To grasp interest and attention of all

    b. To get all participants involved

    c. To be a learning experience

    d. To ease participants and familiarize them with other people

    e. To help participants realize that many people have same concerns

    f. To help participants cope with their home lives

2. Recreational activity and/or topic

    a. Discussion group

        (1) "Parents"

3. Location

    a. A solarium in a psychiatric hospital

4. Age of participants

    a. 15-18 years of age

5. Equipment and/or supplies needed

    a. None

6. Number of participants

    a. 10-15

7. Sex of participants

    a. Male and/or female

8. Amount of time

    a. 30 minutes

9. Organizational pattern

    a. Sitting in a circle or around a table

10. Lead in to activity

    a. "I received a phone call last night from my parents. I don't think they will ever think I've grown up. They ask me all sorts of questions, and it seems that no matter where I live, it isn't far enough away. . . not that I don't love them, it isn't that at all. It just seems that I will always be their baby, and they will always like to take care of me. . . to live a life their way. . . to shelter me. My birthday is next week and they want me to come home. . . I just don't know what to do. I want to go home, yet I want to stay here."

11. Summary

    a. lead into similar problems other participants have with their parents.

    b. how does it feel to be a teen-ager?

        1. At what age does dating begin?

        2. How has a brother or sister been influential?

        3. What are your career interests?

        4. What are your interests?

            a. dress?

            b. parents—how do they dress—today's styles?

12. Evaluation
    a. Were objectives met?
    b. What could have been better?
    c. What was particularly good?
    d. What was particularly bad?

Form 2. Appreciation group

1. Goals of activity
   a. To increase the elderly person's awareness of the outdoors
   b. To increase the elderly person's sensory perceptions
   c. To heighten the elderly person's knowledge of autumn.
   d. To show the vast opportunities for observing nature.
   e. To increase the elderly person's confidence that he can still use his senses and find satisfaction in nature
   f. To heighten the elderly person's appreciation for the value of his life
   g. To get all participants involved
   h. To grasp interest and attention of all.
   i. To be a learning experience.
2. Recreational activity and/or topic
   a. Appreciation group
      (1) "Autumn"
3. Location
   a. A nursing home
4. Age of participants
   a. Senior citizens (over 65 years of age)
5. Equipment and/or Supplies Needed
   a. Slides pertaining to autumn that depict changes in trees, flowers in bloom, harvest, etc.
6. Number of participants
   a. 5-10
7. Sex of participants
   a. Male and/or female
8. Amount of time
   a. 75 minutes
9. Organizational pattern
   a. Seated in a semicircle for slide showing
   b. Walk with partner on nature walk

10. Lead in to activity

    a. Slides or film about autumn (changes in trees, flowers in bloom, harvest, etc.)

    b. Discussion of the autumn changes that we might expect to see around the nursing home or neighborhood (foliage colors, migrating birds, weather changes, etc.)

    c. Short "nature walk" around nursing home or neighborhood to note signs of autumn. Participants will be reminded to use all their senses—smell of leaves, sharpness of wind on face, sound of rustling leaves, colors evident in the trees, flowers still blooming, etc.

11. Summary

    a. What we heard, saw, felt, smelled

    b. The beauty and nature experiences available in our neighborhood

    c. The uniqueness of autumn

12. Evaluation

    a. Were objectives met?

    b. What could have been better?

    c. What was particularly good?

    d. What was particularly bad?

Form 3. One act play

1. Goals of activity

    a. Fun

    b. Participation by all participants

    c. Personal growth gained through participation

    d. Supplement to reading, speaking and mimicry skills

    e. Improve memory

    f. Grasp interest and attention of all

    g. To let participants be successful

    h. To increase the mildly retardate's appreciation of self-worth

2. Recreational activity and or topic

    a. One act play

        (1) "Something Smells Fishy"

3. Location

    a. Auditorium or room with curtain

4. Age of participants

    a. 13-15 (mildly retarded)

5. Equipment and/or supplies needed

   a. Paper and pencil for each participant

6. Number of participants

   a. 10

7. Sex of participants

   a. Male and/or female

8. Amount of time

   a. 75 minutes

9. Organizational pattern

   a. Seated in a semicircle initially

   b. Behind curtain for presentation of play

10. Lead in to activity

   a. "Today we are going to talk about some fishy things! Has anyone ever heard of a man called Noah?" Talk about Noah and the Ark.

   b. Parts of the play will be assigned to each participant. Because some parts require more knowledge than others, leader will give parts that all will be successful in.

   c. Participants will read over their lines.

   d. Group will read their lines in sequence.

   e. Leader will ask participants to write their lines down on paper.

   f. Play itself:

SOMETHING SMELLS FISHY!

NARRATOR: One day a poor fisherman named Noah Raffaela was fishing when a strange thing happened.

NOAH: Hmm, that is strange; I feel a tug on one line and I almost caught a fish on the other!

NARRATOR: Meanwhile down in the ocean . . .

CULPRIT OF COD: Ne-a ha ha ho ho. I am going to drive that funny fisherman simply crazy.

KING OF COD: Culprit of Cod! I thought when you were bailed out of the cod cooler (jail), you would behave. I thought you learned your lesson about playing tricks.

COD FISH ONE AND TWO: Move mouth in disgust and say "Bad, Bad."

NARRATOR: As the conversation goes on, something is happening above the water, too.

NOAH: The same thing keeps on happening to me. Hey, maybe if I see it pull on one line and pick up the other, I will get a fish.

NARRATOR: The pole shakes and shakes.

NOAH: Oh no! I feel the tug on one line pull up the other and the pole that shook fell into the water!

CULPRIT OF COD: Blub, blub, blub, blub (translation): See King of Cod, I did not do anything bad; I just sort of scared him a little.

KING OF COD: Blub, blub, blub, blub (translation): Now you listen here, I know (interrupted)

SEA CRYER: Blub, blub, blub, blub (translation): Now hear this: All fish report to the Great Ruler of Cod. All must attend; Barracuda, shark, goldfish, whales, everyone, and fast, too!

KING OF COD: Well, you can't listen to me now, so let's go. I wonder what the old finnie wants now.

GREAT RULER: Friends, fish, countrymen and women lend me your fins. I come before you to stand behind you to tell you something I know nothing about. I want to make one thing perfectly clear . . . hum, where was I? Oh yeah, I called you here on my fish speakers platform to ask your help in a matter of grave concern. Directly above us is a fisherman. I'm going to bring him down to our specimen aquarium. I want all of you to help me get him down here. This is important to the total security of our water. Will you help me?

MASTER OF FROGS: Croak, croak, croak. I've got just the thing. We'll tip over his boat; but first I'll call Dr. Henry Von Kissingership the Fishchiatrist, and I'll take care of the rest of the details.

TWIN OF SEA CRYER: Blub, blub—good idea!

NARRATOR: And so the fisherman was caught and studied and finally one day he sat and thought.

NOAH: I've got to get away somehow, but the fish say I'll never do it. I think they like me—they're always looking at me and laughing. I'm not funny, am I?

NARRATOR: So from that day on, Noah worked hard on a getaway plan. Then, finally two long years later, Noah finally got away.

KING OF COD: Noah, come with me to the fish lab.

NOAH: Now is my chance to put my plan into action! One, two, three crunch!

KING OF COD: You, blub, blub, blub, blub, you've got me on my bullorbuck bone, now I can't move.

NARRATOR: So Noah got out and as soon as he left the water, he turned gray and old and he found his family and told his story to his grandchildren, but he did not tell a grownup because they would have never believed him.

THE END

11. Summary
   a. Who were some participants in the play?
   b. What did you like about your character?
   c. What did you not like about your character?

    d. Who was your favorite character?

    e. Do you think grownups would believe Noah's story?

12. Evaluation

    a. Were objectives met?

    b. What could have been better?

    c. What was particularly bad?

    d. What was particularly good?

Games of low organization

Many recreational programs place a heavy emphasis on team sports and athletics. Undoubtedly, these activities are valuable and should be included in any recreational program. However, a program should not be set up so as to exclude people who do not or cannot participate in the more vigorous physical activities.

That low-organized games have a place in a well-rounded, person-centered recreational program is fact. Games of low organization can be offered to include many individuals who would otherwise not be participating if these activities were not available. The recreator can use games as a tool to help participants progress toward accomplishing objectives. He should have the necessary skills to lead participants in many activities. The recreator is professionally obligated to serve all segments of society. A repertoire of low-organized games is one way of providing the recreation leader with a needed skill.

DEFINITIONS

• *Pomeroy:* Low-organized games are simple informal games that are played without official rules. They include many of the traditional children's games that vary with local customs and in different sections of the country. They are very popular on playgrounds. They can be played by small or large groups, both indoors or out. [12]

• *Miller and Whitcomb:* "Low organization activities may be described as activities requiring a minimum of organization while allowing for maximum active participation by all . . . in the group."[13]

---

[12] Pomeroy, *Recreation for the Physically Handicapped*, p. 307.

[13] Arthur G. Miller and Virginia Whitcomb, *Physical Education in the Elementary School Curriculum* (Englewood Cliffs, N.J.: Prentice-Hall, 1969), p. 87.

• *Schurr:* "[Low organization games] involve few and simple rules and little or no equipment; they utilize the simple basic skills, they may be adapted to suit the space available, and they may be played by groups of various sizes."[14]

TYPES

The following are five types of low-organized activities:

1. Running and tag games
2. Relays
3. Classroom and inactive games
4. Circle games
5. Simple ball games

CHARACTERISTICS

A. Running and tag games

1. Involve large muscle activity

2. Provide opportunity for each participant to belong to the group and still be "it"

3. Afford participants purposeful, vigorous activity

4. Provide fun and excitement

5. Provide opportunity for participants to express themselves, pretend, and dramatize

B. Relays

1. Consist of teams of no more than six members

2. Require team members to take their turn at the proper time

3. Are an excellent means of reviewing skills

4. Give participants experience of working with and for a team

5. Are physically and emotionally exhausting

6. Require specific instruction

C. Classroom and inactive games

1. Are used when there is no opportunity to use outdoor or gymnasium space

2. Do not require speed in determining winner

3. Require explanation of safety hazards and establishment and maintainence of safety rules

4. Require minimum of space

[14]Evelyn L. Schurr, *Movement Experiences for Children* (New York: Appleton-Century-Crofts, 1967), p. 315.

D. Circle games

1. Provide a confined area for participants
2. Provide excellent formation to explain rules and introduce skills
3. Frequently result in a tendency to exclude persons from active participation
4. Are usually associated with children

E. Simple ball games

1. Afford participants a maximum amount of ball handling and the learning of basic ball skills
2. Develop aim, accuracy, and fine muscle coordination
3. Provide leadup to games enjoyed in later years
4. Are usually self-motivating because of the opportunity to "play ball"

SIGNIFICANCE OF GAMES OF LOW ORGANIZATION IN RECREATION

A low-organized game may be used as a vehicle to improve a person intellectually, physically, socially, and emotionally. Games of low organization can be presented to coincide with and strengthen application of knowledge learned. Most games have a rich cultural heritage that the recreator can capitalize upon to stress an appreciation and knowledge about other lands and people. Games of low organization afford participants an opportunity to use and develop basic skills that can serve as a foundation for games played and enjoyed in later years. Through participation in games, people increase their endurance, flexibility, agility, speed, reaction time, and the capacity to follow directions. Additionally, participants can acquire self-discipline, group spirit, recognition, leadership traits, competitiveness, group cooperation, and sportsmanship.

By their very nature, games of low organization are not for the highly skilled athlete. Rather, they serve as a basis to improve skills, have fun, and ensure that all participate. Recreation is an extremely diverse field. Recreators must strive to present activities that all can engage in and benefit from. Indeed, most low-organized games stress participation rather than winning at all cost. Many people (that is, the very young, the ill, handicapped, and disabled) have not acquired a great deal of proficiency in sports. They should, however, not be excluded from a recreation program. Games of low organization can be used to bridge the gap between work and home and help to foster concepts of self-worth.

CONSIDERATIONS IN CONDUCTING GAMES OF LOW ORGANIZATION

The following are methods that have been successful in conducting low organized games:

1. Know the rules thoroughly
2. Have all equipment ready and accessible
3. Mark lines if necessary
4. Condense rules for presentation in simplest and shortest terms
5. Provide for easy identification for each team
6. Enforce rules immediately
7. Play outside if possible
8. When interest appears to wane, stop the activity
9. Never use walls as turning lines
10. Demonstrate

FORMAT FOR GAMES OF LOW ORGANIZATION

The following are salient features to be included in a format for games of low organization:

1. Name of activity
2. Skills
3. Age of participants
4. Number of participants
5. Equipment
6. Formation
7. Description

Student assignments

This part consists of 11 objectives. You will be called upon to demonstrate your mastery of each objective. Some answers will require written responses. You will be conducting, adapting, and demonstrating activities of low organization throughout this part of the module.

OBJECTIVE	ACHIEVEMENT OF COMPETENCY
1. To define low-organized games.	Write a definition of games of low organization.
2. To describe advantages of leading games of low organization.	Orally describe a minimum of three advantages why recreation personnel should acquire skills in leading games of low organization.

OBJECTIVE	ACHIEVEMENT OF COMPETENCY
3. To determine significance of low-organized games.	Without the aid of references, write a minimum of 200 words in 30 minutes describing the significance of games of low organization in recreation.
4. To describe types of low-organized activities.	Describe the types of low-organized activities in recreation.
5. To indicate characteristics of low-organized activities.	Describe a minimum of four characterisitcs of low-organized activities.
6. To conduct games of low organization.	Without the aid of references, conduct a minimum of two games of low organization.
7. To adapt games of low organization.	Lead a low-organized game and adapt that game for a specific group.
8. To identify types of low-organized games.	Given a list of ten recreational activities, recall and identify a minimum of eight of the types of low-organized games.
9. To develop a portfolio of games of low organization.	Develop a portfolio containing a minimum of 15 games of low organization.
10. To depict considerations in leading games of low organization.	Describe a minimum of seven characteristics to be followed in conducting low-organized games.
11. To develop a format to lead low-organized games.	Without the aid of references, construct a format used to lead low-organized games.

Resources

This part is divided into two sections: (1) a list of reference materials and (2) specific low-organized games.

TEXTBOOKS

ANDERSON, MARIAN H.; ELLIOT, MARGARET E.; and LA BERGE, JEANNE. *Play with a Purpose*. New York: Harper & Row, 1972.

BANCROFT, J. *Games.* New York: Macmillan, 1954.

CORBIN, CHARLES B. *Becoming Physically Educated in the Elementary School.* Philadelphia: Lea and Febiger, 1969.

CRATTY, BRYANT J. *Active Learning Games to Enhance Academic Abilities.* Englewood Cliffs, N.J.: Prentice-Hall, 1971.

FAIT, HOLLIS F. *Physical Education for the Elementary School Child: Experiences in Movement.* Philadelphia: W. B. Saunders, 1971.

MILLER, ARTHUR G., and WHITCOMB, VIRGINIA. *Physical Education in the Elementary School Curriculum.* Englewood Cliffs, N.J.: Prentice-Hall, 1969.

POMEROY, JANET. *Recreation for the Physically Handicapped.* New York: Macmillan, 1964.

SCHURR, EVELYN L. *Movement Experiences for Children.* New York: Appleton-Century-Crofts, 1967.

VANNIER, MARYHELEN, and FOSTER, MILDRED. *Teaching Physical Education in Elementary Schools.* Philadelphia: W. B. Saunders, 1968.

WILLGOOSE, CARL E. *The Curriculum in Physical Education.* Englewood Cliffs, N.J.: Prentice-Hall, 1969.

ARTICLES

GRANDGENETT, RICHARD. "Individualizing PE in the Primary Grades." *Journal of Physical Education and Recreation,* vol. 47, no. 2 (February 1976): 51.

KIRK, JAMES W. "New Games People Are Playing." *Journal of Physical Education and Recreation,* vol. 47, no. 4 (April 1976): 40.

PERRIGO, ROY. "Individualizing PE for Intermediate Grades." *Journal of Physical Education and Recreation,* vol. 47, no. 2 (February 1976): 51-52.

FILM

New Designs in Elementary Physical Education. Washington, D.C.: American Association for Health, Physical Education, and Recreation Film Sales.

SPECIFIC LOW-ORGANIZED GAMES

The low-organized games that follow are representative of many that could have been included. Note that the format is identical for each of the five activities presented.

Form 1. Running and tag game

1. Name of activity: Midnight
2. Skills: Running, tagging, dodging, listening
3. Age of participants: 6-9
4. Number of participants: 8-30
5. Equipment: None
6. Formation: Large playing area with end lines, and defined side lines.
7. Description: One player is the fox and the other players are the chickens. The fox is in his den, a small area marked off at one end of the play space. The chickens approach his den asking, "What time is it?" The fox may answer any clock time. When he answers "Midnight!" that is his signal that he is going to chase the chickens. At the signal, the chickens run for safety. They are safe when they reach a specified area or goal line at the opposite end of the play space. Any who are caught by the fox before they reach safety are taken to his den; and they assist in catching the chickens when the fox again calls the signal. The chickens approach the fox's den and the game continues until all of the players are tagged.

Form 2. Relay

1. Name of activity: Strideball Relay
2. Skills: Running, ball rolling
3. Age of participants: 8-12
4. Number of participants: teams of 6
5. Equipment: One ball for each team
6. Formation: File; players standing with feet in a wide side-stride position
7. Description: Teams stand with legs apart. Each player rolls ball back through his legs. The end player receives the ball, picks it up and runs down the left-hand side of his team to the front of the line. All players move back one space in line and the ball is started again. Team back to starting position first wins.

Form 3. Classroom and inactive game

1. Name of activity: Up Jenkins
2. Skills: Alertness, concentration, eye-hand coordination

54

3. Age of participants: 7-70
4. Number of participants: 6 per team
5. Equipment: A coin
6. Formation: File; teams sitting in a line formation on the floor
7. Description: There are two teams sitting on the floor facing each other. One team is given a coin and begins passing it up and down the line behind their backs. On the signal "Up Jenkins," all hands are raised in the air. On "Down Jenkins," hands must be struck palms down on floor in front of where they are sitting. Other team attempts to guess who has coin.

Form 4. Circle game

1. Name of activity: Circle Soccer
2. Skills: Kicking, trapping
3. Age of participants: 7-10
4. Number of participants: 8-30
5. Equipment: One soccer ball
6. Formation: Circle
7. Description: Participants are in a circle formation. One half group on one half circle and other half composing rest of circle. Each team attempts to kick ball through other half's side. Point scored for every one kicked through below shoulder height. Ball going between two different teams does not count.

Form 5. Simple ball game

1. Name of activity: Fox and Squirrel
2. Skills: Ball handling
3. Age of participants: 6-8
4. Number of participants: 8-10 per group
5. Equipment: One 8 inch ball, one tennis ball
6. Formation: Circle
7. Description: The Fox (8 inch ball) is held in circle opposite Squirrel (tennis ball). On signal, "Go!" both objects are started around the circle, the fox trying to catch the squirrel. The fox may change direction at any time. The squirrel must change direction only to avoid being caught.

Sports

Sports have traditionally maintained a high popularity in recreation programs. People participate in sports because they are fun. Weiskopf indicates that "the urge to play for enjoyment, satisfaction, accomplishment, and fellowship accounts for the majority of participants." [15] Sports are high in participatory and experiential elements; people enjoy engaging in sports activities because they are directly and actively involved. They serve as a means toward physical fitness, competition, and as a "safety valve." These considerations are important ones in twentieth-century America. In a country that is rapidly becoming afflicted with "spectatoritis," sports are in a position of promoting participation by all. Participation enhances a person's physical fitness; sports have been shown to be a positive factor in improving and developing the human body. A person's mental and emotional well-being is directly related to his physical being. An inseperable element of sports is its potential for socialization. This is particularly true in dual and team sports. Many people today desperately need to belong and to become committed to someone or something. Sports can help fill this need. Sports can also be the catalyst for the expression of aggressive, combative, and competitive behavior.

DEFINITIONS

• *Individual sports:* constitute those activities that can be played with satisfaction by a single individual.

• *Dual sports:* are those activities that require two individuals to make playing possible.

• *Team sports:* generally require a minimum of four players on a team. Participants become a team which ordinarily participates against another team.

• *Combative sports:* are those activities that involve one person against another in direct combat.

CLASSIFICATION OF SPORTS

1. *Individual sports:* archery, auto racing, bicycling, boating, bowling, canoeing, casting, creative rhythms and dance, conditioning, curling,

[15]Weiskopf, *A Guide to Recreation and Leisure*, p. 249.

darts, diving, fishing, golf, gymnastics, handball, hiking, horseback riding, hunting, ice skating, roller skating, rope jumping, shooting, skiing, sky diving, sledding, slimnastics, spelunking, squash, swimming, tetherball, track and field, trampoline, weight lifting, yoga

2. *Dual sports:* badminton, billiards, bowling, boxing, croquet, curling, darts, fencing, four square, golf, handball, hopscotch, horseshoes, judo, lawn bowling, paddle tennis, platform tennis, racquet ball, rogue, shuffleboard, squash, table tennis, tandem bicycling, tennis, tetherball, tobogganing, wrestling

3. *Team sports:* baseball, basketball, field hockey, flag football, floor hockey, gator ball, ice hockey, lacrosse, polo, rugby, soccer, softball, speedball, street hockey, swimming, tackle football, team handball, touch football, track and field, volleyball, wrestling

4. *Combative sports:* boxing, fencing, gator ball, judo, karate, wrestling

PROGRAM GOALS

The following are goals to be derived from participation in sports:

1. To develop participants physically, socially, emotionally, and mentally.

2. To educate participants through the activity by helping them to develop as totally functioning individuals while engaging in activities suited for their needs, interests, and capabilities.

3. To develop physical fitness.

4. To develop strength, agility, and coordination.

5. To develop endurance to resist fatigue, perform daily tasks, and meet energy stresses.

6. To promote opportunities for developing self-confidence, sociability, initiative, self-direction, and a feeling of belonging.

7. To promote concepts of sportsmanship.

8. To develop participation in leisure activities to engage in throughout one's life.

9. To develop concepts of health and safety applicable to carryover in later years.

10. To develop proficiencies in those activities commensurate with participation in later years.

11. To provide opportunities for creative thinking, dynamic leadership, and intelligent decision-making.

12. To provide opportunities for individuals to participate in activities that are vigorous, purposeful, challenging, creative, and fun and are consistent with human growth and development of participants.

13. To provide opportunities to "let off steam" in a competitive environment.

LEADUP GAMES

Recreators should recognize that sports activities should be presented in a logical, developmental, and sequential order. This will greatly aid fun aspects of programs. If an activity is too difficult for a specific group of participants, the activity should be modified and presented in a different manner. Recreators should have the competency to determine when specific activities are not meeting the needs of the participants. They should also acquire the skill to present the activity in a manner so that individual participants will be successful. A leadup activity preceding the regular activity is often the only necessary element. In this way individuals will acquire a modicum of skill in which to participate successfully in the regular activity.

Following examples show leadup activities applicable for specific activities.

BOWLING

Since bowling has long been such a favorite pastime in American life, some understanding of the game should be discussed with the participants as early as possible. Many portable bowling games are now manufactured which allow bowling right in the recreation center.

A. *Number of pins*
   1. *Regular bowling.* Ten pins are used, are set up triangularly, and are numbered from one to ten from left to right, number 1 being in the first row; 2 and 3 in the second; 4, 5, and 6 in the third; 7, 8, 9, and 10 in the last. Each pin is worth a point.
   2. *Five pins.* The sets used in school consist of five pins hanging on a crossbar. They are not numbered as in regular bowling according to total number of pins but according to point value which is as follows: 2, 3, 5, 3, 2.
B. *Procedure*
   1. *Regular bowling.* A game is ten frames long. A player takes two

rolls consecutively for a frame. The only exception would be when a strike occurs, and this is explained later.

2. *Five pins.* A game of five pins also consists of ten frames. However, three rolls are taken at one time instead of two. Again, an exception would be when a strike occurs.

C. *Strike*

1. *Regular bowling.* A strike occurs when all ten pins are knocked down on the first roll. It is designated as such: (X).

2. *Five pins.* Since it is impossible to hit all the pins down in one roll, a strike occurs when all pins are down on two rolls.

The method of scoring is very similar. Since three balls are given each frame, three small squares are needed instead of two. And, instead of counting each pin as one point, they each have a value (2,3,5,3,2). Hence, the number fifteen is worked with instead of ten.

Strike = 15 + next two
Spare = 15 + next one

It is still possible to get 30 points per frame so the highest possible score is still 300.

1	2	3	4	5	6	7	8	9	10
2|3|2	5|X	5|5|3	5|5|/	5|2|5	5|5|/				
7	32	45	65	77					

Briefly, frame one shows 2 points on the first roll, 3 on the second, 2 on the third, for a total of 7. A strike was rolled in frame two. Hence, 15 + 5 + 5 or 25 is added to 7 to give a running score of 32. Frame three has 13 points (5 + 5 + 3) added to 32 to give 45.

A spare was rolled in frame four. Hence, 15 + 5 or 20 was added to the 45 to give running score of 65. No running score can be put in frame six until the first ball of frame seven is rolled.

D. *Spare*

1. *Regular bowling.* A spare occurs when all ten pins are knocked down in two rolls. It is signified in the scoring box as (/).

2. *Five pins.* A spare occurs when all five pins are knocked down in three rolls.

E. *Scoring*

1. *Regular bowling.* A game is divided into ten frames or squares each with two smaller squares in the upper left-hand corner. The small squares tell how many pins were knocked down in each frame, whereas the larger square always consists of the total score.

1	2	3	4	5	6	7	8	9	10
2 3	4 5	X	2 6	/	8 /				
5	14	32	40	58					

Frame number one tells us two pins were knocked down on the first ball and three on the second. Hence, there is a total of 5. In frame two, four pins were knocked down on the first and five on the second. Those nine pins were added to the five previous ones to give a running score of 14.

Scoring strikes and spares are where problems occur. The "reward" for rolling a strike is that it not only counts as just 10 total points for that frame but 10 points plus whatever is rolled on the next two balls. A strike was rolled in frame three. Note where the "X" is placed. Now, on the next two balls 8 points were scored. Thus, 10 plus the next two, or 10 plus 8, or 18 is the total score of frame three which is added to total score of frame two to give the running score of 32. Then, since no mark (strike or spare) has recurred, that is added to the 8 in frame four to give running total of 40.

The "reward" for rolling a spare (/) is 10 points plus whatever is knocked down on the next one ball or following ball, as will be the case. In frame five, a spare occurred. Thus, the total score for frame five is 10 points plus the next ball (8) or 18. This gives the running score of 58. Since another spare occurred in frame six, a running score cannot be put in until the next ball is rolled, which will be the first ball in frame seven.

Strike = 10 + next two
Spare = 10 + next one

The highest possible score is attained when a strike is rolled in each frame. This would give the cherished 300 "perfect" game.

CALL NUMBER BASKETBALL (INDOOR–OUTDOOR)

A. *Formation:* Teams are lined up behind their sidelines. Two balls are placed in center of the court, one for each team.

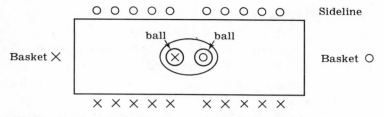

Basket ✕   Sideline   Basket ○

B. *Equipment:* Two basketballs, two deck tennis rings (to hold ball in place), and two basketball goals.

C. *Skills:* Dribbling and shooting

D. *Game:* The object of the game is for a member of one team to make a basket before a member of the opposite team with the corresponding number.

E. *Playing rules*

   1. Each team member has a number corresponding to the number of a player on the opposing team. Once everyone has a number, the team may line up in any order behind their sideline.

   2. The game is started by the leader calling a number.

   3. Players called must pick up their own ball and dribble to their basket.

   4. Players must dribble to their basket before shooting.

   5. If any player loses control of his dribble, he must return to the spot where he lost control and resume play from that spot.

   6. Any basket made by a player who failed to dribble does not count. The player must return the ball to the center of court and proceed to dribble to the basket.

   7. Players may shoot any shot in attempting to make a basket.

   8. Players keep shooting until one of the shooters makes a basket.

   9. If both players make a basket, the player whose ball passes through the rim first, scores for his team. If both players make a basket at the same time, they both score. All play stops after first basket is made.

   10. Once a basket is made, both players return their ball to the center of the court in order to restart the game.

   11. The leader will call the next number and continue this procedure until all numbers have been called.

F. *Scoring*

   1. Each basket counts as one point.

   2. The team with most points at the end of the game wins.

G. *Teaching suggestions*

1. Emphasize dribbling to the basket before shooting.

2. After each game, the leader should reassign numbers in order to give players a chance to dribble and shoot against someone else.

3. Basket shooting can be limited to three shots each or a time limit of thirty seconds.

4. If the game is played in an area without baskets, car tires can be substituted for baskets. Tires should be stacked four (4) high and placed twelve (12) feet from a restraining line. (closer for younger children). Players should shoot from behind the restraining line. If they miss the basket they should retrieve the ball and shoot again after dribbling back to the restraining line. When retrieving the ball, they are not allowed to bounce the ball off the floor into the tires. Two areas of four tires high should be set up for this game.

H. *Variations* This game can be played with four teams instead of two. Two teams would shoot at the same basket. All rules apply to this game as in the other game. In an area without baskets, four car tire baskets can be set up.

LEADUP GAMES

A. *Football goal pass*

Objective: Practice passing, receiving, and pass defense.

Procedure: Two teams. Each team has three goal players and (X) field players. Goal players must remain in the goal area in the rear of their opponents' field. The ball is given to a goal player on one team. To initiate play, he throws a forward pass to one of his field players. Field players can pass to each other but do not score a point unless they complete a pass to one of their goal players. Goal players must receive the ball in their goal area to score. See diagram.

Goal B
Field A
Field B
Goal A

Players in field A pass to players in goal A.

Players in field B pass to players in goal B.

Players in fields A and B attempt to intercept the pass.

B. *Overtake*

Objective: Practice forward pass and receiving.

Procedure: Half the players stand on an outer circle and other half on an inner circle, both circles facing each other. Each circle counts off by two's. All number 1 players in both circles are on one team, and number 2 players are the other team. On signal, a player from one team, standing on outer circle, and a player from opposite team, standing on inner circle, start the balls. Each starter passes to his teammate on the other circle; inner to outer, outer to inner. The ball for each team travels in the same direction around the circle. The team which passes the ball around the circle two times and has the ball in the starter's hands, wins one point. If one team "overtakes" the other while passing, it scores two points. The first team scoring five points wins the game.

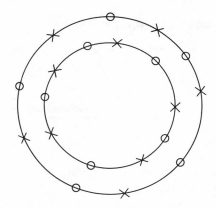

C. *Snatch the football*

Objective: Practice three and four point stances and moving on signal.

Procedure: Two teams line up in parallel lines equidistant from a football placed in the center of the teams. Each player has a number. One number is called. On a whistle or the word "go," both players charge off the line and attempt to bring the football back to their line without being tagged. The opponent must tag with both hands or retrieve the flag (when flag football belts are available).

D. *Quarterback and ends drill*

Objective: Practice for quarterback. Use commands "Down," "Set," "Go!" Practice in centering the ball. Practice for ends in running pass patterns.

Procedure: Arrange squads as shown in the diagram. The first player on both "A" squads will serve as centers. The first player on both "B" squads will serve as quarterbacks. They position themselves between their squads as shown. The next players in all squads become ends— two ends for each quarterback.

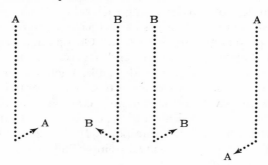

Student assignments

This part consists of nine objectives. You will be called upon to demonstrate your mastery of each objective. Some answers will require written responses.

OBJECTIVE	ACHIEVEMENT OF COMPETENCY
1. To define individual, dual, team, and combative sports.	Write a definition of individual, dual, team, and combative sports.
2. To describe advantages of leading sports activities.	Orally describe a minimum of three reasons why recreation personnel should acquire skills in leading sports activities.
3. To determine significance of sports activities.	Without the aid of references, write a minimum of 200 words in 30 minutes describing the significance of sports activities.
4. To list program goals in sports.	List a minimum of 10 of 13 program goals in sports activities.
5. To indicate advantages of lead-up games.	Orally describe at least three advantages of lead-up games in sports.
6. To identify classification of sports.	Given a list of seven activities, recall and identify a minimum of five sports within each classification.

OBJECTIVE	ACHIEVEMENT OF COMPETENCY
7. To list sports within each category.	List a minimum of four sports within each classification.
8. To construct an activity.	Construct a minimum of one sports activity within each classification.
9. To lead sports activities.	Lead a minimum of four sports activities.

Resources

TEXTBOOKS

ANDERSON, MARIAN H.; ELLIOT, MARGARET E.; and LA BERGE, JEANNE. *Play with a Purpose.* New York: Harper & Row, 1972.

ANDERSON, M. et al. *Physical Education Methods for Elementary Schools.* Philadelphia: W. B. Saunders, 1949.

BANCROFT, J. *Games.* New York: Macmillan, 1954.

CAIN, E., and HUNT, S. *Games the World Around.* New York: Ronald Press, 1941.

DECARLO, T. *Handbook of Progressive Gymnastics.* Englewood Cliffs, N.J.: Prentice-Hall, 1963.

HALSEY, E., and PORTER, L. *Physical Education for Children.* New York: Holt, Rinehart, and Winston, 1958.

HENDMAN, D. *The Complete Book of Games and Stunts.* Englewood Cliffs, N.J.: Prentice-Hall, 1963.

The Recreation Program. Chicago: The Athletic Institute, 1963.

WEISKOPF, DONALD C. *A Guide to Recreation and Leisure.* Boston: Allyn & Bacon, 1975.

WILLGOOSE, CARL E. *The Curriculum in Physical Education.* Englewood Cliffs, N.J.: Prentice-Hall, 1969.

Music

Music is an important function in a well-rounded recreation program. Musical activities are applicable and interesting to every age group. In addition, specific musical activities are easily adapted to meet the needs, abilities, and interests of a large percentage of participants. The full range, thrust, and potential of musical activities can be used to create moods: chamber music for a relaxed mood, "The Farmer in the Dell" for exuberance, or "God Bless America" for patriotism. Musical activities have an eclectic appeal and, depending upon the environment and circumstances, can be used in a myriad of ways. A high percentage of recreational activities take on greater significance when interrelated with music. Some examples are:

1. *singing* "Auld Lang Syne" on the last day of camp
2. *playing* in a musical band at a dance
3. *listening* to stereo music while dining
4. *moving rhythmically* to act out a story
5. *creating* a rhythm-band

Music is successful as a therapeutic tool. The soothing effect that music has on clients in therapeutic recreational settings has influenced the establishment of "Music Therapy" courses in universities throughout the country. Kraus indicates that "music may be used to provide a release for tension and emotional expression, to encourage and stimulate language and communication, to improve group interaction and enhance the self-image of residents." [16] Although the therapeutic value of music has not been substantiated, many medical personnel believe that music is important to the total rehabilitation of many patients.

DEFINITIONS

• *Music:* "Music is a form of human expression of pleasing and melodious combinations of tones." [17] "Music is simply sounds that stir our emotions, please us, or upset us, whether we are making them or listening to them." [18]

• *Singing:* Singing is a generic form of vocal music.

• *Playing:* Playing (i.e., instrumental) music is to make music ". . . through the use of something outside of one's body." [19]

• *Listening:* Listening is an operative quality that elicits an active response and interaction between what is heard and what is thought.

[16]Richard Kraus, *Therapeutic Recreation Service Principles and Practices*. (Philadelphia: W. B. Saunders, 1973), p. 108.

[17]H. Dan Corbin, *Recreation Leadership*. Englewood Cliffs, N.J.: Prentice-Hall, 1959), p. 251.

[18]Tillman, *The Program Book for Recreation Professionals*, p. 179.

[19]*The Recreation Program* (Chicago: The Athletic Institute, 1963), p. 207.

CLASSIFICATION OF MUSIC ACTIVITIES

Although universality is an inherent characteristic of music activities, a simple scheme for classifying the activities is needed. Recreators have categorized music activities in the following six broad areas:

1. singing (vocal)
2. playing (instrumental)
3. listening
4. rhythmic movement
5. creating
6. combined activities[20]

Following is a list of activities within each of the six categories; it is by no means all-inclusive. Rather, it is intended to demonstrate those specific activities that are included within the categories.

1. *Singing:* informal singing, community sings, choruses, quartets and other ensembles, glee clubs, a cappella choirs, madrigal groups, solos, and barbershop quartets.

2. *Playing:* rhythm instruments, simple melody instruments, simple harmony instruments, fretted instruments, bands, orchestras, ensembles and chamber music groups, solos, and duets.

3. *Listening:* incidental hearing, home music, records, radio and television, and live concerts.

4. *Rhythmic movement:* purely rhythmic, simple interpretive singing games, play party games, and folk dances.

5. *Creating:* song making, creative music, Orff instruments, and other music-making.

6. *Combined activities:* folk dancing, musical charades, shadow plays, festivals, seasonal and holiday programs, pageants, caroling, community programs, variety shows, talent shows, sports events (swimming and skating), park concerts, operettas, and opera.[21]

VALUES OF MUSIC ACTIVITIES

Tillman offers a generic, all-emcompassing value of music for the recreator. He indicates that "the ability to set mood in those who receive music as listeners and, more importantly, to allow those who perform or

[20]Ibid., p. 201.
[21]Ibid.

67

create music to express their moods and ideas" is the over-riding value of music that should be derived in a recreation program.[22] Tillman specifies the following as additional values of music activities:

1. Music controls behavior.
2. Music requires cooperation and develops group unity.
3. Music is a background tool for other types of program activities.
4. Music is a therapeutic device.
5. Music is aesthetic.[23]

Musical activities constitute, of course, many of the same values commensurate with the generic field of recreation: enjoyment, fun, participating because of an inner desire to do so, and so forth. The following items are additional reasons for including music activities in recreation programs.

1. To enable each participant to develop his aesthetic potential to the utmost[24]
2. To effectively transmit specific cultural heritage to succeeding generations
3. To provide an outlet for creativity and self-expression
4. To provide participants with a source of enjoyment that is usable throughout life

Student assignments

This part consists of eight objectives. You will be called upon to demonstrate your mastery of each objective. Some answers will require written responses.

OBJECTIVE	ACHIEVEMENT OF COMPETENCY
1. To define music, singing, playing, and listening.	Write a definition of music, singing, playing, and listening.
2. To describe advantages of leading music activities.	Indicate at least five reasons why recreation personnel should acquire skills in leading music activities.

[22]Tillman, *The Program Book for Recreation Professionals*, p. 180.
[23]Ibid.
[24]Abraham H. Maslow, "Music Education and Peak Experience," *Music Educators Journal*, vol. 54 (February 1968): 72ff.

OBJECTIVE	ACHIEVEMENT OF COMPETENCY
3. To determine significance of music.	Write a minimum of 200 words describing the importance of music activities.
4. To describe values of music activities.	List six values of music activities in recreation.
5. To write activities within each classification of music activities.	List a minimum of six activities within singing, playing, listening, and combined activities.
6. To write activities within each classification of music activities.	List a minimum of three activities within rhythmic movement and creating activities.
7. To construct an activity.	Construct a minimum of one music activity within each classification.
8. To lead music activities.	Conduct at least six music activities.

Resources

This part is divided into two sections: (1) a list of reference materials and (2) specific activities.

TEXTBOOKS

ANDRESS, BARBARA et al. *Music in Early Childhood*. Washington, D.C.: Music Educators National Conference, 1973.

BAIRD, PEGGY FLANAGAN. *Music Books for the Elementary School Library*. Washington, D.C.: Music Educators National Conference, 1972.

BOYLE, J. DAVID, comp. *Instructional Objectives in Music*. Washington, D.C.: Music Educators National Conference, 1974.

BUTLER, GEORGE D. *Introduction to Community Recreation*. New York: McGraw-Hill, 1967.

CORBIN, H. DAN. *Recreation Leadership*. Englewood Cliffs, N.J.: Prentice-Hall, 1959.

GARY, CHARLES L., and LANDIS, BETH. *The Comprehensive Music Program*. Washington, D.C.: Music Educators National Conference, 1973.

GRAHAM, RICHARD M., comp. *Music for the Exceptional Child*. Washington, D.C.: Music Educators National Conference, 1975.

KRAUS, RICHARD. *Recreation Today: Program Planning and Leadership*. New York: Appleton-Century-Crofts, 1966.

KRAUS, RICHARD G., and BATES, BARBARA J. *Recreation Leadership and Supervision: Guidelines for Professional Development*. Philadelphia: W. B. Saunders, 1975.

The Recreation Program. Chicago: The Athletic Institute, 1963.

SESSOMS, H. DOUGLAS; MEYER, HAROLD D.; and BRIGHTBILL, CHARLES K. *Leisure Services*. Englewood Cliffs, N.J.: Prentice-Hall, 1975.

SHIVERS, JAY S. *Camping: Administration, Counseling, Programming*. New York: Appleton-Century-Crofts, 1971.

TILLMAN, ALBERT. *The Program Book for Recreation Professionals*. Los Angeles: National Press Books, 1973.

WEISKOPF, DONALD C. *A Guide to Recreation and Leisure*. Boston: Allyn & Bacon, 1975.

WILSON, HARRY R. et al. *Growing with Music*. Englewood Cliffs, N.J.: Prentice-Hall, 1970.

ARTICLES

MASLOW, ABRAHAM. "Music Education and Peak Experience." *Music Educators Journal*, vol. 54 (February 1968).

WENNER, GENE C., et al. "IMPACT". *Music Educators Journal*, vol. 59 (January 1973).

"Arts Impact: Curriculum for Change—A Summary Report." University Park, Pa.: The Arts Impact Evaluation Team, 1973.

"Contemporary Music Project." *Music Educators Journal*, vol. 59 (May 1973).

"Goals and Objectives for Music Education." *Music Educators Journal*, vol. 57 (December 1970).

SPECIFIC MUSIC ACTIVITIES

The music activities that follow are representative of many that could have been included. They illustrate five types of music activities.

Singing: "Throw It Out the Window"*

TRADITIONAL

Home tone: F
Starting note: A (mi, 3)
Key: F Major

Cheerfully

1. Sim - ple Si - mon met — a pie - man, Go - ing to the
2. Lit - tle Miss Muf - fet sat on a tuf - fet, Eat - ing her curds and
3. Old — King Cole was a mer - ry old soul, A mer - ry old soul was

fair,— Said Sim - ple Si - mon to — the pie - man,"Throw it out the
whey!— A - long came a spi - der and sat down be-side her;She threw him out the
he.— He called for his pipe and he called for his bowl;— And threw themout the

win - dow!
win - dow! The win-dow,— the win-dow,— Oh, throw it out the win-dow,"—
win - dow!

D. S. al Fine

In this traditional nonsense song, a novel ending is added to familiar nursery rhymes.

MUSICAL LEARNING

• D. S. al Fine (Dal Segno al Fine) in meas. 12 means go back to the sign ( ) and complete the verse at Fine. Notice that the word "window" is consistently sung to a syncopated rhythm. It is sung this way because of the word rhythm. Syncopated rhythms are used for those words that have a spoken rhythm which closely parallels the melodic rhythm.

PERFORMANCE   This is a good song for chording on both the piano and the autoharp, since only two chords, F and C₇ are used (see p. 81).

It would be easy for the students to make up a second vocal part for this song. By restricting themselves to only the tones of the I chord (F-A-C) and the C₇ chord (C-E-G-B♭), they can compose an interesting and varied part.

You can make up additional verses using Mother Goose rhymes. Try using "Little Jack Horner," or "Hey, Diddle, Diddle." You will have to change the last line of each poem. For example, in "Little Jack Horner," you might have:

He put in his thumb
And pulled out a plum,
And threw it out the window.

*From Growing with Music Book 4 Teacher's Edition by Harry R. Wilson and others. © 1970 by Prentice-Hall, Inc., Englewood Cliffs, N.J. Reprinted by permission.

Playing: "Escalator Song"*

WORDS BY MADELEINE A. DUFAY
NORWEGIAN FOLK TUNE
Record 6, Side B

Home tone: C
Starting note: C (*do*, 1)
Key: C Major

MUSICAL LEARNING

• Use this song to show how a melody grows out of a scale. Write an ascending and descending C major scale on the board. See p. 111. Have the children sing the scale using "la." Have them sing again as you point to the notes of the melody in rhythm. Then ask the class to turn to the "Escalator Song." They should be able to read and sing it easily, since they first learned the sound of the scale upon which the song was built.

SUGGESTED ACCOMPANIMENT
The bell part outlines the scale line used in the melody. Half of the class might sing the bell part while the rest of the class sings the song.

PLAYING INSTRUMENTS

Rhythmically
Bells

Why do stairs in a big es-ca - la - tor   Dis - ap-pear when they get to the top? And when they come down, Ver-y   near the ground, Why don't they ev-er come to a   stop?

*From *Growing with Music Book 2* Teacher's Edition by Harry R. Wilson and others.
© 1970 by Prentice-Hall, Inc., Englewood Cliffs, N.J. Reprinted by permission.

Listening: "Galop"*

When you hear the word comedian, what comes to mind? What is a comedian's job? Can a comedian perform his job in different ways? How would you act if you were a comedian? Do you think a comedian's job is easy? Why?

The first melody of "Galop" follows a short introduction. This melody is repeated immediately and followed by a short section of "whirling" music. Listen carefully for the melody. Here is what it looks like.

You will hear this melody and the whirling music several times before you hear a new musical idea, a B section. By listening carefully for the first melody, the whirling music, the B section, and what follows the B section, it should be easy for you to determine the form of the composition.

Can you name the instruments that stand out in the introduction, the first melody, the whirling music, and the B section? Why do you think the composer chose these particular instruments for each part of the piece? If you were a composer what kind of melodies, rhythm patterns, and instruments would you choose if you were writing music about comedians? Why do you think this piece is in this chapter?

The strongest rhythm pattern of "Galop" is ♩ ♫, two sixteenth notes and an eighth note. Can you find this pattern in "While the Miller Sleeps," on page 91? In "Pawpaw Patch," on p. 48, the same note values may be found but they have been changed around. How have they been changed? Can you substitute the words of the first pattern for the rhythm of the second pattern? What does this show you about the rhythm patterns of words and music?

*From *Growing with Music Book 4* Teacher's Edition by Harry R. Wilson and others. ©1970 by Prentice-Hall, Inc., Englewood Cliffs, N.J. Reprinted by permission.

FROM "THE COMEDIANS"
BY DMITRI KABALEVSKY

Allow the class to discuss freely what the word comedian means to them. Bring out the idea that a comedian sets out to amuse and entertain and that this can be done in many ways — by talking, by dancing, by pantomime. Although a comedian's job may look amusing and easy, it requires years of work and practice to achieve success as a comedian.

The instruments that stand out are:

introduction — xylophone and strings
theme A — trumpet
whirling music — strings
theme B — xylophone

Both the xylophone and the trumpet can produce bright, sharply pointed tones suitable for a musical representation of comedians. Allow the students to explain what musical devices they would use in writing music about comedians.

The rhythm pattern quoted in the last paragraph may be found throughout the 2/4 section of "While the Miller Sleeps." In "Pawpaw Patch," the pattern is reversed (two sixteenth notes *following* an eighth note). The words cannot be switched from one pattern to the other. It should be clear to the students that the rhythm of a song melody is determined by the rhythm of the words.

The form of the piece is Introduction — A — B — A, and should be easily recognized by the class.

Creating: "The Letter 'E' Song";

WORDS BY YVONNE CARR
FRENCH FOLK TUNE

Home tone: G
Starting note: G (*do*, 1)
Key: G Major

PERFORMANCE   The students might isolate various melodic and rhythmic patterns to use in an instrumental accompaniment. For example, the tones in meas. 2, 4 and 12 might be played on bells either as the class sings or as an introduction and coda. The uneven rhythm pattern in meas. 6 might be played on sticks or tambourines while a steady quarter note pattern is played on drums. Encourage the students to make up other accompanying patterns.

MUSICAL LEARNING

- This song is in the key of G major (see p. 102) and might be sung with syllables, letter names, or numbers.
- The melodic movement is by steps, skips, and repeated notes. The students will have no difficulty finding examples of steps and repeated notes. With the exception of meas. 8, 9 and 11, movement by skips occurs across bar lines and is more difficult to see. The students will enjoy hunting out these places.

Vigorously

1. Take the "e" from "ate" and I'm left with "at,"
2. Add an "e" to "mat," and I have a "mate,"

Take the "e" from "rate" and I'm left with "rat," And if the "e" is gone from
Add an "e" to "pat," and I have a "pate," "But if I add an "e" to

"fate,"don't you see I would be left with on - ly "fat," you'll a - gree. } Oh my, what a change, Oh my, what a change, How
"be," you will see, I'll have a bus - y lit - tle "bee," you'll a - gree.

Can you think of other words in which an "e" makes a difference?
The "e" need not come at the end of the word. For example, **bat** and **beat**.

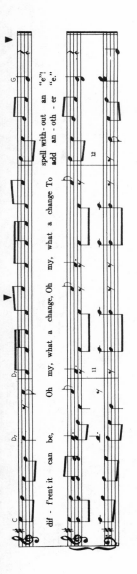

dif - f'rent it can be, Oh my, what a change, Oh my, what a change To spell with-out an "e"; add an - oth - er "e."

"Animal Song"*

WORDS AND MUSIC
BY EMELYN E GARDNER

Home tone: C
Starting note: E (mi, 3)
Key: C Major

Some of the animals mentioned in the song may be unfamiliar to the students. Encourage them to look up any new names in a dictionary.

PERFORMANCE An easy second vocal part appears below. The note values must be adapted to the word rhythms in each verse.

Can you make up other verses using different animals?

Moderately

1. Al - li - ga - tor, hedge - hog, ant - eat - er, bear,
2. Bull - frog, _____ wood - chuck, wol - ver - ine, _____ goose,

rat - tle - snake, buf - fa - lo, an - a - con - da, hare.
whip - poor - will, chip - munk, jack - al, _____ moose.

3. Mud turtle, whale, glow-worm, bat,
   Salamander, snail, and Maltese cat.

4. Polecat, dog, wild otter, rat,
   Pelican, hog, dodo, and bat.

5. House rat, pack rat, white bear, doe,
   Chickadee, peacock, bobolink, and crow.

*Both from *Growing with Music Book 4* Teacher's Edition by Harry R. Wilson and others.
©1970 by Prentice-Hall, Inc., Englewood Cliffs, N.J. Reprinted by permission.

Rhythmic: "Jack and Jill"*

Home tone: C
Starting note: C (do, 1)
Key: C Major

MOTHER GOOSE
MUSIC BY J. W. ELLIOTT

Record 5, Side B

Children enjoy dramatizing these familiar verses from Mother Goose.

PERFORMANCE   Ask the children to choose a place in the classroom which could be the hill. Then ask what kind of steps they would take if they were climbing a big hill.

Rather than suggesting in detail how the action should be carried out, permit the children to make up their own actions.

SUGGESTED ACCOMPANIMENT   Encourage individual children to make up an introduction on the bells showing how Jack and Jill go up the hill (up the scale). Then see if they can make up a coda (or ending) showing how they come down the hill (down the scale). See p. 87.

A descant may be added by playing the bells up and down the scale in the rhythm of two beats per measure (dotted quarter notes).

Using drums or rhythm sticks, the children who are not performing or playing bells may feel the rhythm of the long and short tones by playing the following accompaniment on their desks or table tops.

RELATED ACTIVITIES   The children may enjoy drawing a scene of Jack and Jill climbing the hill. Others may want to draw another scene showing them tumbling down.

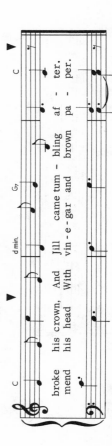

1. Jack and Jill went up the hill   To
2. Up Jack got and home did trot   As
fetch a pail of wa - ter;   Jack fell down and
fast as he could ca - per;   Went to bed to
broke his crown, And Jill came tum - bling af - ter.
mend his head With vin - e - gar and brown pa - per.

*From *Growing with Music Book 2* Teacher's Edition by Harry R. Wilson and others.
© 1970 by Prentice-Hall, Inc., Englewood Cliffs, N.J. Reprinted by permission.

Arts and crafts

Arts and crafts has been used effectively as an outlet for expression, a mode of creativity, and a form of release. Arts-and-crafts activities are part of the total activity offerings in the leisure services. They are highly individualistic. Thus, a high degree of success is easy to build into this phase of the program. Arts and crafts are applicable to all people and to all age levels. They can be offered without taxing financial and/or facility resources, because they are almost unlimited and truely diversified. In addition, many activities in arts and crafts enable people of all ages, ethnic groups, and socioeconomic classes to participate side by side. Arts and crafts use varied media to communicate the participants' emotions. A person's creativity can be expressed in a highly distinctive manner.

A recreator cannot be expected to be highly skilled in all, or even most, areas of the arts-and-crafts program. Rather, he should display those leadership qualities which will enable him to present activities to enhance participants' abilities, knowledge, and self-esteem. However, he should be knowledgeable in certain specific arts-and-crafts activities. The recreator who has the ability to lead many arts and crafts activities will be able to interact positively with recreationists engaging in these activities.

DEFINITIONS

• *Arts and crafts:* "A process of communication rather than a list of activities."[25] Tillman also views arts and crafts as a facilitator of communications: "It is structured for communications in contrast to the emphasis on physical activity in sports."[26]
• *Creativity:* "Closely linked to establishing our identity."[27] The majority of arts and crafts activities are high in creativity.
• *Sculpture:* "the carving of a solid material with sharp tools such as chisels, drills, burrs, or axes."[28]
• *Printing:* "A print is an original art work, the impression resulting from placing paper, fabric, or other flat materials in direct contact with another surface that has been treated with inks or paints."[29]

[25] *The Recreation Program*, p. 16.
[26] Tillman, *The Program Book for Recreation Professionals*, p. 153.
[27] *Ibid.*, p. 155.
[28] Edward L. Mattil, *Meaning in Crafts* (Englewood Cliffs, N.J.: Prentice-Hall, 1971), p. 27.
[29] Ibid., p. 55.

- *Modeling:* "working with malleable or plastic materials using the hand or simple tools such as spatulas or modeling tools."[30]
- *Ceramics:* "An activity in which objects are formed of clay and hardened by heat."[31]
- *Papier-mâché:* "Paper that is softened and to which paste, sizing, or resin is added to give it strength and hardness when it dries."[32]

CLASSIFICATION OF ARTS-AND-CRAFTS ACTIVITIES

A mere listing of a myriad of arts-and-crafts activities cannot constitute a complete catalog of those activities. In all likelihood there cannot be a compilation of every activity classified as arts and crafts because what an individual experiences before, during, and after an arts-and-crafts activity should be of a progressive and ever-evolving nature. The variety and individuality inherent within each specific classification emphasizes this. Therefore, the listing that follows is an attempt to present a wealth of activities generally considered to fall within arts and crafts. "No arts and crafts activity can remain static, but must provide continuously a chain reaction to new and increasingly significant fields of expression for the individual."[33] Macramé is an example of this concept. A beginner may engage in a sampler and a more advanced person may create a large wall hanging. Of course, most macramé activities will fall between these two extremes. The degree of difficulty will depend upon the needs, interests, and abilities of the participants.

Activities include: Aluminum foil, basket-making, beadwork, block printing, blueprinting, book binding, braiding, candlemaking, cardboard construction, carving, cards and Christmas decorations, cement craft, ceramics, chair caning, china painting, chip carving, clay modeling, collage, crepe-paper craft, découpage, drawing, embossing, etching, fabrics, feltwork, finger painting, flower arrangements, furniture refinishing, graphics, jewelry making, knitting, leatherwork, macramé, marionettes, metalwork, mosaics, needlework, oiled paper, origami, painting, papier-mâché, photography, picture framing and matting, plastic craft, pottery, printing, puppetry, pyrography, raffia, rugs, sculpture, silk-screen fabrics, sketching, stenciling, stitchery, tin craft, tie-dyeing, upholstery, weaving, woodwork, and yarn figures.

---

[30]Ibid., p. 27.
[31]Ibid., p. 152.
[32]Ibid., p. 171.
[33]*The Recreation Program*, p. 17.

VALUES IN ARTS AND CRAFTS

Weiskopf indicated that the following six values result from involvement in arts and crafts activities:

1. Appreciation and recognition
2. Personal satisfaction
3. Pride and accomplishment
4. Creative expression
5. Working with the hands
6. Formation of hobbies[34]

Kraus emphasized that arts-and crafts activities are vital to one's personal worth. "Arts-and-crafts activities fill the important need of all human beings to explore their own resources, to manipulate the environment, and to create something that is beautiful, personally expressive, decorative, or useful."[35]

Bottorf indicated that the following values can be derived from participating in arts-and-crafts activity:

1. Release of tension
2. A therapeutic agent
3. Satisfaction in accomplishment, in personal endeavor and success
4. Development of initiative, self-reliance and orderly thinking
5. Development of a feeling of individual personal worth and respect[36]

Student assignments

This part consists of eight objectives. You will be called upon to demonstrate your mastery of each objective. Some answers will require written responses. You will be conducting and participating in a variety of arts and crafts activities throughout this part of the module.

OBJECTIVE	ACHIEVEMENT OF COMPETENCY
1. To define arts and crafts.	Write a definition of arts and crafts.
2. To define creativity.	Write a definition of creativity.

[34]Weiskopf, *A Guide to Recreation and Leisure*, p. 233.

[35]Richard Kraus, *Recreation Today: Program Planning and Leadership* (New York: Appleton-Century-Crofts, 1966), p. 215.

[36]Edna A. Bottorf, cited in H. Dan Corbin, *Recreation Leadership* (Englewood Cliffs, N.J.: Prentice-Hall, 1959), p. 167.

OBJECTIVE	ACHIEVEMENT OF COMPETENCY
3. To identify arts-and-crafts activities.	Given a list of definitions for five arts-and-crafts activities, recall and identify a minimum of four of the activities.
4. To construct an arts-and-crafts activity.	Construct at least one arts-and-crafts activity.
5. To describe importance of arts-and-crafts activities in recreation.	Without the aid of references, write a minimum of 200 words in 30 minutes describing the significance of arts-and-crafts activities in recreation.
6. To lead an arts-and-crafts activity.	Without the aid of references, conduct a minimum of one arts-and-crafts activity.
7. To describe values in arts-and-crafts activities in recreation.	Orally describe a minimum of five values in arts-and-crafts activities in recreation.
8. To identify arts-and-crafts activities.	List a minimum of 20 arts-and-crafts activities.

Resources

This part is divided into two sections: (1) a list of textbooks and (2) specific arts-and-crafts activities.

TEXTBOOKS

BUTLER, GEORGE D. *Introduction to Community Recreation*. New York: McGraw-Hill, 1967.

CORBIN, H. DAN. *Recreation Leadership*. Englewood Cliffs, N.J.: Prentice-Hall, 1959.

CORBIN, H. DAN, and TAIT, WILLIAM J. *Education for Leisure*. Englewood Cliffs, N.J.: Prentice-Hall, 1973.

KRAUS, RICHARD. *Recreation Today: Program Planning and Leadership*. New York: Appleton-Century-Croffs, 1966.

KRAUS, RICHARD G., and BATES, BARBARA J. *Recreation Leadership and Supervision: Guidelines for Professional Development*. Philadelphia: W. B. Saunders, 1975.

MATTIL, EDWARD L. *Meaning in Crafts*. Englewood Cliffs, N.J.: Prentice-Hall, 1971.

MITCHELL, A. VIOLA, and CRAWFORD, IDA B. *Camp Counseling*. Philadelphia: W. B. Saunders, 1964.

The Recreation Program. Chicago: The Athletic Institute, 1963.

SHIVERS, JAY S. *Camping: Administration, Counseling, Programming*. New York: Appleton-Century-Crofts, 1971.

TILLMAN, ALBERT. *The Program Book for Recreation Professionals*. Los Angeles: National Press Books, 1973.

WEISKOPF, DONALD C. *A Guide to Recreation and Leisure*. Boston: Allyn & Bacon, 1975.

SPECIFIC ARTS-AND-CRAFTS ACTIVITIES

The two arts-and-crafts activities that follow are representative of many that could have been included. They illustrate two types of arts-and-crafts activities.

Feltwork

1. Decorative felt plaque (frog)

    a. Materials needed—coordinating colors according to individual preference

        (1) one roll of cloth tape 1½" wide

        (2) one ceiling tile 9" X 11"

        (3) three different felt colors

        (4) two plastic button back Wiggle Eyes

        (5) one piece of 3" yarn

        (6) one ½" fabric daisy

        (7) glue

        (8) one pom pom 4" diameter

        (9) scissors

      (10) one 1" ring

      (11) one 1" fabric daisy

    b. Directions

        (1) trace and cut pattern pieces

        (2) trim ceiling tile with cloth tape around borders

        (3) place felt pieces on tile in desired arrangement

        (4) glue felt pieces to tile

        (5) tape ring to center of back of tile for hanging finished product

Base of
Pom Pom
(cut 1)

Frog's
Body
(cut 1)

Lily Pad
(cut 1)

Lily Pad
(cut 1)

Legs
(cut 2)

Arms (cut 2)

Flower
Base (cut 1)

Flower Stem (cut 1)

Leaf
(cut 2)

2. Ecology plaque

    a. Materials needed

        (1) glue

        (2) one piece of wood 6″ X 6″

        (3) assorted dried beans and spices

        (4) one 1″ ring with screw for hanging

(5) sandpaper

(6) stain (wood)

(7) spaghetti—approximately six trands for each plaque

b. Directions

(1) distress the wood, sand rough edges, stain

(2) attach ring at center top

(3) outline a design with the spaghetti

(4) cover small section with glue and place beans or spices on top, continue until the whole piece of wood is covered with dried beans and spices

Dance

Dance has served mankind as a form of expression since antiquity. It provides man with the need to move as a response to rhythmic experiences. Kraus indicates that dance has "met certain basic needs of society, . . . the need to worship, to educate in communal customs, to express tribal or national loyalties, to engage in courtship, to assist in the therapeutic process, to become creatively involved in artistic expression, and, finally, as a social or recreational form."[37] Weiskopf wrote that "during the last two decades, there has been a spectacular increase in the number of persons and groups participating in various kinds of dancing."[38]

There is great variety in dance. Furthermore, there are individual gradations within each dance activity. Because of these two characteristics, dance has appeal for all ages. It can develop socialization, has spectator value and can be used to interrelate to other aspects of the total recreation program. Recreators should recognize that dance can be offered all year. Dance has been used effectively in therapeutic recreational programs (for example, wheelchair dancing and square dancing for the blind). In addition, dance can be used in a variety of special events throughout the year such as a special talent show or a recital. Clubs can be easily established for special-interest areas, such as a folk dance club or a social dance club.

[37]Kraus, *Recreation Today: Program Planning and Leadership*, p. 196.

[38]Weiskopf, *A Guide to Recreation and Leisure*, p. 236.

Personnel in the leisure services must make a concerted effort not to duplicate already existing dance programs offered by public, voluntary, or private agencies. This rule applies, of course, to all programming in the leisure field. It is especially important here because dance is extremely diversified.

Dance allows creative self-expression for a large segment of the population. A recreator who is able to discern concepts inherent in dance, who has acquired competencies needed to lead certain dance activities, and who believes in the values of dance will be able to offer a viable dance program to many people.

DEFINITIONS

- *Dance:* "Dance is spontaneous expression, but it is also the primordial urge to move in rhythm."[39] Dance movement endeavors to convey feelings and ideas; i.e. communicate with others.
- *Folk dance:* "survived long enough to have become a part of the traditional social customs of a society."[40]
- *Round or couple dance:* a large number of American folk dances performed by a couple.[41]
- *Square dance:* requires no routine of steps and entails a constant change of partners and interrelationship of couples.[42]
- *Modern dance:* "creative expression and communication of ideas through movement."[43]
- *Creative rhythms for children:* provide opportunities for a variety of experiences in expression through movement.[44]
- *Tap, clog, character dance:* based on sounds and participant's responses to them, ranges from extensive movement to sound patterns with the feet.[45]

CLASSIFICATION OF DANCE ACTIVITIES

Dance is a unique activity because it is a creative activity that is high in socialization. Characteristics of a dance program are that it is an extremely

[39]Tillman, *The Program Book for Recreation Professionals*, p. 166.
[40]*The Recreation Program*, p. 42.
[41]Ibid., p. 44.
[42]Ibid., p. 43.
[43]Ibid., p. 52.
[44]Ibid., p. 48.
[45]Ibid., p. 54.

diversified, eminently individualistic, and highly interrelated program area. Following is a consolidated list of dance experiences that comprise many dance activities: Acrobatic, ballet, block dances, character dance, circle dance, classic dance, clog, concert dance, creative rhythms for children, dance mixers, ethnic dance, eurhythmics, folk dance, gymnastic dance, Hawaiian dance, interpretive dance, jazz dance, Latin American dance, longways dance, modern dance, pageants, record hops, rock dance, round dance, social or ballroom dance, solo dance, song play, square dance, talent shows, tap dance, tinikling.

VALUES OF DANCE

Weiskopf lists the following values that are obtained by participating in dance:

1. Fun and enjoyment
2. Release of tensions
3. Contribution to mental and physical well-being
4. Development of poise, self-confidence, and personal adequacy
5. Socialization
6. Appreciation of various cultures[46]

Tillman emphasizes the following values of dance:

1. Physical activity
2. Creativity
3. Appreciation of beauty
4. Incorporation with other recreation events
5. Relaxation and escape
6. Service to others
7. Rhythm and coordination
8. Opportunity for new adventure and new experience[47]

A further value, and one tangentially related to many of the above values, is the tremendous opportunities that dance provides for corecreational activities.

[46]Weiskopf, *A Guide to Recreation and Leisure,* p. 237.
[47]Tillman, *The Program Book for Recreation Professionals,* pp. 168–70.

Student assignments

This section of the module consists of seven objectives. You will be called upon to demonstrate your mastery of each objective. Some answers will require written responses. You will be conducting and participating in a variety of dance activities throughout this part of the module.

OBJECTIVE	ACHIEVEMENT OF COMPETENCY
1. To define dance.	Without the aid of references, write a definition of dance.
2. To identify types of dances.	Recall and identify a minimum of four types of dances.
3. To describe importance of dance activities in recreation.	Write a minimum of 200 words describing the significance of dance activities in recreation.
4. To construct a dance activity.	Construct a minimum of one dance activity.
5. To conduct a dance activity.	Conduct a minimum of one dance activity.
6. To describe dance activities.	Orally describe a minimum of 15 dance activities.
7. To describe values in dance activities in recreation.	List a minimum of seven values in dance activities in recreation.

Resources

This part is divided into two sections: (1) a list of reference materials and (2) specific dance activities.

TEXTBOOKS

BUTLER, GEORGE D. *Introduction to Community Recreation*. New York: McGraw-Hill, 1967.

DE GRAZIA, SEBASTIAN. *Of Time, Work and Leisure*. New York: The Twentieth Century Fund, 1962.

FAIT, HOLLIS F. *Special Physical Education, adapted, corrective, developmental*. 3rd ed. Philadelphia: W. B. Saunders, 1971.

KRAUS, RICHARD. *Recreation Today: Program Planning and Leadership.* New York: Appleton-Century-Crofts, 1966.

KRAUS, RICHARD G., and BATES, BARBARA J. *Recreation Leadership and Supervision: Guidelines for Professional Development.* Philadelphia: W. B. Saunders, 1975.

The Recreation Program. Chicago: The Athletic Institute, 1963.

SESSOMS, H. DOUGLAS; MEYER, HAROLD D.; and BRIGHTBILL, CHARLES K. *Leisure Services.* Englewood Cliffs, N.J.: Prentice-Hall, 1975.

SHIVERS, JAY S. *Camping: Administration, Counseling, Programming.* New York: Appleton-Century-Crofts, 1971.

TILLMAN, ALBERT. *The Program Book for Recreation Professionals.* Los Angeles: National Press Books, 1973.

WEISKOPF, DONALD C. *A Guide to Recreation and Leisure.* Boston: Allyn & Bacon, 1975.

ARTICLES

BUSCH, JO ANN. "Everybody Teaches, Everybody Learns." *Journal of Physical Education and Recreation*, vol. 47, no. 2 (February 1976): p. 55.

CHAPLIN, LINDA. "Teaching Dance Improvisation Creatively." *Journal of Physical Education and Recreation*, vol. 47, no. 4 (April 1976): p. 42.

SPECIFIC DANCE ACTIVITIES

The dance activities that follow are representative of many dances that could have been included. They illustrate four types of dance activities.

Hansel and Gretel: German Song Play

Formation: Double circle, partners facing.

MEASURES	SONG
Music A	**1.**
1–2	Little playmate, dance with me,
3–4	Both your hands, now give to me,
5–6	Heel and toe, away we go,
7–8	Round and round the merry row.
Music B	**2.**
1–8	Tra-la-la-la-la-la-la, etc.

Music C	**3.**
1–2	With your feet go tap, tap, tap,
3–4	With your hands go clap, clap, clap,
5–6	Heel and toe, away we go,
7–8	Round and round the merry row.

Music C	**4.**
1–2	With your head go nip, nip, nip,
3–4	With your fingers snip, snip, snip,
5–6	Heel and toe, away we go,
7–8	Round and round the merry row.

DANCE

Music A	**1.**
1–4	BOW to partner, JOIN HANDS in skater's position, right hands joined over left and FACE COUNTERCLOCKWISE.
5–6	PLACE HEEL FORWARD, POINT TOE BACKWARD, then dance THREE light RUNNING STEPS FORWARD.
7–8	REPEAT pattern of Measures 5–6 with other foot.

Music B	**2.**
1–8	SKIP COUNTERCLOCKWISE, singing.

Music C	**3.**
1–4	TAP FOOT three times, then CLAP OWN HANDS three times,
5–8	REPEAT pattern of measures 5–8.

Music C	**4.**
1–4	NOD HEAD three times, then SNAP FINGERS, overhead 3 times.
5–8	REPEAT pattern of measures 5–8.

Repeat entire song play with partner or at the end; children in outer circle move foward one place to new partner.

Virginia Reel (Simplified)

Formation: Column of four, five, or six couples, facing forward, girl on partner's right.

Starting position: Partners facing.

1.

1–4   FORWARD AND BACK. All walk forward three steps, bow to partner on fourth count (counts 1–4), walk four steps backward to place (counts 5–8).

5–8   FORWARD AND BACK AGAIN.

2.

9–12   RIGHT ELBOW SWING. Partners hook right elbows, swing once around and return to place with eight walking or skipping steps (counts 1–8).

13–16   LEFT ELBOW SWING. Once around with partner, returning to place (9–16).

3.

1–4   TWO HAND SWING. Partners join both hands, swing once around clockwise and return to place with eight walking or skipping steps (counts 1–8).

5–8   DO-SI-DO. Partners walk forward passing right shoulders, then, without turning, move to the right, passing back to back, and walk backwards to place, passing left shoulders (9–16).

4.

9–12   HEAD COUPLE: SASHAY DOWN. Head couple, with both hands joined, sashays down the center to the foot of the set with eight slides (counts 1–8).

13–16   HEAD COUPLE: SASHAY BACK. Head couple sashays back to place with eight slides (9–16).

5.

1–8   CAST OFF. Head boy turn left, head girl turn right, and each lead line to foot of set (counts 1–16).

6.

9–16   FORM AN ARCH AND THE OTHERS GO THROUGH. Head couple at foot of set, join and raise both hands to form an arch. Second couple lead others under the arch, advancing to become new head couple (1–16).

Repeat entire dance with each new head couple.

Tinikling (Philippines)

Requirements for the dance: Two long bamboo poles about nine feet long. The poles rest on a block of wood about two inches thick and 30 inches long. Two players sit on the floor, holding one pole in each hand, and strike the poles together and apart in this rhythm:

Count 1: Strike poles together in middle.
Counts 2, 3: Strike poles apart on block of wood twice.

Maintain a steady rhythm: in-out-out; in-out-out. Players may either slide or slightly lift poles in shifting positions.

Step 1: Dancers stand outside poles so that the right hip is near pole 1. In starting the dance, the first count is usually just a pause.

Count 1: Pause—poles are struck in middle.
Counts 2, 3: Leap sideways into middle onto right, left foot. (Poles are apart.) Count 1: Leap sideways onto right foot, outside pole 2. (Poles are together.) Count 2, 3: Leap sideways into middle onto left, right foot. (Poles are apart.) Continue in this manner.

The step may also be done with dancers standing outside pole 2, facing the other way.

On the eighth measure, dancers can turn in the middle with the two steps so as to face the other way for a repeat of the figure. This can be made more difficult by turning each time.

Step 2: Dancers move continuously clockwise around and in between the poles in this manner: Count 1, 2, 3, 4: Walk forward outside pole 1 with a right, left, right, left.

Counts 5, 6: Leap between poles—right, left—and finish outside pole 2, still facing clockwise.
Counts 1, 2, 3, 4: Walk outside pole 2 with right, left, right, left.
Counts 5, 6: Leap between poles—right, left—and finish outside pole 1.

Continue in this manner.

Step 3: The two dancers join hands as they face each other.

Count 1: Jump astride both poles as they are struck together in center.
Counts 2, 3: Jump in middle, landing on both feet twice at the same time as the poles are struck apart twice.

Rustic Reel: American progressive trio dance

Formation: Trios facing trios in circle or column. Trios formed by boy and two girls.

Starting Position: Boy standing between his two partners, hands joined in lines of "threes."

MEASURES	
	1.
1–8	FORWARD AND BACK and REPEAT. Four steps forward toward opposite trio and four steps backward to place (measures 1–4), and repeat (5–8).
	2.
1–8	SASHAY RIGHT. Each boy joins both hands with his opposite right-hand girl and sashays to his right with eight slides (measures 1–4), then returns to place with eight slides (5–8).
	3.
1–8	SASHAY LEFT. Each boy joins both hands with his opposite left-hand girl and sashays to his left with eight slides (measures 1–4), then returns to place with eight slides (5–8).
	4.
1–4	FORWARD AND BACK.
5–8	FORWARD AND PASS. All walk forward eight, passing opposite by right shoulder, to meet a new line of three.

Repeat entire dance with each new set of threes.

Dramatics

Drama is an important aspect of cultural life. It is a creative activity that communicates and maintains cultural heritage. Thus, drama can be used as a means to foster an understanding between people of different religious and racial backgrounds. Kraus indicates that drama "expresses man's hopes and dreams, his view of life, his tragic or humorous episodes or experiences. Thus, it reflects, interprets, and enriches life."[48]

Many recreational activities can be easily correlated with drama. Furthermore, there is a tremendous range of dramatic activities for participants to engage in—from the simple to the complex. This enables people of all age levels, educational backgrounds, and socioeconomic levels to participate and enjoy dramatic activities on an individual basis. For example, a group of preschool children may engage in "pretending" activities while a group of senior citizens produce and perform a play before an audience. There are, of course, numerous dramatic experiences that fall between these extremes. A characteristic of drama is that it is an artistic medium that allows creative self-expression.

Drama has significant appeal for both performer and audience alike. It has, historically, been an essential ingredient in leisure service programs. Recreators have successfully used drama to depict specific events and to preserve aspects of cultural life within the community. Dramatic activities have been used as a concluding special event in a number of leisure programs. In whatever ways this medium is used, it is unquestionably a vital and needed activity. An all-encompassing dramatic program should be highly diversified and totally person-centered. Therefore, recreators should possess abilities to lead people in a wealth of dramatic activities.

DEFINITIONS

• *Drama:* "self-expressive creativity because it allows man to interpret his environment and feelings to others with techniques and styles that not only communicate but entertain."[49]

• *Creative play:* a form of make-believe that focuses around some experience that the participant is familiar with.[50]

• *Creative drama:* the performers devise their own gestures, lines, and actions.

• *Formal drama:* set plays, with lines to be memorized and rehearsals in which the formal drama is prepared for an audience.[51]

• *Monologue:* one speaker maintains a simple characterization.[52]

[48]Kraus, *Recreation Today: Program Planning and Leadership*, pp. 181-82.
[49]Tillman, *The Program Book for Recreation Professionals*, p. 189.
[50]Dorothy W. Lynds; cited in H. Dan Corbin, *Recreation Leadership*, p. 213.
[51]*The Recreation Program*, p. 73.
[52]Ibid., p. 79.

- *Monodrama:* one person, through a series of dramatic monologues, impersonates several characters who tell the story.[53]
- *Shadow play:* figures are cut out of cardboard and are mounted on sticks and held so that their shadows are thrown on a screen.[54]
- *Play:* a story acted before an audience by players on a stage, and it is usually the final goal of any drama program.[55]

CLASSIFICATION OF DRAMA ACTIVITIES

Drama has universal appeal for both performer and audience, and many different dramatic activities can be presented which are geared to the age of participants. Therefore, to make an all-inclusive list of drama activities is, at best, an arduous task. The following activities constitute a compilation of drama activities that recreators can draw from: adult repertory theater, arena productions, blackouts, burlesques, ceremonials, charades, children's theater, choral speaking, community theater, creative dramatics, dance drama, demonstrations, dramatic games, dramatizations, dumb crambo, experimental theater, festivals, formal drama, grand opera, imaginative play, impersonation, light opera, marionettes, mask making, monodrama, monologue, musical comedy, observance, one-act play, operetta, pageant, pantomime, paper-bag dramatics, peepshow box, plays, play reading, puppetry, radio and television broadcast, scenery making, shadow play, skit, sociodrama, storytelling, stunt, tableaux, theater parties, theater-in-the-round, and variety show.

VALUES OF DRAMATIC ACTIVITIES

Mitchell and Crawford indicate that children receive the following benefits from participating in dramatic activities:

1. An opportunity to imitate
2. A chance to pretend, imagine, and exaggerate
3. Practice in group cooperation
4. Self-discipline and self-direction
5. Poise, good enunciation, and proper voice projection
6. Fun[56]

[53] Ibid.
[54] Ibid., p. 82.
[55] Ibid., pp. 77-78.
[56] A. Viola Mitchell and Ida B. Crawford, *Camp Counseling* (Philadelphia: W. B. Saunders, 1964), p. 120.

Tillman emphasizes that drama provides "a chance to achieve a very personal, original expression without the pressure of rigid standards."[57] He specifies the following positive aspects of drama activities:

1. Creativity
2. Understanding others (empathy)
3. Appreciation and development of voice and body movements as art forms
4. Socialization
5. Release emotions
6. Physical exercise
7. Interrelationship with other recreation program areas
8. Therapeutic[58]

The values to be derived from dramatic activities are reliant upon the specific activities offered. For example, paper-bag dramatics can be used as a creative and self-expressive activity. Participants can create their own puppets, write a skit, make the scenery and perform in front of an audience. Furthermore, paper-bag dramatics can have other, quite varied, objectives, that is, release of tension, tolerance toward specific groups of people, development of poise and self-control, and entertainment for an audience. Personnel in the leisure services should acquire competencies to present a well-rounded program of dramatic activities. An extensive and varied amount of dramatic activities should be offered that is commensurate with the needs, interests, and abilities of all people. As an artistic medium, drama can help recreators plan more effectively for large numbers of people.

Student assignments

This part consists of seven objectives. You will be called upon to demonstrate your mastery of each objective. Some answers will require written responses. You will be conducting and participating in a variety of dramatic activities throughout this part of the module.

OBJECTIVE	ACHIEVEMENT OF COMPETENCY
1. To define drama.	Write a definition of drama.
2. To identify types of dramatic activities.	Recall and identify a minimum of five types of dramatic activities.

[57]Tillman, *The Program Book for Recreation Professionals*, p. 190.
[58]Ibid., pp. 190-91.

OBJECTIVE	ACHIEVEMENT OF COMPETENCY
3. To describe importance of dramatic activities in recreation.	Write a minimum of 200 words describing the significance of dramatic activities in recreation.
4. To construct a dramatic activity.	Construct a minimum of one dramatic activity.
5. To conduct a dramatic activity.	Conduct a minimum of one dramatic activity.
6. To list dramatic activities.	List a minimum of 25 dramatic activities.
7. To describe values in dramatic activities in recreation.	List a minimum of ten values in dramatic activities in recreation.

Resources

This part is divided into two sections: (1) a list of reference materials and (2) a specific dramatic activity.

TEXTBOOKS

BUTLER, GEORGE D. *Introduction to Community Recreation*. New York: McGraw-Hill, 1967.

CORBIN, H. DAN. *Recreation Leadership*. Englewood Cliffs, N.J.: Prentice-Hall, 1959.

CORBIN, H. DAN, and TAIT, WILLIAM J. *Education for Leisure*. Englewood Cliffs, N.J.: Prentice-Hall, 1973.

GRAY, PAULA GROSS. *Dramatics for the Elderly*. New York: Teachers College Press, 1974.

KRAUS, RICHARD. *Recreation Today: Program Planning and Leadership*. New York: Appleton-Century-Crofts, 1966.

KRAUS, RICHARD G., and BATES, BARBARA J. *Recreation Leadership and Supervision: Guidelines for Professional Development*. Philadelphia: W. B. Saunders, 1975.

MITCHELL, A. VIOLA, and CRAWFORD, IDA B. *Camp Counseling*. Philadelphia: W. B. Saunders, 1964.

The Recreation Program. Chicago: The Athletic Institute, 1963.

SESSOMS, H. DOUGLAS; MEYER, HAROLD D.; and BRIGHTBILL, CHARLES K. *Leisure Services*. Englewood Cliffs, N.J.: Prentice-Hall, 1975.

SHIVERS, JAY S. *Camping: Administration, Counseling, Programming.* New York: Appleton-Century-Crofts, 1971.

TILLMAN, ALBERT. *The Program Book for Recreation Professionals.* Los Angeles: National Press Books, 1973.

WEISKOPF, DONALD C. *A Guide to Recreation and Leisure.* Boston: Allyn & Bacon, 1975.

ARTICLES

MORGAN, DAVID. "Combining Orff-Schulwerk with Creative Dramatics for the Retarded." *Therapeutic Recreation Journal*, vol. 9, no. 2 (1975): 54–56.

SPECIFIC DRAMATIC ACTIVITY

The dramatic activity that follows is representative of many dramatic activities that could have been included.

Paper-bag dramatics

    A. Materials needed
       1. One bag for each group of participants
         a. Each bag is filled with specific paraphernalia
         b. Contents of each bag is determined by the instructor and is reliant upon the size of each group (usually included in each bag are simple materials and costumes)
    B. Directions
       1. Each group is given a bag full of materials
       2. Each group must use contents of their bag to produce a skit

---

MODULE 3

First aid and safety

Rationale

We live, work, and play in a highly mobile society. One of people's greatest joys is the satisfaction derived from traveling. This travel, quite naturally, takes people to unfamiliar places. In case of an accident or injury, an individual may not know where to go for aid. Therefore, it is essential—both for his own safety and the safety of others—that he obtain skills in first aid.

There has been an explosion in the amount of leisure pursuits. A great many people find enjoyment and satisfaction in camping and other "back-to-nature" experiences, such as backpacking, camp crafts, mountain climbing, and other activities. Many of these activities take place away from good medical care. It is vital for a person to have first aid skills when physicians and/or hospitals are not readily accessible.

It is essential that everyone acquire knowledge of first aid. First aid is the immediate care given to the victim of an accident or injury. Such care does not replace that of a trained medical practitioner. In many instances, a competent first aider can save a life by knowing correct procedures to follow until the services of a physician can be obtained. A knowledge of

97

first aid is an especially vital skill for the recreator. A person in the field of recreation comes into contact daily with large groups of people. Many activities in recreation have a moderate or high amount of risk. Therefore, the competent recreator should have skills to ensure the safety of participants engaged in a recreation program.

DEFINITIONS

• *First aid:* the immediate and temporary care given to the victim of an accident or injury until the services of a physician can be obtained. It is the initial step in the general care of the injured.

• *Emergency care:* "Emergency care performed by an emergency medical technician goes a step further; it not only continues the care begun by the first aider but also packages, extricates, and transports the ill or injured to a medical facility."[1]

• *Definitive professional care:* Continues at the point where emergency care stops. Definitive professional care provides assistance "in the form of medication, intravenous fluids, sutures, surgery, and other medical procedures necessary to maintain and restore the individual."[2]

GENERAL ASPECTS OF SERIOUS FIRST AID TREATMENT

There are five directions a first aider should follow for serious first aid treatment:

1. Give the urgently necessary first aid
2. Have the victim lie down
3. Check for injuries
4. Plan what to do
5. Carry out the indicated procedures

Give the urgently necessary first aid. First aider should establish priorities and render help first to those injuries where time is essential; stopped breathing, severe bleeding, poisoning, and so forth.

Have the victim lie down. First aider should not disturb the patient. In the majority of cases involving administering first aid to people seriously injured, the victim will be lying down. However, the guiding princi-

---

[1]Pamela Bakhaus doCarmo and Angelo T. Patterson, *First Aid Principles and Procedures* (Englewood Cliffs, N.J.: Prentice-Hall, 1976), p. 3. Reprinted by permission.
[2]Ibid.

ple should be that the seriously ill or injured person should be "in the position best suited to his condition or injuries."[3] The victim should not become too hot or too cold. Generally speaking, blankets are of more help beneath, than on top of, the patient.

Check for injuries. First aider should establish what happened, the victim's reactions pertaining to the accident or injury, and his own ideas about the extent of his injuries. First aider should examine the victim by checking the vital signs. All injuries should be treated. A first aider should not merely treat the most obvious injuries and not think to probe for additional injuries that might be less obvious but as dangerous.

Plan what to do. The first aider should always have a reason for what he does. He should not overreact. Rather, he should plot a course of events to follow in order to render efficient first aid.

Carry out the indicated procedures. Upon completion of examination of the victim, the first aider should proceed to administer the appropriate first aid. Analysis of vital body signs should indicate the necessary procedural methods to follow.

LEGAL LIABILITY

Many recreation agencies have established that no first aid can be rendered by any person except a physician. Recreators should conform to agencies' rules and regulations concerning first aid procedures. Personnel in the leisure services should recognize that regulations pertaining to first aid vary from agency to agency and from state to state. Recreators should become aware of specific first aid procedures to follow in each agency with which they are affiliated.

Kraus and Bates indicate that first aid should be offered only under the following two circumstances: (1) if the injury is a minor one, of a type that the recreation leader is equipped for and authorized to deal with, and (2) if it is an emergency situation requiring immediate action while more expert medical assistance is on the way.[4] They reemphasize that recreation leaders should be strictly limited to first aid rendered to injured or ill persons. Recreators can be sued if they apply incorrect first aid techniques. For this reason, people are often reluctant to assist the ill or injured. However, this fear is generally unsubstantiated. DoCarmo and

[3]American Red Cross, *Advanced First Aid and Emergency Care* (Garden City, N.Y.: Doubleday, 1973), p. 22.

[4]Richard Kraus and Barbara J. Bates, *Recreation Leadership and Supervision: Guidelines for Professional Development* (Philadelphia: W. B. Saunders, 1975), p. 250. Reprinted by permission.

Patterson wrote that "court records show no case where a lay first aider, acting in good faith, assisted an ill or injured individual, and was successfully sued thereafter."[5] The first aider should recognize that once he elects to render assistance he is responsible for his actions. Thus, to minimize the possibility of a lawsuit, the first aider should:

1. Recognize and care for the life-threatening injuries or illnesses immediately

2. Recognize his own limitations and see that the emergency medical system is activated as quickly as possible

3. Follow recognized accepted first aid procedures when caring for an injured or ill individual

4. Proceed to care for the individual carefully, explaining to the individual, if necessary, what is being done to assist him[6]

The fear of liability suits has served to deter medical personnel from assisting injured or ill people. To help alleviate this situation, most states have enacted Good Samaritan laws. Only nine states do not have these laws. Generally speaking, the lay first aider is not protected by these laws. However, "if he follows the points listed . . . and works to the best of his ability, the first aider need not be afraid of being sued."[7] It is recommended that every recreation department formulate definitive procedures that recreators should follow in the event of an accident or illness. Inservice staff meetings should address this issue on a regular basis.

PREVENTIVE SAFETY

All recreation facilities should afford participants safe areas in which to participate. Recreators should be safety-conscious and conduct leisure activities in a safe environment. In addition, recreation personnel should be trained in basic first aid techniques. The following rules are essential for safe recreation:

1. Adequate supervision and leadership should be available for recreational activities.

2. Areas for recreational use should be properly designed and carefully located.

[5]doCarmo and Patterson, *First Aid Principles and Practices,* p. 14. Reprinted by permission.
[6]Ibid.
[7]Ibid.

3. Supplies and equipment should be inspected regularly and thoroughly.

4. Safety rules should be enforced for all activities.

5. All hazards (for example, open ditches and broken glass) should be eliminated.

6. Walls should never be used as end points in races.

7. Stones or rocks should never be used for bases.

8. Supplies and equipment should be used for their intended purposes.

9. Medical recommendations for activities should be observed.

10. Boundary lines should be clearly marked.

11. Proper clothing should be worn while engaging in recreational activities (for example, high heels should not be worn when participating in running activities, loose clothing should not be worn when using power tools).

12. Activities should be stopped before fatigue becomes a factor.

VALUE OF FIRST AID TRAINING TO SELF

1. Ability to administer first aid to oneself
2. Ability to direct others to give proper care
3. Development of safety consciousness

VALUE OF FIRST AID TRAINING TO OTHERS

1. Ability to administer first aid to family members, coworkers, acquaintances and strangers
2. Ability to give first aid instruction to others
3. Promotion of proper safety attitudes to others

VALUE OF FIRST AID TRAINING FOR RECREATION PERSONNEL

The overwhelming majority of first aid that personnel in the leisure services will be called upon to deliver will be of a minor nature. A large percentage of situations requiring first aid intervention can be handled effectively by the individual or his family. However, all personnel in the leisure services must be conscious of safety factors that can deleteriously affect an activity. A leisure activity, which has an inherent ingredient of fun, can be ruined if it is presented in an unsafe manner. A safe environment will contribute significantly to the voluntary, enjoyable, and self-fulfilling aspects of a re-creative experience.

Leisure services personnel must be able to recognize injuries and illnesses of a life-threatening nature. In addition, personnel should be able to maintain victims until medical assistance becomes available. "Properly applied first aid techniques can restore breathing and heart beat, control hemorrhage, prevent or reduce shock, protect open wounds from contamination, minimize fracture damage, and comfort the stricken person."[8]

VITAL SIGNS

The first aider should recognize specific vital signs. These are indicators of changes within the body due to injury or illness. Upon arriving at the scene of an accident, the first aider should examine each individual for injuries, and the quickest and best examination is to check the vital signs. The following are seven vital signs which should be checked:

1. Pulse. If it cannot be felt at the wrist, check at the carotid artery at the neck.

2. Respiration. Feel for air exchange, look and listen to the rate and depth of breathing.

3. Skin. Observe the skin's color, temperature, and moistness.

4. Pupils of the eye. Observe for dilation, constriction, unequalness, and response to light.

5. State of consciousness. Determine whether the individual is conscious, incoherent, or unconscious.

6. Ability to move. Determine if the individual is able to move the arms and legs or react to external stimuli.

7. Reaction to pain. Ask the individual whether he feels pain or discomfort, and if so, where.[9]

The first aider is able to objectively evaluate the seriousness of the injuries by the vital signs. Thus, he can quickly establish priorities in the care of the victims.

PRIORITIES FOR FIRST AID CARE

The first aider must establish an order of priority for the care and treatment of injured persons. Ideally, the first aider will be able to make logical decisions based upon his examination and observation of the accident and victims involved. doCarmo and Patterson indicate that:

[8]Ibid., p. 2.
[9]Ibid., p. 9.

Highest priority for receiving attention are individuals who have an obstructed airway, are having difficulty breathing, or have ceased to breath. Closely aligned to respiratory difficulty are cardiac arrest and extremely irregular or weak heart action. Uncontrollable hemorrhage, severe head injuries, open chest or abdominal wounds, poisonings, heart attacks, and severe shock should also receive first priority. Second priority injuries include burns, fractures, and spinal injuries. Lowest priority should be assigned to minor fractures, minor bleeding wounds, and obvious death.[10]

FIRST AID PROCEDURES AT THE SCENE

The first aider's presence of mind at the scene of an injury is of tremendous importance. The wrong words spoken to the wrong person at the wrong time may induce shock. The first aider should seek professional medical assistance, such as an ambulance, emergency squad, hospital, or physician, by telephone. He should instruct helpers carefully. As the first aider proceeds to care for the most severely injured, he should keep the following points in mind:

1. Do not move an injured individual from the position in which found. The only exception would be where that position might endanger the life of the individual or the first aider.

2. Determine whether the individual is breathing by opening the airway and feeling for an air exchange. Also feel for the pulse at the neck (carotid) artery. If no pulse is found and there is no breathing, institute cardiopulmonary resuscitation immediately. If breathing and pulse are found, continue to maintain an open airway.

3. Protect the individual from possible harm from bystanders and surroundings.

4. Cover the victim to help prevent shock.

5. Loosen any tight or constricting clothing.

6. Apply necessary bandages and splints, if available.

7. Talk to the individual to comfort and reassure him.

8. Do not attempt to diagnose or judge the injuries or illness; just care for the indicators exhibited.

9. Do not talk to bystanders about the condition of the individual.

10. Remain in charge until the injured or ill individual can be turned over to qualified persons, namely: police, rescue squad, or family.

11. Do not look in wallets or purses for identification. If medical identification is present it will be around the wrist or neck.

[10]Ibid., pp. 9–12.

12. Keep the situation as found, especially if a police investigation will be necessary.

13. Recognize your own limitations and see that the emergency medical system has been activated.[11]

WOUND

A wound is a break in the skin or mucous membrane. There are four classifications of wounds:

1. Abrasions (made by rubbing or scraping)
2. Incisions (sharp cuts that tend to bleed freely)
3. Lacerations (jagged wounds)
4. Punctures (pointed object run through the skin)

The following is the first aid treatment for wounds in which bleeding is not severe:

1. Wash hands thoroughly with clean water and soap.
2. Cleanse the injury thoroughly with plain soap and boiled water cooled to room temperature, or with clean running tap water and soap, applying the soap and water with a sterile dressing.
3. "Apply a dry sterile or clean dressing [that is, material placed directly over the wound] and bandage it firmly in place."[12]
4. "Caution the victim to see his physician promptly if evidence of infection appears."[13]

TRAUMATIC SHOCK

Traumatic shock is a depressed condition of many of the body functions due to failure of enough blood to circulate through the body following serious injury. The symptoms of traumatic shock are:

1. Dilated pupils
2. Vacant and lackluster eyes
3. Nausea and vomiting
4. Weak (but very rapid) or absent pulse
5. Shallow irregular breathing at increased rate
6. Pale, cold, and/or moist skin

[11]Ibid., p. 12.
[12]American Red Cross, *Advanced First Aid*, p. 38.
[13]Ibid.

The following is the first aid treatment for traumatic shock:

1. Position of patient
   a. Keep patient lying down (note: if there is difficulty breathing, the patient's head and chest should be elevated).
   b. Raise the foot of the bed or stretcher eight to twelve inches.
2. Heat administration
   a. Do not add heat, merely prevent a large loss of body heat.
   b. Place a blanket beneath him (note: do not induce sweating; it is better if the patient is slightly cool than very warm).
3. Fluid administration
   a. Fluids are of value in traumatic shock.
   b. If patient vomits or is nauseous or unconscious, do not give fluids.
   c. Plain water, neither hot nor cold, is the best fluid (½ glass of water at 15 minute intervals).
   d. Never give alcoholic drinks.

POISONING BY MOUTH

The following is the first aid treatment for poisoning by mouth:

1. Give first aid without delay; obtain medical advice by telephone as quickly as possible concerning antidotes. Save the label or container in order to identify the poison.

2. Give the victim milk or water to dilute the poison; four glasses or more with adults should be administered.

3. Induce vomiting promptly if indicated on label of poison.

4. Administer "universal antidote" or medicinal charcoal.

EPILEPTIC SEIZURES

The following is the first aid treatment for epileptic seizures:

1. Do not restrain the person in his convulsions.

2. Protect him from injury (for example, push away objects which he may strike against).

3. Do not obstruct breathing.

4. When seizure subsides, loosen the clothing about the neck and allow him to lie flat and rest with his head turned to the side.

BURNS

There are three types of burns:

1. Thermal
2. Sunburn
3. Chemical

Burns are classified in the following manner:

1. First degree: skin is reddened
2. Second degree: blisters develop
3. Third degree: deep destruction of underlying growth cells.

Burns are classified according to depth or degree.
The following is the first aid treatment for burns of the skin:

1. Thermal burns
   a. Treat for shock.
   b. Relieve pain and prevent further contamination by the application of a thick, sterile dressing (the dressing should be dry).
      1) apply the dressing in at least four, and preferably six, layers.
   c. Do not rupture blisters.
   d. Do not expose to direct sunlight until healing has occurred.
2. Mild sunburn
   a. Commercial preparations may relieve pain. Do not use butter or oleomargarine.
   b. Wash hands before applying the material.
   c. Use a dressing if blistering appears.
   d. Do not expose to direct sunlight until healing has occurred.
3. Chemical burns
   a. Wash away the chemical completely with large quantities of water.
   b. Follow directions on a label if they are available.
   c. Do not apply additional chemicals to the burn.
   d. Do not expose to direct sunlight until healing has occurred.

HEART ATTACK

The following is the first aid treatment for heart attack:

1. Faintness
   a. A lying-down position is best.
   b. Raising the legs is helpful.
2. Shortness of breath
   a. Raise the head and chest until patient is comfortable.
   b. Provide adequate ventilation, guarding against drafts and cold.
3. Acute pain
   a. A lying-down position is best.
   b. Comfort the patient by speaking encouragingly.
4. When a person has a heart attack his chest may hurt, he may have difficulty in breathing, and he may pass out. The first aider should attempt to determine if the heart attack victim has special medicine. Give him medicine only if he is awake. Call the victim's physician, who may be able to give specific first aid instructions.

FOREIGN BODY IN THE THROAT

The following is the first aid treatment for a foreign body in the throat:

1. Let the patient attempt to cough up the object (do not probe into the throat with the fingers or slap him on the back if he is conscious).
2. Do not distract and alarm the patient from his attempt to cough and breathe effectively by asking him questions.
3. Take the patient to a physician or the nearest hospital emergency ward.
4. If the patient stops breathing, give artificial respiration and try to clear the airway with fingers.

BANDAGING

There are six types of bandages:

1. Anchoring a bandage
2. Circular-turn bandage
3. Recurrent-turn bandage
4. Closed-spiral-turn bandage
5. Figure-of-8 bandage
6. Arm sling

The following are the first aid procedures for the six types of bandages:

1. Anchoring a bandage

    a. "Place the end of the bandage on a bias at the starting point.

    b. Encircle the part, allowing the corner of the bandage end to protrude.

    c. Turn down the protruding tip of the bandage and encircle the part again."[14]

2. Circular-turn bandage

    a. Encircle the part with each layer of bandage superimposed on the previous one.

    (1) Use of the circular-turn bandage is limited to covering parts of uniform width, such as the head, neck, and toe.

3. Recurrent-turn bandage

    a. The first fold is placed over one side of the part being covered; the next fold covers the opposite side of the part being covered, and each succeeding fold is working toward the center.

    b. Bandage must be held in place by circular bandage at the folds of the recurrent turns.

    c. Recurrent turns of bandage wind back and forth over a part.

4. Closed-spiral-turn bandage

    a. Each turn of the bandage overlaps one-third to one-half the width of the preceding one.

    b. No areas of skin or dressing should be visible between the turns of a closed-spiral-turn bandage.

    c. A closed-spiral-turn bandage may be used to bandage a part that varies in width.

5. Figure-of-8 bandage

    a. The figure-of-8 bandage consists of two special loops of bandage, one up and one down, crossing each other and forming an 8.

    b. The turns are of the criss-cross variety.

6. Arm sling

    a. "Place one end of the bandage on the uninjured side and let the other end hang down in front of the chest. Carry the point behind the elbow of the injured arm.

    b. Carry the second end of the bandage up over the shoulder and tie the two ends together at the side of the neck (not over the spine).

[14]Ibid., p. 207.

c. Bring the point of the bandage forward and pin it to the front of the sling. If a pin is not available, twist the point of the bandage until it is snug at the elbow and tie a single knot."[15]

BLEEDING

The following are four methods for controlling bleeding:

1. Direct pressure
2. Finger pressure on the brachial artery
3. Hand pressure on the femoral artery
4. The tourniquet

The following are the first aid techniques for controlling bleeding:

1. Direct pressure

   a. Place the cleanest material available against the bleeding point and apply firm pressure with your hand (note: elevate the bleeding part to help stop bleeding).

2. Finger pressure on brachial artery

   a. Put pressure on the brachial artery against the underlying bone.

   b. This will diminish the flow of blood to the upper extremity below the pressure point.

3. Hand pressure on the femoral artery

   a. Put pressure with the heel of the hand on the femoral artery in the mid-groin against the underlying pelvic bone.

   b. This will diminish bleeding in the lower extremity below the pressure point.

4. The tourniquet

   a. Wrap the material tightly twice around the limb, above the wound and between the body and the wound; tie a half knot.

   b. Place a short stick or similar material on the half knot and tie a full knot.

   c. Twist the stick to tighten the tourniquet until the flow of blood ceases.

   d. Secure the stick in place with the loose end of the tourniquet, another strip of cloth, or other improvised material.

   e. A tourniquet should only be used as a last resort, that is, when a

[15]Ibid., pp. 173–74.

life is in jeopardy. A tourniquet left on for an extended period of time causes the death of tissues and the part may have to be amputated. The decision a first aider has to make is "to risk sacrifice of a limb in order to save a life."[16]

ARTIFICIAL RESPIRATION

The following are the first aid procedures for artificial respiration:

1. Mouth-to-mouth artificial respiration
   a. Place patient on his back in a supine position.
   b. Clear the mouth of any foreign matter with the fingers.
   c. Press the tongue forward.
   d. Use fingers of both hands to lift the lower jaw from beneath and behind so that it juts out; hold the jaw in this position with one hand and tilt the head back to help clear the passageway.
   e. Make a leakproof seal by holding the nostrils shut.
   f. Place mouth over the patient's and exhale with a smooth steady action until the chest rises.
   g. Upon observing the chest rising, remove mouth from patient's in order to allow the victim's lungs to empty.
   h. Alternate between breathing into the patient's mouth and allowing his lungs to empty.
   i. Repeat this approximately 12 times per minute.
2. Manual (back pressure-arm lift method) artificial respiration
   a. Position of subject
      (1) Subject is in a face-down, prone position.
      (2) Patient's elbows are bent and hands are placed one upon the other.
      (3) Subject's face is turned to the side with cheek placed upon his hands.
   b. Position of first aider
      (1) Kneel on either the right or left knee, or both knees if more comfortable.
      (2) Hands are placed upon the flat of the patient's back so that the palms lie just below an imaginary line running between the armpits.
      (3) The fingers should be spread downward and outward, and the tips of the thumbs should touch slightly.

[16]Ibid., p. 37.

c. Compression phase

(1) Rock forward, keeping elbows straight, until the arms are vertical.

(2) The upper part of the first aider's body should exert slow, steady, even pressure downward upon the hands.

e. Expansion phase

(1) First aider should rock backward enabling the patient's arms to be drawn toward the first aider.

(2) Patient's arms should be drawn upward and toward the first aider; first aider should feel resistance at the subject's shoulders.

(3) Lower the patient's arms to the ground.

f. Repeat compression and expansion phase 12 times per minute at a steady rate.

Student assignments

This part consists of 27 objectives. You will be called upon to demonstrate your mastery of each objective. Some answers require written responses. Some responses will be of a demonstrable nature; that is, you will demonstrate mastery of a specific first aid technique. The objectives of the module are similar, but not identical, to that used in the "Standard First Aid Course" used by the American Red Cross.

OBJECTIVE	ACHIEVEMENT OF COMPETENCY
1. To describe the value of first aid training.	Write the value of first aid training to yourself and others.
2. Describe first aid directions in serious first aid treatment.	Orally describe first aid directions to follow in serious first aid treatment.
3. To identify types of wounds.	Identify a minimum of four types of wounds.
4. To demonstrate first aid treatment of a wound.	Demonstrate first aid competencies of a wound in which bleeding is not severe.
5. To identify symptoms of traumatic shock.	Identify a minimum of three symptoms of traumatic shock.
6. To demonstrate first aid treatment in traumatic shock.	Demonstrate a proficiency in administering first aid treatment to a person in traumatic shock.

OBJECTIVE	ACHIEVEMENT OF COMPETENCY
7. To demonstrate first aid in poisoning.	Demonstrate first aid treatment for poisoning by mouth.
8. To describe types of burns.	Describe a minimum of three types of burns.
9. To identify classifications of burns.	Identify a minimum of three classifications of burns.
10. To demonstrate first aid for thermal burns.	Demonstrate first aid treatment for thermal burns of the skin.
11. To list first aid procedures in epileptic convulsions.	List a minimum of five first aid procedures to follow in cases of epileptic convulsions.
12. To describe first aid procedures in heart attack.	Describe a minimum of two first aid procedures to follow in heart attack cases with regard to the following: a. faintness, b. shortness of breath, and c. acute pain.
13. To describe first aid procedures for an object lodged in the throat.	Describe a minimum of three first aid procedures to follow for an object lodged in the throat.
14. To demonstrate first aid of anchoring a bandage.	Demonstrate the correct first aid technique of anchoring a bandage.
15. To demonstrate first aid of the circular-turn bandage.	Demonstrate the correct first aid technique of the circular-turn bandage.
16. To demonstrate first aid of the closed-spiral-turn bandage.	Demonstrate the correct first aid technique of the closed-spiral-turn bandage.
17. To demonstrate first aid of the figure-of-8 bandage.	Demonstrate the correct first aid technique of the figure-of-8 bandage.
18. To demonstrate first aid of the recurrent-turn bandage.	Demonstrate the correct first aid technique of the recurrent-turn bandage.

OBJECTIVE	ACHIEVEMENT OF COMPETENCY
19. To demonstrate first aid of an arm sling.	Demonstrate the correct first aid technique of applying an arm sling.
20. To demonstrate first aid for controlling bleeding.	Demonstrate a minimum of four first aid techniques for controlling bleeding.
21. To demonstrate first aid for mouth-to-mouth artificial respiration.	Demonstrate the correct first aid technique for administering mouth-to-mouth artificial respiration.
22. To demonstrate first aid for manual artificial respiration.	Demonstrate the correct first aid technique for administering manual artificial respiration (that is, back pressure-arm lift method).
23. To describe concepts in preventive safety.	Describe a minimum of eight concepts in preventive safety in recreation.
24. To write the vital signs.	Write a minimum of six of the seven vital signs.
25. To write priorities for first aid care.	Write at least 100 words describing priorities for first aid care.
26. To describe legal liability.	Orally describe legal liability in first aid care.
27. To write first aid procedures to follow at the scene of an accident.	Write a minimum of 10 of 13 first aid procedures to follow at the scene of an accident or injury.

Resources

This part is divided into two sections: (1) a list of textbooks and films and (2) a problem-solving activity.

TEXTBOOKS

AMERICAN RED CROSS. *Advanced First Aid and Emergency Care.* Garden City, N.Y.: Doubleday, 1973.

———. *Basic First Aid, Books 1–4.* Garden City, N.Y.: Doubleday, 1971.

BANNON, JOSEPH J. *Problem Solving in Recreation and Parks.* Englewood Cliffs, N.J.: Prentice-Hall, 1972.

DOCARMO, PAMELA BAKHAUS, and PATTERSON, ANGELO T. *First Aid Principles and Procedures.* Englewood Cliffs, N.J.: Prentice-Hall, 1976.

First Aid: Contemporary Practices and Principles. Minneapolis: Burgess Publishing, 1972.

First Aid Textbook. Garden City, N.Y.: Doubleday, 1965.

KRAUS, RICHARD, and BATES, BARBARA J. *Recreation Leadership and Supervision: Guidelines for Professional Development.* Philadelphia: W. B. Saunders, 1975.

FILMS

Catalog of Films and Slides. Boston: Greater Boston Red Cross, 1973.

Champions on Film. "Artificial Respiration," "Control of Bleeding," "Physical Shock," "Wounds," "Fractures and Dislocations," "Transportation of the Injured." 745 State Circle, Ann Arbor, Michigan, 48104.

Standard First Aid Series 10. Boston: Greater Boston Red Cross.

The $30,000 lawsuit*

SITUATION

This Stillwater Park District has been sued in Warren County Circuit Court for $30,000 damages for injuries received by a ten-year-old girl on allegedly unsafe playground equipment in Wood Lake Park. The suit was filed by Philip Stonquest of 515 John Street on behalf of his daughter, Kathleen, and himself.

It is alleged that the girl fell sixteen feet last June 16 while playing on a "swing and pipe" slide in the park. The complaint described the playground equipment as a steel ladder and a slanting steel pole (or pipe) on which children could slide to the ground after climbing the ladder. It is alleged that the device was dangerous because there was "no safe means by which the children could get from the top of the ladder to the slide." It charged that the park district failed to maintain equipment in a safe condition.

According to the complaint, the child sustained a fractured arm, internal injuries, and other external injuries when she fell. The suit asked for $25,000 damages for the child's injuries. The father also asked $5,000 for medical and hospital expenses.

*Joseph J. Bannon, *Problem Solving in Recreation and Parks*, © 1972, p. 337. Reprinted by permission of Prentice-Hall, Inc., Englewood Cliffs, New Jersey.

PROBLEM

What is the difference between a governmental and a proprietary function? How would it apply in this case? Do you think the equipment as described is dangerous and unsafe? State your reasons and the criteria you used to determine this. Devise a checklist that would assist in keeping playground equipment safe and in good condition. How often should playground equipment be checked? Who should check the equipment? Search the court decisions that have been made in your state that are similar to the case presented here.

MODULE 4

Activity requirements for human growth and development

Methods and materials

The field of recreation is extremely diverse. What is recreation to one person is not necessarily recreation to another. Recreators should have the ability to plan meaningful activities to include all people. They should recognize that some activities are better suited to one age group than to another. For example, senior citizens would probably enjoy an arts-and-crafts project more than they would playing a vigorous athletic team sport in a formal atmosphere.

The recreator should understand that different age groups have various traits which affect their life styles. A viable, person-centered recreation program should meet the needs of all people. Quite often, recreators only plan activities for one group of people; they do not plan their program to include all people. A recreator who has the skills needed to plan programs for all people is a valuable addition to any recreation staff.

To effectively plan and carry out a viable recreation program, the leader must be aware of factors that influence the success of a recreation program: the age, sex, and skill of people, the size of the group, and activities that meet the individuals needs at a specific time. It is important that a recreator recognize why an activity is planned for a specific person. An activity should have a goal and an objective which is consistent with an individual's needs. Activities are instruments that a recreator has at his command. He should realize that some activities are better suited for one individual than for another. Consequently, he should not offer activities in a haphazard fashion. A recreation leader usually does not offer an activity just for activity's sake. Rather, he should have the ability to select an activity that is in harmony with the objectives set forth for each person.

CONCEPTS OF ACTIVITY ANALYSIS

When an activity is analyzed, it is broken down into all of its component parts. This affords the recreator an opportunity to determine what specific elements predominate within an activity. By such analysis, a recreator will become aware of unique qualities inherent within an activity. He will, therefore, be able to select and offer activities suitable for specific groups of people. Recreators should, of course, recognize that many variables could be superimposed upon participants and their "success" in various recreation experiences. Therefore, it is essential that recreators learn to analyze activities.

FUNCTIONS OF ACTIVITY ANALYSIS

Activity analysis is used primarily as a means to match a patient's needs with the rehabilitation objectives set forth by a rehabilitation team. Historically, many recreators perceived activity analysis as constituting the sole domain of the therapeutic recreator. However, knowledge of activity analysis is a valuable competency for all recreators. It is to the recreation leader's advantage to be able to break down an activity into its component parts. This process helps to ensure more continuity in activity offerings.

Activities are the media through which individuals experience the satisfactions which give activities their recreational value and significance. Through forms of activity, an individual can satisfy his recreation desires and interests. In order to optimally plan activities, a recreator should know the varied activities that are commonly considered recreation and the satisfactions and benefits they give many people. In addition, by being able to "see" the various ingredients inherent in a specific activity, the recreator will be able to plan those activities that will greater benefit a participant. If recreators acquire the skills of analyzing activities, they will be able to objectively evaluate their activity program.

ADAPTING AREAS AND ACTIVITIES FOR RECREATION

Four concepts are significant in the adaptation of areas and activities to recreation. First, the recreator must be aware of where the participant is along a continuum of acquired skills. The recreator is then able to take the participant from where he is to where he wants to go; or in the case of a disabled or handicapped person, where the recreator wants the participant to go.

The second concept is that, in a recreational setting, the activities are merely tools—methods and materials—which the recreator has at his disposal. The recreation leader should start an activity program so that fun, success, and a sense of accomplishment are built into the program.

The third concept is that any activity can be adapted to meet the needs of all the participants. The major limitations are the leader's own innovativeness and his commitment to serve all segments of society.

The fourth concept is that the materials which are adapted—rules, space, supplies, and equipment—should be done so in a developmental and sequential order. Activities are built upon previously acquired skills that participants have already mastered. Therefore, those activities that are offered have a higher probability of being successful to participants than might otherwise be the case.

Understanding these concepts aids recreation leaders in using techniques that have proved valuable for years. Furthermore, the recreation leader should understand that all four concepts are usually applied simultaneously.

Pomeroy has specified procedures that recreation leaders should follow in adapting activities to recreational programs. She indicates that "usually activities must be slowed down."[1] Recreation leaders should explore various methods (for example, trial and error) of adapting activities. She offers the following several ways to adapt activities for groups:

1. Use the "assembly line" process, when working on group projects, by encouraging each individual to contribute according to his particular physical/mental/emotional ability. In a sewing club, for example, only one person may be physically capable of using a sewing machine; two people may be able to use scissors, while others may pin, measure, and so on.

2. Suggest types of activities that can include everyone; i.e., pantomime plays, puppetry, primitive dance, pottery, and so on.

3. Structure activities in such a manner that individuals may participate by using their toes, one hand, one arm, and so on.

4. Encourage groups and individuals to work out their own adaptations. Some handicapped individuals and groups can adapt activities for

---

[1]Janet Pomeroy, *Recreation for the Physically Handicapped* (New York: Macmillan, 1964), p. 81.

themselves. For example, in one program the recreation leader demonstrated the game of deck tennis as it is normally played to a group of severely handicapped children, and then suggested that the group work out their own adaptations. The fact that some were in wheelchairs, and some were on crutches presented a problem. However, they were all able to play successfully.[2]

Although all of Pomeroy's adaptations were for the physically handicapped participant, all of the concepts and methods can be modified to include all people.

The following list illustrates five specific ways that volleyball can be adapted to meet the individual needs of senior citizens:

1. Lower the net from 8 feet to 6 feet.
2. Make the playing surface (the court) smaller.
3. Adapt the volleyball; for example, use balloons, nerf balls, bladder balls, and so forth.
4. Adapt the rules; for example, newcomb, elementary newcomb, bounce newcomb, no serve, serve from in close, and so forth.
5. Players may be restricted to only playing a certain place or position on the court.

VALUES OF RECOGNIZING AGE-GROWTH CHARACTERISTICS

There are several reasons why recreation personnel must determine age-growth characteristics for recreation:

1. Age of participants is a factor in planning recreation programs to meet interests and needs.
2. A recreator can use knowledge of age-growth characteristics as a means to motivate individuals to become actively involved in programs.
3. A recreator can better classify a group of participants.
4. A recreator can provide activity offerings which are more nearly suited to an individual's needs.
5. A recreator can use age-growth characteristics as a general guide for *initiating* programs geared to individual needs of participants.

A CLASSIFICATION SCHEME FOR CATEGORIZING AGE GROUPS

The following classification and list of specific recreational activities should be used for various age groups. These activities are illustrative rather than hard and fast.

[2] Ibid.

1. Infant (birth–2½ years of age): storytelling, "peek-a-boo" chasing games, crude constructive play, toys, and equipment play

2. Preschool (3–5 years of age): blocks, singing and dancing games, rhythmics, simple crafts, simple circle games, and impersonation play

3. Early childhood (6–8 years of age): rivalry games, mimetics, individual activities, rhythmics, and story play

4. Late childhood (9–11 years of age): group games, leadup athletic games, trips, outings and explorations, and relays

5. Early adolescence (12–14 years of age): group games, handicrafts, mountain climbing, skiing, social clubs and parties, and reading

6. Late adolescence (15–19 years of age): athletic and team games in a formal atmosphere, social games and parties, reading, music, and dramatics

7. Young adults (20–34 years of age): hobbies, art, social clubs, music, dramatics, individual and team sports, and spectator activities

8. Middle-age (35–65 years of age): crafts, parties and dances, individual sports, spectator sports, hobbies, and social clubs

9. Senior citizens (over 65 years of age): social clubs, hobbies, excursions and group sightseeing tours, arts and crafts, physical fitness, discussion and appreciation groups.

CHARACTERISTICS OF AGE GROUPS

A. Infants (birth–2½ years of age)
1. Physical traits
   a. Very rapid, but declining, rate of growth
   b. Instability of physiological processes
   c. Development of physiological equilibrium (that is, crawling, creeping, walking)
   d. Development of eye–hand coordination
   e. Establishment of satisfactory rhythms of rest and activity
2. Mental traits
   a. Development of preverbal and verbal communication
   b. Mimicking what is spoken
   c. Rudimentary concept formation
   d. Awareness of the alive as opposed to inanimate, and the familiar as opposed to unfamiliar
3. Social traits
   a. Establishment of self as a very dependent being

    b. Development of rudimentary social interaction

    c. First adjustments to the expectations of others

    d. Adjustment to adult feeding demands

    e. Adjustment to adult cleanliness demands

    f. Adjustment to adult attitudes toward genital manipulation

B. Preschool (3–5 years of age)

  1. Physical traits

    a. Rapid body growth

    b. Development of speech

    c. Development of muscular coordination

    d. Much motor activity

    e. Manipulation of materials

  2. Mental traits

    a. Rapid brain growth

    b. Active imagination

    c. Development of purposeful activity

    d. Strengthening of memory

    e. Responsiveness to suggestion

  3. Social traits

    a. Frequent association with adults

    b. Loyalty to family

    c. Imaginary friends and acquaintances

    d. Frequent exaggeration

    e. Affection and sympathy

C. Early childhood (6–8 years of age)

  1. Physical traits

    a. Slow growth rate

    b. Prevalence of disease and fatigue

    c. Improvement of motor coordination

    d. Impulsiveness and restlessness

  2. Mental traits

    a. Search for reality

    b. Very little interest in school work

    c. Good memory

    d. Questioning of attitudes

  3. Social traits

    a. Imitation and rivalry among playmates

    b. Small appreciation of moral values

    c. Very impressionable (that is, assumes mannerisms and habits of elders)

    d. Sensitivity to failure

D. Late childhood (9–11 years of age)

  1. Physical traits

    a. Stability in growth rate and physiological processes

    b. Good motor control

    c. Appearance of sex differences

    d. Immunity to disease and fatigue

    e. Good muscular coordination

  2. Mental traits

    a. Increased objective thinking, decreased reasoning

    b. Questioning

    c. Refinement and development of perception

    d. Advanced emotions

    e. Mental alertness

    f. Striving for reality and truth, understanding of real causal relations

  3. Social traits

    a. Movement into peer-centered society

    b. Rebelliousness, cynicism, and selfishness

    c. Development of time morality and rule learning

    d. Marked separation of boys and girls

    e. Desire to impress others, especially peers of the same sex

E. Early adolescence (12–14 years of age)

  1. Physical traits

    a. Rapidly increasing growth rate and increasing glandular activity culminating in sexual maturity

    b. Muscular with clumsiness and awkwardness

    c. Very susceptible to fatigue

    d. Respiration, temperature, and pulse of adult

  2. Mental traits

    a. Selective memory

    b. Creative imagination

    c. Abstract, logical thinking

    d. Strong emotions with little control

e. Development of ideals of right and wrong, altruism, and ambition

3. Social traits

a. Strong rebellion against adults, period of greatest conflict between parent and child

b. Strong identity with peers in a new heterosexual grouping

c. Consciousness of opposite sex with shyness, compensated by showing off and teasing

d. Behavior according to a shifting peer code (easily influenced)

F. Late Adolescence (15–19 years of age)

1. Physical traits

a. Physical growth nearing maximum

b. Development of physical balance and coordination

c. Strong sexual drive

d. Excessive physical activity for some, nonexistent physical activity for others

2. Mental traits

a. Strong selective memory

b. Mental alertness

c. Enlarged mental horizon

d. Escape of reality by daydreaming

e. Very opinionated and stubborn

3. Social traits

a. Defiance of adults; extreme group loyalty

b. Mixed social groupings

c. Social consciousness toward the group

d. Affectionate with a possible marriage partner

e. Formulation of a workable belief and value system

G. Young adult (20–34 years of age)

1. Physical traits

a. Maturity almost fully completed

b. Muscular endurance

c. Mastery of motor and senses

d. Restless when idle

2. Mental traits

a. Permanent habits and interests

b. Abstract reasoning and practical thinking

      c. Responsibility for self leading to development of unified personality

      d. Evaluation of ideas

   3. Social traits

      a. Marriage and family ties

      b. Work efficiency for financial gains through a vocation

      c. Ambitious and reliable

      d. Very mobile, more educated and more aware than previous group of young adults

      e. Civic activity

H. Middle-age (35–65 years of age)

   1. Physical traits

      a. Maturity fully completed

      b. Concern about general health

      c. Motor reflexes diminished

      d. Less excessive physical activity

      e. Frustration in not being able to physically keep up with others at work or at home

   2. Mental traits

      a. Mentally alert

      b. Mental horizons reliant upon experiences, discussion, and reading

      c. Development of vocation and definite work pattern

      d. Diminished abstract reasoning

   3. Social traits

      a. Desire for status

      b. Desire for financial security

      c. Civic responsibility and community service

      d. Responsible, and frustration, in trying to do things with their teenage children

I. Senior citizens (over 65 years of age)

   1. Physical traits

      a. Declining health and ability

      b. Physical deterioriation

      c. Loss of mobility

      d. Greater amount of sleep needed

   2. Mental traits

      a. Loss of memory

     b. Senility

     c. Diminished abstract reasoning

     d. Escape of reality by daydreaming

  3. Social traits

     a. Resistance to change

     b. Social isolation (friends are deceased)

     c. Lack of self-worth

     d. Fixed low income

CHARACTERISTICS OF SPECIFIC HANDICAPPED GROUPS

General characteristics and specific recreation activities for eight handicapped groups are:

A. Visually impaired and blind

  1. Vision deviates from the normal (A person is classified as blind if he can see at a distance of 20 feet what a normal person can see at 200 feet. A visually impaired person can see at a distance of between 70 and 200 feet what a normal person can see at 200 feet.)

  2. Normal life span

  3. Usually no other limiting physical disabilities

  4. Severely limited social life, limited mobility

B. Hearing impaired and deaf

  1. Hearing deviates from normal (A person with a hearing loss above 60 decibels is considered deaf. An average person has a hearing loss of between five and six decibels.)

  2. Weak in language and verbal communication

  3. Poor balance and tendency to become dizzy

  4. Adequate motor skills

C. Senior citizens (over 65 years of age)

  1. Loss of memory

  2. Declining health and ability

  3. Social isolation

  4. Lack of self-esteem

  5. A fixed low income

  6. Escape from reality by daydreaming about the past

D. Mentally ill

  1. Difficult interpersonal relationships

  2. Deficient in social skills

E. Mentally retarded
1. Some degree of below-normal intellectual functioning
2. Socially inadequate
3. Ineffective in applying whatever he has learned to problems of ordinary living
4. Lack of coordination, less resistance to fatigue, lower levels of strength, a poor self-image, and poor body articulation

F. Epileptic
1. Disturbance in the brain causing a convulsion or spasm
2. Pattern of recurrent seizures, not a specific disease entity
3. Two types: cause unknown (idiopathic) and definite causes (symptomatic)
4. Many kinds; two most frequent: petit (small) mal and grand (large) mal
5. Controlled by medication

G. Cerebral palsy
1. Brain damaged
2. Inability to control muscular movements
3. Lack of balance, awkward and shambling gait, tremors, guttural speech and grimacing
4. Frequently complicated by the occurrence of convulsions, behavior disturbances, and/or mental retardation

H. Physically handicapped
1. A physically handicapped person possesses the same needs (i.e. recognition, success, approval, self-worth, etc.) as the "normal" person
2. Poor social skills, isolation from peer-group relationships
3. Physical deficit, but otherwise normal
4. Frequent emotional, psychological, physiological, and social deviance

Implications and adaptations in recreation for the visually impaired and the blind

1. The visually handicapped have the same basic needs as the "normal" individual.
2. The recreator should use as many of the visually handicapped person's senses as he can.
3. The leader should strive to let the visually impaired do whatever he can to help himself.

4. Normal recreational activities should be used whenever and wherever possible for carryover.

5. Emphasis should be placed on developing confidence and self-esteem through the activities.

6. There are several adaptive techniques and equipment for working with visually handicapped people:

   a. Special table and board games (for example, chess and checkers) with sunken or perforated squares

   b. Cards marked in Braille

   c. Crossword puzzles with plastic tiles of Braille letters

   d. A sighted person who acts as a partner of the visually impaired

   e. Different surfaces and materials for boundaries; for example, a concrete surface for out-of-bounds and a wood surface for in-bounds; heavy painted lines for out-of-bounds markers

   f. Larger, lighter, and more colorful balls than those used with normally sighted people with bells, buzzers, or rattles for easy location.

7. The kinesthetic sense should be used a great deal.

Recreational activities for the visually impaired and the blind

1. Wrestling
2. Sculpture and carving
3. Music
4. Radio listening
5. Political groups
6. Religious organizations
7. Ethnic organizations[3]
8. Roller skating to music
9. Archery
10. Golf
11. Track and field
12. Bowling
13. Fishing
14. Social, folk, square, and modern dancing
15. Marching
16. Body building

[3]Robert P. Overs, Elizabeth O'Connor, and Barbara DeMarco, *Guide to Avocational Activities*, vol. I, no. 58 (Milwaukee: Curative Workshop of Milwaukee, May 1972).

17. Modified stunts and tumbling
18. Basketball goal shooting
19. Light exercise to music
20. Boating
21. Swimming[4]
22. Games and relays
23. Outdoor recreational activities, such as camping, hiking, boating and sailing[5]

Implications and adaptations in recreation for the hearing impaired and deaf

1. Recreator should stand close to the person he is working with.

2. In active games hearing handicapped should have a "hearing-partner" whenever possible.

3. The recreator should limit climbing and apparatus activities if the person has balance difficulties.

4. The recreator should directly face the participant at his eye level and speak slowly and clearly.

5. Hand gestures, visual aids or other methods of nonverbal communication may be used.

6. The recreator should use as many of the hearing handicapped person's senses as he can.

Recreational activities for hearing impaired and deaf people

1. Throwing games
2. Target and skill games
3. Running games
4. Table and board games
5. Card games
6. Model racing games
7. Puzzles
8. Boating, sailing, canoeing
9. Horseback riding

[4]Maryhelen Vannier and Hollis F. Fait, *Teaching Physical Education in Secondary Schools* (Philadelphia: W. B. Saunders, 1964), p. 356.

[5]Arthur S. Daniels and Evelyn A. Davies, *Adapted Physical Education* (New York: Harper & Row, 1965), p. 270.

10. Physical fitness sports such as jogging, running, weightlifting, and gymnastics

11. Roller skating

12. Water sports, such as swimming, skiing, diving, skin diving

13. Winter sports, such as skiing, skating, sledding, tobogganing, snowmobiling, snowshoeing

14. Archery

15. Bowling, lawn bowling, bocci

16. Rifle, pistol, trap or skeet shooting

17. Raising, caring for, and propagating plants

18. Badminton

19. Croquet

20. Reading and literature appreciation activities

21. Traveling

22. Dance[6]

Implications and adaptations in recreation for the epileptic

1. Recreators should know first aid procedures for epileptic seizures.

2. Recreation activities that require body contact, climbing, or are highly emotional are not advisable for epileptics.

3. Swimming activities should be offered only if supervision is possible.

4. Activities that would result in injury if the participant lost consciousness (for example, horseback riding, bicycling, rifle and pistol shooting, and apparatus work) should be avoided.

5. Fatiguing activities should be avoided.

Recreational activities for the epileptic

1. Folk, social, tap, and modern dance

2. Bowling

3. Fly and bait casting

4. Table and card games

5. Hiking

6. Archery

7. Golf

[6]Overs, O'Connor, and De Marco, *Guide to Avocational Activities*, vols. I and II.

8. Tennis

9. Badminton

10. Social recreational activities

11. Basic sport skills

12. Team games in which body contact has been largely eliminated, such as volleyball[7]

13. Individual and dual sports, such as shuffleboard, bowling, table tennis, horseshoes, tennis and squash.[8]

Implications and adaptations in recreation for the mentally ill

1. Mentally ill people digress from the normal in terms of interpersonal relationships with others, that is they feel worthless, inferior, and deficient in social skills and are overly sensitive to real or imagined social slights.

2. Recreation can be used as a vehicle to teach skills that will contribute to alleviating personal, social, and emotional demands of everyday life.

3. Recreational activities should provide outlets that are constructive to the participants' needs.

4. Recreation for mentally ill people should enable participants to engage in resocialization activities.

5. Recreation programs for mentally ill people should serve to release creative self-expression, develop a sense of recognition and pride in accomplishment, release hostility, and be fun.

6. Recreation in a psychiatric setting should provide programs that can be carried over into each person's home or community.

7. Recreational activities for mentally ill people should foster a need to belong, provide opportunities to meet people, and offer an environment free of competitive pressures.

8. Activities should be informal, should be less structured, and should provide opportunities for social learning within a group.

Recreational activities for the mentally ill

1. Shuffleboard

2. Casting

---

[7]Vannier and Fait, *Teaching Physical Education in Secondary Schools*, pp. 353–54.
[8]Daniels and Davies, *Adapted Physical Education*, p. 232.

3. Croquet
4. Horseshoes
5. Ring toss
6. Bowling
7. Weightlifting
8. Bag punching[9]
9. Grooming
10. Coffee and conversation
11. Psychodrama
12. Dance therapy
13. Drama and poetry
14. Cooking
15. Small crafts
16. Movies
17. Exercise group[10]

Implications and adaptations in recreation for the mentally retarded

1. Verbal directions should be few and simple.

2. As many of the participants' senses as possible should be stimulated.

3. Kinesthesis and demonstration should be used.

4. Activities should be offered on a developmental basis and broken down into small, progressive and sequential steps.

5. The mentally retarded have a shorter attention span and usually cannot work toward a goal as well as the mentally normal; therefore, activities should not be too challenging and long in duration.

6. The mentally retarded often perform best the first couple of times a skill is practiced.

7. Repetition, drill, and review of skills are needed more with the mentally retarded than with the mentally normal.

8. Recreational activities should be appropriate for the chronological age of the participants.

[9]Vannier and Fait, *Teaching Physical Education in Secondary Schools*, p. 165.

[10]Richard Kraus, *Therapeutic Recreation Service Principles and Practices* (Philadelphia: W. B. Saunders, 1973), p. 79.

Recreational activities for the mentally retarded

1. Sports and physical fitness, such as bowling, skating, swimming, volleyball, track and field, and roller skating

2. Creative experiences, such as arts and crafts, music, dance, and drama

3. Games, such as quiet table games, active equipment games, social games and mixers, active outdoor or gymnasium games

4. Social activities, such as club activities, parties, dances, trip programs, and dinners

5. Training in living skills, such as cooking, sewing, repair of simple equipment, and trips using public transportation

6. Special events and trips

7. Camping, such as day camping, residential camping, two- or three-day vacation camping[11]

8. Running games

9. Throwing games

10. Indoor games

11. Model racing games

12. Professional sports observation

13. Bicycling

14. Boating, sailing, canoeing

15. Archery

16. Fishing and trapping of acquatic animals

17. Animal care, training, breeding, and exhibiting

18. Farming, fishing, and forestry activities

19. Photography

20. Drama

21. Sculpture and carving activities[12]

Implications and adaptations in recreation for senior citizens

1. Recreational activities should strive to afford participants a feeling of usefulness and a sense of self-worth and dignity.

2. Transportation should be provided to and from the activity.

3. Recreational activities that help in social interaction and facilitate self-expression should be offered.

[11]Ibid., pp. 105–11.
[12]Overs, O'Connor, and De Marco, *Guide to Avocational Activities*, vols. I and II.

4. Recreational activities should be offered free of charge.

5. Recreational activities should contribute to meaningful social relationships with others.

6. Recreational activities should be offered that are suitable for participants' functioning capacity.

7. Recreational activities should be of a challenging and interesting nature—physically, mentally, emotionally, and socially.

Recreational activities for senior citizens

1. Arts and crafts
2. Music
3. Dramatics
4. Dance
5. Religious services
6. Films
7. Hobbies
8. Social programs
9. Games, such as adapted bowling, golf, shuffleboard
10. Trips and outings
11. Camping
12. Horseshoes
13. Card games
14. Reading
15. Service projects[13]

Implications and adaptations in recreation for the cerebral palsied

1. The recreator should provide slow, repetitive movements in a sequence to help movement skills of the cerebral palsied.

2. Highly competitive activities accompanied by continuous excitement should not be offered.

3. Recreational activities that help in social interaction and facilitate self-expression should be offered

4. Activities that involve fine finger dexterity are not as good as the free, large motor movements that aid in movement exploration.

5. Activities that produce tension and require a quick response should not be offered.

[13]Kraus, *Therapeutic Recreation Service Principles and Practices,* p. 155.

6. Activities that stress methods of relaxation, body control, and accuracy of movement are valuable.

Recreational activities for the cerebral palsied

1. Swimming
2. Social, square, folk, and tap dancing
3. Horseshoes
4. Games of low organization
5. Shuffleboard
6. Leadup games to sports
7. Bowling
8. Archery
9. Golf
10. Fly and bait casting
11. Table tennis
12. Campcraft activities including fishing
13. Games requiring movement accuracy such as hitting or kicking stationary objects[14]

Implications and adaptations in recreation for the physically handicapped

1. Recreational activities should be presented that enhance social interaction, self-expression, and personality development.

2. Recreational activities should develop self-esteem and personal accomplishment.

3. Recreational activities should afford the physically handicapped an opportunity to participate actively in their community.

4. The physically handicapped can learn and deepen personal interests through appropriate recreational activities.

5. The recreator will often have to adapt areas, facilities, and rules to provide meaningful activities for the physically handicapped.

6. The physically handicapped are eager to compete with the nondisabled.

7. Individuals with physical limitations are often well integrated members of the nondisabled in social groups.

8. Wherever and whenever possible, recreational activities should be offered that are suitable for the chronological age of the participants.

[14]Vannier and Fait, *Teaching Physical Education in Secondary Schools*, p. 352.

Recreational activities for the physically handicapped

1. Drama
2. Music
3. Dance
4. Arts and crafts
5. Special events
6. Clubs and interest groups
7. Active games and sports
8. Social recreation
9. Outings and trips
10. Day camping[15]
11. Swimming
12. Quiet games
13. Nature[16]

Student assignments

This part consists of nine objectives. You will be called upon to demonstrate your mastery of each objective. Some answers require written responses. Some responses will be of a demonstrable nature; that is, you will be conducting, adapting, and demonstrating activities suitable for specific ages, interests, and abilities.

OBJECTIVE	ACHIEVEMENT OF COMPETENCY
1. To describe concepts of activity analysis.	Orally describe at least two concepts of activity analysis.
2. To write the functions of activity analysis.	Write a minimum of 100 words describing the functions of activity analysis.
3. To describe why a recreator should be able to recognize age-growth characteristics in recreation.	Orally describe advantages for recognizing age-growth characteristics in the field of recreation.

[15]Pomeroy, *Recreation for the Physically Handicapped*, pp. 178–344. Pomeroy identifies these 10 activities as appropriate for the physically handicapped and discusses them in depth.

[16]Kraus, *Therapeutic Recreation Service Principles and Practices*, pp. 128–37.

OBJECTIVE	ACHIEVEMENT OF COMPETENCY
4. To write a scheme categorizing age groups.	Write a classification scheme categorizing age groups from infants to senior citizens.
5. To describe and adapt a recreational activity.	Describe one recreational activity and adapt the activity for three age groups.
6. To list recreational activities for specific age groups.	List a minimum of three recreational activities applicable for each age group.
7. To describe characteristics of age groups.	List a minimum of three characteristics of each age group identified.
8. To describe characterisitcs of diagnostic groups.	List a minimum of three characteristics of each diagnostic group identified
9. To describe and adapt a recreational activity.	a. List one recreation activity. b. Orally describe how the activity can be adapted for at least three diagnostic groups identified.

Resources

This part is divided into two sections: (1) a list of reference materials and (2) two problem-solving activities.

TEXTBOOKS

ADAMS, RONALD C.; DANIEL, ALFRED N.; and RULLMAN, LEE. *Games, Sports and Exercises for the Physically Handicapped*. Philadelphia: Lea and Febiger, 1974.

AVEDON, ELLIOT M. *Therapeutic Recreation Service: An Applied Behavioral Science Approach*. Englewood Cliffs, N.J.: Prentice-Hall, 1974.

BANNON, JOSEPH J. *Problem Solving in Recreation and Parks*. Englewood Cliffs, N. J.: Prentice-Hall, 1972.

CORBIN, H. DAN, and TAIT, WILLIAM J. *Education for Leisure*. Englewood Cliffs, N.J.: Prentice-Hall, 1973.

DANIELS, ARTHUR, and DAVIES, EVELYN A. *Adapted Physical Education*. New York: Harper & Row, 1965.

FAIT, HOLLIS. *Physical Education for the Elementary School Child: Experiences in Movement*. Philadelphia: W. B. Saunders, 1971.

———. *Special Physical Education: Adapted, Corrective, Developmental*. Philadelphia: W. B. Saunders, 1966.

GORDON, IRA J.; GUINAGH, BARRY; and JESTER, R. EMILE. *Child Learning Through Child Play*. New York: St. Martin's Press, 1972.

JERSILD, ARTHUR T. *Child Psychology*. Englewood Cliffs, N. J.: Prentice-Hall, 1968.

KRAUS, RICHARD. *Recreation Today: Program Planning and Leadership*. New York: Appleton-Century-Crofts, 1966.

———. *Therapeutic Recreation Service Principles and Practices*. Philadelphia: W. B. Saunders, 1973.

MILLER, ARTHUR G., and WHITCOMB, VIRGINIA. *Physical Education in the Elementary School Curriculum*. Englewood Cliffs, N.J.: Prentice-Hall, 1969.

POMEROY, JANET. *Recreation for the Physically Handicapped*. New York: Macmillan, 1964.

RATHBONE, JOSEPHINE, and LUCAS, CAROL. *Recreation in Total Rehabilitation*. Springfield, Ill.: Charles C. Thomas, 1970.

RICHARDSON, HAZEL A. *Games for the Elementary School Grades*. Minneapolis: Burgess, 1951.

STEIN, THOMAS A., and SESSOMS, H. DOUGLAS. *Recreation and Special Populations*. Boston: Allyn & Bacon, 1973.

VANNIER, MARYHELEN, and FAIT, HOLLIS F. *Teaching Physical Education in Secondary Schools*. Philadelphia: W. B. Saunders, 1964.

FILMS

Dehumanization and the Total Institution. New York: New York University Film Library Catalogue.

Physical Education for Blind Children. Long Beach, Calif.: Charles Buell.

Recreational Activities for Mentally Retarded Children. New York: National Association for Retarded Children.

The Therapeutic Community. Ann Arbor, Mich.: University of Michigan Television Center and Division of Gerontology.

Therapy Through Play. Albertson, N.Y.: Human Resources Center.

PAMPHLETS

OVERS, ROBERT P.; O'CONNOR, ELIZABETH; and DEMARCO, BARBARA. *Guide to Avocational Activities*, vols. I and II, nos. 5A and 5B. Milwaukee: Curative Workshop of Milwaukee, May 1972.

SHRINER, MILDRED. "Growing Up." Chicago: National Easter Seal Society for Crippled Children and Adults.

"Aids and Appliances for the Blind." New York: American Foundation for the Blind.

"Cerebral Palsy." New York: United Cerebral Palsy Association.

"Doctor, only through early diagnosis can you control cerebral palsy." New York: United Cerebral Palsy Association.

"Education." Washington, D.C.: Epilepsy Foundation of America.

"Employment." Washington, D.C.: Epilepsy Foundation of America.

"Epilepsy." Washington, D.C.: Epilepsy Foundation of America.

"Facts About Blindness." New York: American Foundation for the Blind.

"Facts on Mental Retardation." New York: National Association For Retarded Children.

"Family Information." Washington, D.C.: Epilepsy Foundation of America.

"Hello World." Washington, D.C.: The President's Committee on Mental Retardation.

"How to Provide for Their Future." New York: National Association For Retarded Children.

"Legal Information." Washington, D.C.: Epilepsy Foundation of America.

"New Facts About Older Americans." Washington, D.C.: US Department of Health, Education and Welfare, Office of Human Development, Administration on Aging.

"Q:A." New York: United Cerebral Palsy Association.

"Retirement Roles and Activities." US Department of Health, Education and Welfare, *1971 White House Conference on Aging, Sectional and Session Reports*.

"They Need You Now." New York: National Association for Retarded Children.

"Tomorrow is Today." New York: United Cerebral Palsy Association.

"To Your Future . . . with Love." Washington, D.C.: The President's Committee on Mental Retardation.

"What Do You Do When You See a Blind Person." New York: American Foundation for the Blind.

"Who is the Visually Handicapped Child?" New York: American Foundation for the Blind.

"Youth—NARC Orientation Handbook." New York: National Association for Retarded Children.

What kind of a program for Downsville?*

SITUATION

You are presently serving as a state recreation and park consultant. You have just received a request from the community of Downsville (pop. 31,500) asking that you assist the city's recreation committee in improving recreation opportunities. Downsville is located in the west central part of the state.

It is the center of an agricultural area about forty miles in diameter. The economy of the area is generated in three main areas: agriculture, manufacturing, and retailing. The annual median family income is $8,100. About 20 percent of the population is black. Below is a chart describing the population:

POPULATION CHART

AGE	1970	PERCENTAGE	1980	PERCENTAGE
Under 5	4,171	9.7	4,770	9.7
5–19	11,200	26.0	12,340	25.0
20–44	13,000	30.3	16,990	34.6
45–64	8,753	20.4	8,957	18.3
65–over	5,867	13.6	6,103	12.4

Downsville's founders were conscious of the need for open space and planned Laken Park and Woodworth Park in the original layout of the community. Realizing the need to maintain these park areas, Downsville citizens created the post of park director nearly fifty years ago. During this fifty-year period, eleven new parks were established and park acreage increased from 10 acres to 690 acres. Other facilities in the city of Downsville include:

1. Municipal indoor swimming pool —operated jointly by the city and the Y.M.C.A.

2. Lake Sagamore and Lake Vinton —these are two country clubs owned by the railroad. The man-made lakes serve a large segment of the Downsville population.

3. Camp WA-NO-ME—this area is also owned by the railroad and is located across from Lake Sagamore. It is the only resident camp within twenty miles of Downsville. The camp provides an area in which school camping could be established. All buildings would need to be winterized.

4. Sun Lake—this is a small private lake built by Sun Products for its employees. The area boasts family picnicking, swimming, and playground facilities. However, presently only 60 residents of Downsville have access to it.

*Joseph J. Bannon, *Problem Solving in Recreation and Parks*, © 1972, pp. 277–78. Reprinted by permission of Prentice-Hall, Inc., Englewood Cliffs, New Jersey.

5. Rainbow Swim and Tennis Club—this facility is located on the south side of the community and is only open to members. Approximately 400 families pay a fee of $300 per year to use this facility.

6. Rod and Gun Club—this facility is located on ten acres of undeveloped land two miles outside the city limits.

7. Downsville Country Club—this area provides an eighteen-hole golf course, tennis courts, and a swimming pool for its members. Family membership fees are $1,200 per year. This club serves only a very few of the citizens of Downsville.

8. School facilities—located in Downsville are ten elementary schools, two junior high schools, and one high school.

At present the city provides no funds for conducting a recreation program. The Downsville Citizens' Recreation Committee is very concerned about this and has asked you to assist in organizing a program that might be proposed to the mayor and council for funding.

PROBLEM

What kind of a program would you recommend for the citizens of Downsville? How would you assess the needs of the community? Does the population chart reveal any significant characteristics that would be helpful in planning the program? What kind of a relationship should be developed with the schools? Do you think the school facilities would provide good playground locations? What kind of a staff would be required to implement your program? Would it be possible to apply for federal grants that would assist in implementing the program? What would be the total cost of implementing the recommended program? What state enabling legislation would you recommend for the administering of the program? Why? How would you involve the citizens in the planning of the program? Is citizens' involvement important? Why? To what extent would you allow the citizens to become involved in the decision-making process? Be specific.

WHAT ADDITIONAL INFORMATION WOULD BE HELPFUL IN SOLVING THIS PROBLEM?

Case # 14*

Fredrick Sturbridge, male, white, age 17, single

Diagnosis: cerebral palsy

*Elliot M. Avedon, *Therapeutic Recreation Service: An Applied Behavioral Science Approach* (Englewood Cliffs, N.J.: Prentice-Hall, 1974), pp. 232–33. Reprinted by permission.

General appearance and condition: Obese, multiple disability which has affected ambulation and intelligence; uses wheelchair; well-dressed, obvious dental caries, poor general hygiene, some visual problems.

Social history: Middle-income family, special education in public school when family can arrange it. Parents are in their 50's; child is dependent in all areas; mother is impatient; father concentrates on his work, doesn't spend much time with the boy; child is and will be vocationally and socially dependent; spends considerable time by himself with nothing to do, no friends; parents lack knowledge and imagination, and are at a loss.

Educational history: It is difficult to determine how retarded Freddy is. He has learned to read on approximately a third-grade level and should enjoy newspaper pictures and headlines. He may be able to read content such as is found on the sports page. He has been taught to take certain responsibilities in the home.

Recreation report: Because he has no friends and his parents take little interest in him, he spends almost all day watching television, or the people who go by his window. (He lives in a first-floor flat.) Parents say he has been taught to use crutches but he doesn't practice with them, and they find it too much trouble to insist since "he is in that condition." He has gone on vacation to his grandfather's farm each summer, but he says it's just like being at home only he spends some time outside. His father tried to take him out a few times to watch some sporting events, but there was some difficulty about the fire laws and the wheelchair. When asked about such things as a windowbox garden, or swimming, or a camp for disabled children, his mother said they all seem like things that might interest Freddy, but she or his father wouldn't know where to begin.

QUESTIONS

1. Do you feel that Freddy should remain at home or be institutionalized? Explain your answer.
2. What makes Freddy as dependent as he is?
3. If you were assigned to this case, what would you do in the event that Freddy must remain at home?

MODULE 5

Concepts of interpersonal communications and group processes

Principles of communications

The recreation profession is a human-service field dealing with a very special commodity—people. It is recognized that an effective leader has the ability to establish rapport with participants while, at the same time, giving instructions to them. Many times a recreator will explain procedures to follow, only to find that things were done in the exact opposite manner. Why does this happen? Where does the fault lie? We would probably say that "There was a breakdown in communications," and we would probably be correct. A recreator should strive to obtain skills to communicate effectively with people. He will be a more efficient and productive person and the participants will have a better time if communication channels are open.

Recreation is for everybody. Recreation is everybody's right. It is not something to be arbitrarily taken away at someone's whimsical discretion. There are people who want to engage in recreational experiences but who have serious limitations in their ability to communicate effectively with others (for example, the person who does not speak English, who is aphasic, or who is deaf). The recreator is professionally obligated to serve all segments of society. A recreator who possesses skills to communicate verbally and nonverbally with people, who has the ability to speak clearly and concisely, and who has acquired an aptitude for listening effectively to people can serve individuals in a rewarding and efficient manner.

Many recreation personnel are people-oriented; they enjoy working with and for people. Recreators often deal with people on an individual basis. However, the nature of recreation, with its emphasis on activities, lends itself ideally to working with groups. Thus, most recreation personnel work with groups of people. Therefore, a knowledge of group processes is an important component of the competencies recreation personnel need.

DEFINITIONS

• *Communication:* "the process of transferring one's ideas, facts, or theories through the use of language, gestures, and vocal intonation to another person or group of persons. . . . Thinking beings are able to convey their thoughts and emotions to others."[1]

• *Interpersonal communication:* "the transmission of information, ideas, emotions, skills, etc., by the use of symbols—words, pictures, figures, graphs, etc. It is the act or process of transmission that is usually called communication."[2]

• *Active communication:* "transmission of information, consisting of discriminative stimuli, from a source to a recipient."[3]

• *Compulsory group:* a group in which membership is compelled; a person has to join.

• *Motivated group:* a group which a person may join voluntarily, however; there are elements of pressure and there are desires for being formally approved for membership.

• *Voluntary group:* a group which people join because of an interest; they want to join because of an inner desire to do so.

---

[1]Thomas A. Scheidel, *Speech Communication and Human Interaction.* (Glenview, Ill.: Scott, Foresman, 1972), pp. 6 and 7.

[2]Bernard Berelson and Gary A. Steiner, *Human Behavior: An Inventory of Scientific Findings* (New York: Harcourt Brace Jovanovich, 1964), p. 254.

[3]Theodore M. Newcomb, "An Approach to the Study of Communication Acts," in *Communication and Culture,* Alfred G. Smith, ed. (New York: Holt, Rinehart and Winston, 1966), p. 66.

- *Decision-making:* "the process by which individuals and/or groups of individuals attempt to adjust their ideas and actions to outside factors which are believed likely to have influence on them."[4]
- *Group dynamics:* "a group of persons who are *psychologically* aware of their interindividual relationships and who are *moving toward a goal that they have agreed upon collectively.*"[5]

PROCESS OF GROUP DYNAMICS

Group dynamics has developed from a multiple origin, that is, no one discipline can be credited with fostering concepts of group dynamics. Sociologists and psychologists alike have surmised that the essential difference between the behavior of an individual and that of a group is that the individual has no established relationship with others, whereas a group of individuals always behaves in a social context.[6] The presence of other people elicits a different pattern of responses than those which characterize the behavior of an isolated individual.

Behavior itself, whether individual or collective, is dynamic. The leisure field includes many opportunities for people to participate in group activities. These group endeavors can function as a dynamic whole, as an interdependence on specific integral parts, or as an arena to readily identify individuals with others in a cooperative relationship. Recreators should recognize that the latter can be used as a motivating factor to satisfy needs in the individual.

The existence of the interaction of one person with others in a recreational activity forms a network of relationships that brings out individual action in a spontaneous manner. Bonner indicates that:

> Their interactions are integrated in such a way that their psychological tensions are shared. The "togetherness" of the group as a dynamic structure is due to a "circular" reaction in which there is a high degree of self-intensification in each member of his own "excitement" as he finds it reflected in others.[7]

The reciprocity of shared feelings and camaraderie that may be stifled in individuals can be freely expressed within a group-oriented recreational function. Recreation includes activities that an individual voluntarily participates in for enjoyment and personal satisfaction. Thus, the basic condi-

---

[4]*Looking into Leadership.* (Washington, D.C.: Leadership Resources, 1966), p. 3.

[5]Hubert Bonner, *Group Dynamics Principles and Applications* (New York: Ronald Press, 1959), p. 45.

[6]Ibid., pp. 28–29.

[7]Ibid., p. 45.

tion of group behavior is present in a recreational activity that includes experiences of an interactive, complementary, and friendship nature.

SIGNIFICANCE OF INTERPERSONAL COMMUNICATIONS AND GROUP PROCESSES

Communication should be instrumental in creating better understanding between people. However, this does not instinctively happen. Communication is very hard to achieve. People have a tendency to judge, to evaluate, to approve, or disapprove before they understand what the other person is saying. People are often inclined to react first by forming an evaluation of what has been said and then to evaluate it from their own point of view. Many times people talk "at" a person rather than "with" a person.

In the majority of occurrences involving more than one person, there is a need to have the ability to communicate. The field of recreation is no exception to this need. Indeed, because of many features inherent within the field of recreation, the ability to communicate is extremely important. Recreators often realize how vital communication is when leading an activity. They should also recognize the importance of articulating the virtues of their program and the recreation field to other people. Recreators are professionally obligated to help people understand the role of recreation in their own lives. People must be helped and guided to understand the importance of a quality recreative experience that can challenge their capabilities and contribute to the total quality of their lives. In addition, the capacity to effectively communicate with people serves a practical purpose when the recreation program is being evaluated and budgets are being proposed. Recreators must defend their programs, describe why money is needed, and articulate the values derived from participating in recreational activities.

OBJECTIVES OF COMMUNICATIONS AND GROUP PROCESSES

1. To develop a recognition of specific ways to communicate effectively with people

2. To acquire a knowledge of determinants of successful verbal communications

3. To develop a knowledge of determinants of successful nonverbal communications

4. To define interpersonal communications

5. To develop an awareness of methods for effective verbal communications

6. To define group dynamics

7. To develop an awareness of methods for effective nonverbal communications

8. To recognize the nature and types of groups

9. To develop a knowledge of the following seven methods of organizing groups:

    a. "buzz group"

    b. interview

    c. small group discussion

    d. role playing

    e. symposium

    f. dialogue

    g. panel discussion

FOUR DETERMINANTS OF EFFECTIVE VERBAL COMMUNICATIONS

1. Vocabulary

    a. clarity of voice

    b. organization of presentation

2. Attitudes

3. Voice tone and volume

4. Effective listening

1. *Vocabulary.* Several problems could ensue if a recreator failed to acquire appropriate vocabulary: omission of important ideas, long rambling speeches that confuse, or a loss of attention by participants.

    a. Clarity: a sentence that is organized, grammatically correct, and meaningful may lose its impact if it is spoken too softly, rushed, or articulated poorly.

    b. Organization: a recreator often has to explain how to follow specific procedures (rules, regulations, next step in an arts and crafts project) in leading an activity. A person who rambles confuses participants by jumping from one thought to the next, inserting last-minute ideas, failing to summarize.

2. *Attitudes.* Many recreators maintain a professional, caring attitude toward participants, programs, and the recreation field. Many participants will be able to detect if a recreator has a positive attitude toward them or to the program. The attitude that the recreation professional is able to relay to participants may determine the success of a program.

3. *Voice tone and volume.* An expression as short as "oh" can be used to express many emotions and/or attitudes. Tone is a voice quality. Therefore, a person can reverse the meaning of spoken words by the tone and/or volume of words.

4. *Effective listening.* It requires skill to listen effectively to others. Many times people do not listen openly because they are afraid of the possible influence this may have on their attitudes. People are certain that they know what a person is going to say before he says it. Thus they do not listen because they have a preconceived notion of what will be said.

TWO DETERMINANTS OF SUCCESSFUL NONVERBAL COMMUNICATIONS

1. Pantomime
2. Metacommunication

1. *Pantomime.* Pantomine is used as a substitute for verbal communication. It is a conscious effort to communicate by acting out a particular situation, using gestures to express attitudes, emotions, and activities. Pantomime can be useful with the following four types of people:

    a. non-English speaking
    b. aphasic
    c. elderly
    d. deaf

2. *Metacommunication.* Metacommunication adds to verbal messages. Actions that accompany words modify and alter their meanings. Facial expressions may be used to indicate anger, pity, superiority, or terror without a word being spoken. The way a person sits and stands in relation to another and the manner in which his arms and legs move communicate messages that can confirm or contradict verbal statements.

Nonverbal communication can either confirm, clarify, or contradict verbal communication. Nonverbal communication is used to relay messages and facilitate effective interaction. Recreation personnel should be aware that nonverbal and verbal communication have an equal impact on the individuals with whom they work.

WORK-ORIENTED GROUP

A work-oriented group is a group concerned with exploring problems and making plans and recommendations for carrying out tasks. Specific functions carried out by a leader and/or members of the group are:

1. Initiating: starting and keeping the group action moving (for example, steps to be taken next and emphasizing group goals).

2. Regulating: influencing the direction of the group's work (for example, summarizing and restating goals).

3. Informing: bringing opinion, fact, and information to the group's attention.

4. Supporting: creating an emotional climate which is conducive to holding the group together.

5. Evaluating: helping group evaluate its decision, goals, and/or procedures.

PROGRAM-ORIENTED GROUP

Most recreation personnel lead an activity-oriented or program-oriented group more often than they lead a work-oriented group. In the program-oriented group (for example, teaching a crafts activity, leading a dance, or planning a special event) the leader is in need of sound judgement in order to achieve the group's goals. In a program-oriented group the leader of the group or members of the group may assume any of the following five roles:

1. Policy-maker: helping the group to determine goals, meeting time and place, membership, and so forth.

2. Planner: helping the group develop definite plans for activities and projects.

3. Organizer: helping the group to formulate specific plans for action.

4. Resource person: lending informational support to the group.

5. Stimulator: helping the group to stay motivated by ideas and suggestions.

GROUP PROCESSES

Seven methods of organizing groups are:

1. "Buzz Group"
2. Interview
3. Small group discussion
4. Role playing
5. Symposium

6. Dialogue

7. Panel discussion

CHARACTERISTICS OF A "BUZZ GROUP"

1. A "buzz group" is used to break a large group into small segments to facilitate discussion.

2. A "buzz group" is an informal device that is easy to set up and guarantees total participation by all members of the group.

3. A "buzz group" might be selected as a group dynamics process in order to consider many separate aspects of a subject problem or to provide limited support to individuals to bring about their participation in the total group process.

4. A "buzz group" may be set up by the "count off" procedure; if there is a large group of 60 people, the group counts off from one to ten—all number one's are in one group, number two's in another group, etc.

5. There does not have to be a chairman, but group members agree on who is to report the results of the discussion.

CHARACTERISTICS OF A DIALOGUE

1. A dialogue is an informal, conversational, and interpersonal discussion carried on in front of a group by two knowledgeable people on a specific subject.

2. A dialogue permits direct and easy communication of information and viewpoints by the participants.

3. A dialogue allows expression of two points of view.

4. A dialogue is relatively simple in form and easy to plan and carry out.

5. A dialogue might be used to create interest and/or focus attention on a specific subject or problem.

6. A dialogue is a good method to quickly set a group framework for thought and discussion and to give basic facts needed for general group discussion.

7. A dialogue helps unskilled speakers present their ideas.

CHARACTERISTICS OF A PANEL DISCUSSION

1. A panel discussion is an informal or formal conversational discussion before an audience by a selected group of persons under the direction of a moderator.

2. A panel discussion can focus on and raise different points of view, different facts, and different attitudes on a subject or problem.

3. A panel discussion divides responsibility by requiring some pre-meeting thought and fact gathering from individual panel members.

4. A panel discussion can never be completely controlled by the moderator because the panel members can ignore questions and directions.

5. The direction of the discussion can be maintained somewhat because panel members have previously met and discussed the scope of the discussion.

6. The moderator will set the ground rules prior to introduction of the panel.

7. A panel discussion permits maximum interaction and interstimulation between panel members.

8. A panel discussion affords the panel members an opportunity for active and dramatic presentation of the subject matter within a competitive framework.

CHARACTERISTICS OF AN INTERVIEW

1. An interview is the questioning of an expert on a given subject by an interviewer who represents the group.

2. There is mutual support and sharing of responsibility between the expert and the interviewer.

3. The interviewer sets the level of discussion, the speed with which areas are developed, and the direction of development.

4. It is much more difficult for the expert to evade points of concern to the group if the interviewer continues to question in those areas.

5. An interview is more formal than a dialogue, and less formal than a lecture or a speech.

6. The interviewer becomes a bridge between the expert and the group.

CHARACTERISTICS OF A SYMPOSIUM

1. A symposium is a group of talks, speeches, or lectures presented by several individuals on the various aspects of a particular subject or problem.

2. A symposium allows for a systematic and relatively complete expression of ideas without interruption.

3. A moderator often controls the time and the subject matter to be covered.

4. A symposium is a comparatively formal manner of presentation which is relatively easy to organize.

5. A symposium does not allow for a great deal of interaction between the participants.

6. A symposium is limited in developing audience involvement.

CHARACTERISTICS OF ROLE PLAYING

1. Role playing provides for informality.

2. Role playing is flexible, permissive, and affords an opportunity for experimentation.

3. Role playing enhances participation by providing psychological involvement of the individual and the group.

4. Role playing provides a concrete "doing experience" which can be used as a basis for discussion (that is, showing rather than telling).

5. Role playing releases inhibitions as the role players enact their feelings through the guise of another person.

6. Role playing is relatively easy to plan and is done with a minimum of props.

CHARACTERISTICS OF SMALL GROUP DISCUSSION

1. A small group discussion allows a great deal of interaction and stimulation between members of the group.

2. A small group discussion places responsibility on all members to participate and to be prepared with ideas and facts.

3. A small group discussion permits leadership responsibility to be shared by all who contribute.

4. A small group discussion affords all members an opportunity to broaden their viewpoints.

5. A small group discussion allows members to think as a group.

6. A small group discussion encourages members to listen, reason, and contribute.

Student assignments

This part consists of 17 objectives. You will be called upon to demonstrate your mastery of each objective. Some answers require written responses. Some responses will be of a demonstrable nature, that is, you will be constructing and leading a variety of groups relative to their organizational structures.

OBJECTIVE	ACHIEVEMENT OF COMPETENCY
1. To describe types of groups.	Describe a minimum of two types of groups.
2. To demonstrate group processes.	a. Demonstrate a minimum of three group processes in the work-oriented group. b. Demonstrate a minimum of three group processes in the program-oriented group.
3. To describe characteristics of a "buzz group."	a. Describe a minimum of three characteristics of a "buzz group." b. Construct and lead a "buzz group."
4. To describe characteristics of a dialogue.	a. List a minimum of five characteristics of a dialogue. b. Construct and lead a dialogue.
5. To describe characteristics of a panel discussion.	a. List a minimum of six characteristics of a panel discussion. b. Construct and lead a panel discussion.
6. To describe characteristics of an interview.	a. Describe a minimum of three characteristics of an interview. b. Construct and lead an interview.
7. To describe characteristics of a symposium.	a. List a minimum of four characteristics of a symposium. b. Construct and lead a symposium.
8. To describe characteristics of role playing.	a. Describe a minimum of four characteristics of role playing. b. Construct and lead a role playing group.
9. To describe characteristics of small group discussion.	a. Describe a minimum of four characteristics of small group discussion.

	b. Construct and lead a small group discussion.
10. To identify group processes.	Given an illustrated drawing, plus three characteristics for each of the seven group process techniques identified, match a minimum of five of the specific group process techniques depicted by the drawings.
11. To define interpersonal communication.	Write a definition of interpersonal communication.
12. To describe significance of interpersonal communication.	Write a minimum of 100 words describing the significance of concepts of interpersonal communication for the field of recreation.
13. To describe determinants of verbal communication.	Orally describe a minimum of three determinants of successful verbal communication.
14. To demonstrate methods for verbal communication.	Demonstrate a minimum of four methods for effective verbal communication.
15. To describe determinants of nonverbal communication.	Orally describe a minimum of two determinants of successful nonverbal communication.
16. To demonstrate methods for nonverbal communication.	Demonstrate a minimum of four methods for effective nonverbal communication.
17. To describe feelings in a series of exercises.	Describe feelings, verbally and nonverbally, in a series of exercises.

Resources

This part is divided into two sections: (1) a list of reference materials and (2) two problem-solving activities.

TEXTBOOKS

ALEXIS, MARCUS. *Organizational Decision Making*. Englewood Cliffs, N.J.: Prentice-Hall, 1967.

BEAL, GEORGE M.; BOHLEN, JOE M.; and RAUDABAUGH, NEIL. *Leadership and Dynamic Group Action*. Ames, Iowa: Iowa State University Press, 1972.

BERELSON, BERNARD, and STEINER, GARY. *Human Behavior: An Inventory of Scientific Findings*. New York: Harcourt Brace Jovanovich, 1964.

BERNE, ERIC. *Games People Play*. New York: Grove Press, 1971.

BONNER, HUBERT. *Group Dynamics Principles and Applications*. New York: Ronald Press, 1959.

BOSMAJIAN, HAIG. *The Rhetoric of Nonverbal Communication*. Glenview, Ill.: Scott, Foresman, 1971.

CARTWRIGHT, DORWIN, and ZANDER, ALVIN. *Group Dynamics Research and Theory*. White Plains, N.Y.: Row, Peterson, 1956.

DANFORD, HOWARD. *Creative Leadership in Recreation*. Boston: Allyn & Bacon, 1964.

GIFFIN, KIM, and PATTON, BOBBY R. *Fundamentals of Interpersonal Communication*. New York: Harper & Row, 1971.

JAMES, MURIEL, and JANGEWARD, DOROTHY. *Born to Win*. Reading, Mass.: Addison-Wesley, 1971.

KRAUS, RICHARD. *Recreation Today: Program Planning and Leadership*. New York: Appleton-Century-Crofts, 1966.

KRUPER, KAREN R. *Communication Games*. New York: The Free Press, 1973.

Looking Into Leadership. Washington, D.C.: Leadership Resources, Inc., 1966.

MYERS, GAILE, and MYERS, M. T. *The Dynamics of Human Communication*. New York: McGraw-Hill, 1973.

NEWCOMB, THEODORE M. "An Approach to the Study of Communication Acts." *Communication and Culture*. Edited by Alfred G. Smith. New York: Holt, Rinehart and Winston, 1966.

SCHEIDEL, THOMAS A. *Speech Communication and Human Interaction*. Glenview, Ill.: Scott, Foresman, 1972.

TANNENBAUM, ROBERT; WESCHLET, IRVING R.; and MASSARIK, FRED. *Leadership and Organization: A Behavioral Science Approach*. New York: McGraw-Hill, 1961.

TILLMAN, ALBERT. *The Program Book for Recreation Professionals*. Los Angeles: National Press Books, 1973.

TUBBS, STEWART, and MOSS, SYLVIA. *Human Communication: An Interpersonal Perspective*. New York: Random House, 1974.

WENBURG, JOHN R., and WILMOT, WILLIAM W. *The Personal Communication Process*. New York: Wiley, 1973.

ARTICLES

BILLINGS, C. R. "Understanding Meta-Decisions: The Key to Effecting Organizational Change." *Journal of Educational Data Processing*, nos. 4–5 (1974): 3–64.

FALLON, K. D. "Participatory Management: An Alternative in Human Service Delivery Systems." *Child Welfare*, 53 (November 1974): 555–62.

GIAMMATEO, MICHAEL. "6 Bits of Information Problem." *Investigating Your Environment Series*. Portland, Ore.: US Forest Service, 1973.

PROBLEM-SOLVING ACTIVITIES

The following are two specific activities that students can engage in. Both activities are designed to depict both group dynamic concepts and verbal and nonverbal communication.

Express your feelings

Do these five exercises individually. Below are some feelings you may have experienced. For each of these five experiences you are to report verbally and nonverbally ways that you express such feelings. The nonverbal response should indicate how you might express such feelings by actions without using words.

1. When you feel very aggravated with a member of the same sex, but reluctant to say so openly, how do you usually express your feelings?

Verbally?

Nonverbally?

2. An instructor says or does something to you that deeply hurts your feelings, how do you usually express your feelings?

Verbally?

Nonverbally?

3. When you feel totally bored on a date, how do you usually express your feelings?

Verbally?

Nonverbally?

4. When you are working in a job and doing the very best you can do and your boss tells you that you are a very inadequate worker, how do you usually express your feelings?

Verbally?

Nonverbally?

5. Your parents ask you to do something that you are afraid you cannot do very well. You do not wish them to know that you feel inadequate, how do you usually express your feelings?

Verbally?

Nonverbally?

---

6 Bits of information problem*

INSTRUCTIONS

1. Divide participants into groups of six.

2. Each participant will receive one part of the problem.

3. Group must adhere to the following directions:

  a. There is a problem to solve.

  b. Each participant can *tell* other members of the group what is on the paper but must not *show* it to others in their group.

4. As this activity progresses the group leader will:

  a. 5-8 minutes into the problem write on the board "TRUST"

  b. 8-12 minutes into the problem write on the board "VISUAL DISPLAY"

  c. 12-15 minutes into the problem write on the board "MATRIX"

5. After the groups have finished the problem the group leader will ask the following three questions:

  a. What kept your group from solving the problem initially?

  b. What helped your group to solve the problem later?

  c. What were some characteristics of this problem-solving exercise?

6. The group leader will discuss the importance of effective listening in this problem-solving exercise.

  a. Did a form of polite (ritualistic) listening occur? (This is when people listen but do not care about the words spoken because the words have no significance.) Ritualistic listening may occur when two people meet on the street and one person says "How are you?" to the other and does not care what the other replies because the response has little meaning.

  b. Real listening is important. This form of listening transpires when statements become meaningful. This usually happens when people interrupt and say "What did you say?" or "Say that again!"

*Michael Giammateo, "6 Bits of Information Problem," *Investigating Your Environment Series,* Portland, Ore.: U.S. Forest Service, 1973.

[1]Although you may tell your group what is on this slip, you may not pass it around for others to read.

[2]Although you may tell your group what is on this slip, you may not pass it around for others to read.

INFORMATION

The Dinosaurs had Tom for a teacher during the third period.

Dick and Belinda did not get along well and so they did not work together.

During the first period the Team Leader taught the group that Harry liked best.

INFORMATION

All teachers taught at the same time and exchanged groups at the end of each period.

Each teacher liked a different group best.

During the second period each teacher taught the group he liked best.

Each teacher taught every group during one of the first four periods of the day.

[3]Although you may tell your group what is on this slip, you may not pass it around for others to read.

[4]Although you may tell your group what is on this slip, you may not pass it around for others to read.

INFORMATION

The Freznel Elementary School Intermediate Unit had two teacher's aides, four teachers, and four instructional groups of students. Each instructional group had chosen its own name.

Sybil was the Team Leader for the Intermediate.

INFORMATION

Your group members have all the information needed to find the answer to the following question. Only one answer is correct. You can prove it.

IN WHAT SEQUENCE DID THE APES HAVE THE VARIOUS TEACHERS DURING THE FIRST FOUR PERIODS?

Some of the information your group has is irrevelant and will not help solve the problem.

[5]Although you may tell your group what is on this slip, you may not pass it around for others to read.

[6]Although you may tell your group what is on this slip, you may not pass it around for others to read.

INFORMATION

Belinda and Ralph disagreed about how it would be best to handle the Bombers who always had trouble settling down to work.

Dick preferred to work with the Champs over all other groups.

Although the Team Leader had been at Freznel School for five years, this was a shorter period of time than for the other team members.

INFORMATION

The Team Leader taught the Dinosaur the second period.

Harry worked with the Bombers in the third period.

Sybil had been at Freznel School a shorter period of time than any of the other teachers in the Intermediate Unit.

MODULE 6
Field visits and discussion

General statement

Professional laboratory experience should begin in the first year of college. Kraus and Bates indicate that:

> Early field exposures provide an excellent means of screening out disinterested, apathetic or poorly equipped students, and of giving students a realistic picture of the field that will help them in making hard career decisions. Field experiences may also help to confirm the judgement of advisors by demonstrating that certain students have a high level of interest and ability and should be strongly encouraged—or to tell students that recreation is the field in which they really should carry on their life's work. Such knowledge should not have to wait until the end of the student's junior or senior year.[1]

[1] Richard G. Kraus and Barbara J. Bates, *Recreation Leadership and Supervision: Guidelines for Professional Development* (Philadelphia: W. B. Saunders Company, 1975), p. 117. Reprinted by permission.

One component of the field work experience is field visitations to recreation agencies. These on-site visits bring students closer to the realities of a professional environment. This early exposure can help supplement, complement, and reinforce classroom activities.

Field visitations should afford students an opportunity to bridge the gap between the didactic and the practical. Students are provided with guided observations of recreation programs in operation. Students should visit a vast array of recreation agencies in order to become exposed to a wide variety of philosophies, program/agency objectives, staffing patterns, and so forth.

Field visitations/observations help to ensure that students will be familiar with a variety of recreation agencies prior to their field work assignment. Students should be able to objectively and subjectively evaluate specific agencies. In addition, they should have opportunities to thoroughly discuss the salient features of each agency and indicate specific methods for improving each agency. Students should be able to ascertain the operational effectiveness and efficiency of various recreation agencies. This introductory method of observation is a means of orienting students to a vast array of agencies offering leisure services.

DEFINITIONS

- *Field visits/observations:* student visits to an agency to learn about the operational efficiency and service delivery system of the agency.
- *Recreator:* a paid professional leading a recreation program.
- *Recreationist:* a participant in a recreation program.
- *Leisure service agencies:* The following are agencies that provide leisure services: public agencies on federal, state, and local levels, voluntary agencies, college union, armed services, Red Cross, schools, industrial agencies, private agencies, therapeutic agencies.

Student assignments

This part consists of 19 objectives. You will be called upon to demonstrate your mastery of each objective. Some answers require written responses.

OBJECTIVE	ACHIEVEMENT OF COMPETENCY
1. To describe the type of agency visited.	Differentiate between types of agencies and describe the type of agency visited.

OBJECTIVE	ACHIEVEMENT OF COMPETENCY
2. To describe number of people who are served by the agency in a year.	Write the number of people who are served by the agency in a year.
3. To describe the makeup of the population within the agency.	Write the makeup of the population within the agency visited.
4. To describe the number of recreation personnel employed in the agency.	Write the number of recreation personnel employed on a full-time and/or part-time basis in the agency.
5. To identify the number of volunteers who assist with the leisure program.	List the number of volunteers who assist with the leisure program.
6. To identify interaction between recreators and recreationists.	List at least one example of an interaction between recreators and recreationists.
7. To explain the relationship between recreation staff and other department(s) within the agency.	Verbally explain the relationship between recreation staff and other department(s) within the agency.
8. To explain whether or not the agency has a recreation department.	Verbally explain whether or not the agency has a recreation department.
9. To construct the recreation department's philosophy of recreation.	Verbally explain the recreation department's written philosophy of recreation.
10. To write objectives of the leisure services provided.	Write a minimum of two objectives of the leisure services provided.
11. To describe the differences between philosophy and objective.	a. Apply some of the major concepts of recreation to clarify the differences between philosophy and objectives.

b. Verbally explain the differences between philosophy and objectives. |
| 12. To identify recreation activities observed during the visit. | Write at least 50% of the recreation activities observed during the visit. |
| 13. To identify the person(s) who plan(s) the recreation program. | List the person(s), by title or name, who plan(s) the recreation program. |

OBJECTIVE	ACHIEVEMENT OF COMPETENCY
14. To identify the person(s) who lead(s) the recreation program.	List the person(s), by title or name, who lead(s) the recreation program.
15. To describe how the recreation department evaluates programs.	Write a summary of how the recreation department evaluates programs.
16. To describe future goals of the recreation department.	Write a summary of a minimum of two future goals of the recreation department.
17. To describe facilities, supplies, and equipment needed to expand the recreation program.	Given the scope of activities offered during the visit, list one additional facility and two additional supplies and equipment needed to expand the recreation program.
18. To identify why a person would or would not like to be employed in the agency's recreation department.	List a minimum of three reasons why a person would or would not like to be employed in the agency's recreation department.
19. To describe the operational efficiency of an agency.	Apply some of the major concepts of recreation and evaluate the operational efficiency of an agency based on an understanding of the concepts.

Resources

This part is divided into three sections: (1) a list of textbooks, (2) field visitation instruments, and (3) two problem-solving exercises. There is no text presently that deals exclusively with field visitations. As a result, a variety of resources must be used.

TEXTBOOKS

BANNON, JOSEPH J. *Problem Solving in Recreation and Parks.* Englewood Cliffs, N.J.: Prentice-Hall, 1972.

BUTLER, GEORGE D. *Introduction to Community Recreation.* New York: McGraw-Hill, 1967.

CORBIN, H. DAN, and TAIT, WILLIAM J. *Education for Leisure.* Englewood Cliffs, N.J.: Prentice-Hall, 1973.

HANSON, ROBERT F., and CARLSON, REYNOLD E. *Organizations for Children and Youth*. Englewood Cliffs, N.J.: Prentice-Hall, 1972.

HEITMANN, HELEN M., and KNEER, MARIAN E. *Physical Education Instructional Techniques: An Individualized Humanistic Approach*. Englewood Cliffs, N.J.: Prentice-Hall, 1976.

HJELTE, GEORGE, and SHIVERS, JAY S. *Public Administration of Recreational Services*. Philadelphia: Lea and Febiger, 1972.

KRAUS, RICHARD. *Therapeutic Recreation Service Principles and Practices*. Philadelphia: W. B. Saunders, 1973.

KRAUS, RICHARD G., and BATES, BARBARA J. *Recreation Leadership and Supervision: Guidelines for Professional Development*. Philadelphia: W. B. Saunders, 1975.

SESSOMS, H. DOUGLAS; MEYER, HAROLD D.; and BRIGHTBILL, CHARLES K. *Leisure Services*. Englewood Cliffs, N.J.: Prentice-Hall, 1975.

WEISKOPF, DONALD C. *A Guide to Recreation and Leisure*. Boston: Allyn & Bacon, 1975.

FIELD VISITATION INSTRUMENTS

Agency Evaluation Sheet, see pages 163–64.

Guideline for Field Visits (GFV), see pages 165–66.

Agency Evaluation sheet

Agency evaluation should include three major sections. The first section should cover objective data on the agency, department, or program. The second section should cover a "gut reaction" evaluation of the agency. The third aspect of the evaluation should focus on specific ways and means to improve the agency's recreation program.

SECTION 1—OBJECTIVE DATA

A. Agency
  1. What type of agency is it?
  2. What are its major services?
  3. What is the number of participants served in a year?
  4. What is the makeup of the population?
B. Recreation Department
  1. Where is recreation on the agency Table of Organization (TO)?
  2. What is the departmental TO?

3. What is the number of recreation personnel? Paid? Volunteer?

4. What job levels are represented in the departmental TO?

5. What are the basic qualifications for staff at varying levels?

C. Recreation Program

1. What is the basic philosophy of the recreation department? Is it written down?

2. What are the objectives of the recreation services provided?

3. What is the scope of the recreation department's program?

4. When are activities offered?

5. Who plans the program?

6. When and how are recreation programs evaluated?

7. Who evaluates the recreation program?

8. What criteria are used in evaluating programs?

9. What are the major problems the department faces in planning and/or conducting programs?

10. What are some of the future goals of the department?

SECTION II—OBSERVER'S EVALUATION OF AGENCY

Based on data in Section I and on your observations of the facilities, personnel, and programs observed, what are *your* feelings about:

1. The tone or "feel" of the agency and recreation department?

2. Do you think recreation personnel enjoy their jobs? Would you like to work there? Why? Why not? If yes, in what position? What is the desirability of working in the agency or department?

3. What are the relationships among recreation staff and the department's relationship with other departments and participants in the program?

4. What are the interactions between participants in programs and their responses to activities?

5. Are the facilities, supplies, equipment and/or materials available for conducting the program adequate?

6. Please add whatever reactions you personally had in relation to your visit.

SECTION III—OBSERVER'S RECOMMENDATIONS

Based on the data obtained from sections I and II, make specific recommendations on how to improve the agency's recreation program.

Guidelines for field visits (GFV)

A. Agency
   1. What type of agency is it?
     a. Correctional institution
     b. Special hospital
     c. General hospital
     d. Boarding homes for sheltered care
     e. Homes for the aged
     f. State schools
     g. State institutions
     h. Nursing homes
     i. Community recreation department
     j. Industrial recreation
     k. Voluntary
     l. Armed service
     m. Private
     n. Public
     o. Red Cross
     p. Schools
     q. Other

   2. What is the number of people served in a year?
   3. What is the makeup of the population?
     a. Preschool
     b. Preadolescent
     c. Adolescent
     d. Late adolescent
     e. Young adult
     f. Middle age
     g. Senior Citizens
     h. Male
     i. Female
     j. Other

B. Recreation Department
   1. Does the agency have a recreation department?
   2. How many recreation personnel are employed on a full-time basis?
   3. How many recreation personnel are employed on a part-time basis?
   4. How many volunteers assist with the recreation program?

5. What are relationships among recreation staff and relationships with other departments within the agency?

C. Recreation Program

1. Is there a written philosophy of the recreation department?

2. What are at least two objectives of the recreation services provided?

3. What is the scope of the agency's recreation program?

4. Who leads the recreation activities (title or name)?

5. Who plans the recreation program (title or name)?

6. Are the facilities, supplies, and equipment sufficient for carrying out the program?

a. List one additional facility needed to expand the recreation program.

b. List two additional supplies and equipment needed to expand the recreation program.

7. What interaction(s) among participants and recreation staff was evident?

8. Does the recreation department have an evaluation of programs?

9. Does the recreation department have future goals? If yes, name two.

D. Personal reactions in relation to the visit

1. Would *you* like to work in the recreation department of this agency? If yes, list a minimum of three reasons why you would like to work in this agency. If no, list a minimum of three reasons why you would not like to work in this agency.

2. What were your "feelings" about the agency?

Whom shall I work for?*

SITUATION

You have recently been interviewed for the position of director of parks and recreation for four communities in the state.

In the first community, Owensville, the recreation and park services are operated by a park district. The park district consists of a five-member board elected by the citizens of the district. Enabling legislation permits the district to levy 20 cents per $100 assessed valuation for recreation programs. It also has the power to issue bonds for 5% of the total assessed valuation. As director of recreation and parks you would be responsible to the five elected board members.

*Joseph J. Bannon, *Problem Solving in Recreation and Parks*, © 1972, p. 222. Reprinted by permission of Prentice-Hall, Inc., Englewood Cliffs, New Jersey.

In the second community, Cartersville, the recreation and park services are conducted under auspices of the mayor and council. All funds for services are derived from the general appropriation fund of the city. As director you would be directly responsible to the mayor. However, a recreation and park advisory board is appointed and all activities of the department must first be reviewed by the advisory board. The mayor retains veto power over this group.

In the third community, Jamestown, all recreation and park programs are operated through the board of education. State enabling [legislation] permits the board to levy a tax of 25 cents per $100 of assessed valuation for recreation programs. The amount levied for recreation purposes may not be used for any services other than recreation. Capital improvements under this system must be approved by the board of education. As director you would be directly responsible to the superintendent of schools.

In the fourth community, Glens Falls, the recreation and park services are operated by the mayor and council. However, a city manager is employed to direct all the activities of the city. The city is permitted to levy a tax of 20 cents per $100 assessed valuation for the recreation and park services; the funds generated by this tax must be used exclusively for this purpose. As director you would be responsible to the city manager.

The salary and fringe benefits for each position are about the same and therefore of no consideration in your decision.

PROBLEM

Under which system do you feel you could be most effective? Why? What are the advantages and disadvantages of operating under the park district, the mayor and council, the board of education, the city manager?

Personnel policies at the next meeting*

SITUATION

You have just accepted a position of director of recreation and parks in a city with a population of 50,000. The previous director has recently retired. Due to illness during his last five years in office, he was unable to make necessary changes in program, personnel, and finance. At the first meeting with the board you are requested to review and update the existing personnel policies. Board members reported that a number of problems arose last year that could have been settled without much difficulty if the policies had been updated. One problem in particular dealt with suspension procedure; another, concerning employment practices, indicated that the department was violating a number of state and federal laws.

*Joseph J. Bannon, *Problem Solving in Recreation and Parks*, © 1972, pp. 223–24. Reprinted by permission of Prentice-Hall, Inc., Englewood Cliffs, New Jersey.

PROBLEM

Write personnel policies that you could recommend to the board. Write policies for the following: employment practices, time and attendance, overtime, vacations, absences, absence due to armed-service obligation, special leave, jury duty, dismissal and suspension, grievances, staff training, salary policy, and retirement.

MODULE 7

Techniques of leadership and supervision

Principles and practices

In the provision of leisure services, personnel are responsible for developing and conducting programs that satisfy the leisure needs and interests of people. The program is people-oriented rather than product-oriented, although defined products may result from participation. Leadership is needed at all levels in an organization, but this module is designed primarily to investigate techniques used in face-to-face leadership with participants in leisure programs. Supervision of these programs by middle management personnel will also be studied. Basic concepts of leadership and supervision will be discussed. Leadership styles, methods, and techniques will be analyzed. The functions of supervisors will be learned and an *elementary examination* of the supervisory process will be made.

DEFINITIONS

• *Leadership:* an ability to influence others to work toward the achievement of a defined goal. Leadership involves two or more people.

169

• *Supervision:* is a process in which an individual directs and controls the provision of leisure programs, sharing this process with those whom he supervises.

OBJECTIVES

1. To examine concepts of leadership and their application to leisure services.

2. To identify various leadership roles.

3. To define characteristics of a leader.

4. To learn the duties and responsibilities of leaders in leisure services.

5. To learn leadership styles and when and how they are used in leisure services.

6. To define principles of leadership in leisure services.

7. To examine methods for evaluating leadership.

8. To learn leadership needs of varying categories of program and the leadership skills required for each category.

9. To define the duties and responsibilities of supervisors in leisure services.

10. To learn the fundamental principles of supervision and apply them to leisure services.

11. To learn the components of the supervisory process in leisure services.

12. To examine the methods of evaluating leisure service leadership.

LEADERSHIP

In leisure services, leadership is an important ingredient. People who use leisure services in communities are seeking ways to satisfy their leisure needs and interests. They may need varying kinds of help including information about the availability of resources, assessment of their needs and/or interests so that they may make wise choices of leisure pursuits, skill learning that permits them to engage in activities, organization of activities to enable them to gain the greatest benefit from participation, and interpretations of concepts of leisure. From interpretations, people may be able to develop philosophies of living that help them to put work and leisure into perspective and live to their fullest and most effective capacities.

Sources of leaders

Over many years there has been a continuing controversy about what makes a leader. Many studies have been conducted to define the traits of leaders, but none have developed a universally accepted set of characteristics. Today, it is generally accepted that a leader must have a variety of characteristics depending on individual situations.

Appointed Leadership. Leaders are appointed in many situations by an authority. In leisure services a department superintendent appoints leaders to assume certain roles in accordance with the authority given to him. Another example is a club president who appoints a member to be chairman of a fund-raising event.

Elected Leadership. Government in a democratic society is an example of elected leadership. The people who are to be governed elect the person or persons whom they want to govern them. A simple example is a club which elects the officers who will operate the club for the benefit of the members.

Emergent Leadership. A person may emerge as a leader in a group which has formed to achieve a certain goal. For example, in a sport an individual may become the leader because of great skill in the activity or because he knows about other groups that want to play. This person is selected as "captain" to organize the group to play and to find others with whom to play.

Charismatic Leadership. This type of leadership is the result of a combination of personality traits and certain talents which attract people to follow a given individual. Frequently these individual characteristics are subtle blends that defy accurate analysis. Many military officers have been described as charismatic leaders who could inspire their troops to unbelievable heights of valor.

Whatever the source of leadership, it must be understood that it must be related to the specific situation. It is dependent on the needs of the group to be served, the organizational structure within which the group functions, what the group wants to achieve and the personal characteristics of the leader.

The "power" concept in leadership

A dictionary definition of power is that "it is the ability or capacity to do or act or to effect something."[1] There are many ways in which this definition is interpreted. In a purely mechanical sense it is the energy expended to perform a certain act. Power can also be interpreted as influence: a certain conglomeration of factors such as money, social status,

[1]C. L. Barnhart, *The American College Dictionary* (New York: Random House, 1963), p. 950.

a position of authority, or a combination of these factors. Power may be based also on intellectual capacity, (the ability to act as an outcome of superior knowledge). In addition, it may be a moral or emotional capacity that exerts a pressure that causes a reaction from others. Power can be physical—the ability to subdue another through physical strength.

In leisure services leadership, all of these types of power may be found with the possible exception of mechanical energy. It could be argued that some may not be valid in leadership in leisure services; yet, it is probable that instances of the use of each type could be found in the conducting of programs.

Leadership roles

The leader in leisure services plays many roles. There are three main categories:

1. Face-to-face leadership and contact with participants

2. Supervision of face-to-face leaders and direct leadership of representatives of participants (such as a youth council)

3. Administrative or executive leadership, where the major focus is on the leading of policymaking, planning, developing, controlling, and evaluating of services.

Direct, face-to-face leadership is often considered (erroneously) as the major leadership role. But unless there is leadership at each level in the organizational structure, the potential for maximum service will be lessened.

Leadership tasks

1. The leader is a guide and an "enabler." As a guide the leader helps the participant to take a desirable direction. He outlines alternatives and provides resources so that the participant may make a choice.

2. The leader is a coordinator. Various segments of a program must be put together if the experience is to be meaningful for the participants. For example, if a group is going on a day trip to a nearby park, the leader should coordinate the time of departure and the method of transportation so that the group has an unhurried, safe trip to its destination.

3. The leader is a teacher. Frequently, participants need to learn skills in order to enjoy the activity. The leader must be able to teach the skills.

4. The leader encourages and stimulates participants to reach their highest level of capacity in a given experience. For this role he must understand how to motivate people and what kinds of stimuli are needed in different situations. In addition, he must recognize that individuals react differently in different situations.

5. The leader promotes good morale. A leader must be able to accept each person for what he is. In group leadership it is necessary for the leader to help the group to accept each individual in the group and to acknowledge the contribution that each person makes to the goals of the group.

6. The leader helps in the decision-making process. It is necessary to make decisions in every leadership situation. In some cases, the leader weighs the alternatives and makes the decision. At other times the group makes the choice through some established process, such as "majority rules."

Leadership challenges

Many challenges confront the person who assumes a leadership role. These challenges may take several forms.

1. Risk may be necessary when leadership is challenged. For example, a children's group may challenge the leader because he limps. The leader must take the risk of performing a physical skill (rope jumping) to show the children that he is physically capable of leading them. Once this has been accomplished, the group will be ready to accept him as a leader. When a leader takes a risk and accepts a challenge, he must recognize that, if he fails to meet the challenge, his potential for leading the group lessens and may lead to total ineffectiveness with that *particular* group.

2. The leader must present a positive image for the group. One of the problems of boys who live in poverty areas is the one-parent, female-dominated household in which there is no positive male adult figure to follow. An example of the extent to which this problem is recognized is the relatively new trend of seeking male teachers for preschool groups. In the past this field employed women teachers almost exclusively. A man must present a positive image so that the children will want to emulate him.

3. The leader may also be a target. A leader who takes a stand on a controversial issue is constantly challenged by those who oppose his commitment. He must be able and willing to present logical, factual arguments to support his point of view.

Unless leaders are willing to accept these types of challenges, it is questionable that they have chosen a field that suits them.

Leadership characteristics

To carry out the many tasks of a leisure services leader, the individual must have certain innate or learned characteristics. The most fundamental of these is that the individual like people. A sincere liking for people as human beings who have worth and dignity is essential; it enables a leader to relate to people and work with them to achieve goals that are important to them and to himself. He should also recognize that many goals can be achieved through group effort that cannot be achieved through individual effort. Tillman makes the statement that "leadership itself is a life style assumed by individuals to fulfill their personal needs, and, if properly managed, provides greater opportunities of fulfillment for others than they could manage as individuals on their own."[2] Leadership might also be considered as fulfillment of the individual's need to be needed. All of these are ways of characterizing a leader.

In addition to these basic characteristics, there are certain other traits that are essential for leaders in leisure services:

1. Knowledge that the needs of others should take precedence over personal needs

2. Knowledge that will assist the individuals served to achieve their goals

3. Ability to accept each person for what he is

4. Ability to interpret goals of the group and help them to achieve those goals

5. Ability to motivate others into action

Leadership relates to specific situations. A person who can lead a basketball team to success may not be able to lead a successful discussion. Leaders in leisure services must be able to motivate everyone in a group to accept the goals of the group and to assist the group as a whole to define the methods to be used to achieve those goals. In addition, the leader helps the group to indicate how the responsibilities for the tasks to be completed for goal achievment will be assigned to the group members, including the leader. In doing this the leader must urge each individual to perform at his best to enhance the potential for reaching the defined goal. At the same time, the leader must also help the group recognize that its goal may not be possible. For example, a leader of a sports team urges the highest level of performance for the team, but at the same time helps the team recognize that they may not achieve their goal of winning a game because another team has a higher level of performance and will win.

[2]Albert Tillman, *The Program Book for Recreation Professionals* (Los Angeles: National Press Books, 1973), pp. 42–43.

Leadership techniques

All leadership is based on the ability to correctly define the goals of the group and to establish the necessary relationships with the group to achieve the goals as well as the ability to:

1. Communicate ideas to the group. The leader must recognize that both verbal and nonverbal communications are conditioners of the action taken by the group. The leader who says "Let's go," but makes no move to any action, probably will evoke no action on the part of the group. To implement action toward a goal, a leader implies the actions that are needed, uses persuasion to show the correctness of the suggested actions, and prophesizes the successful outcome of the action as a means of inspiring the group. To reinforce the suggested plan, a leader repeats the process to be followed and asks for questions about the plan at each step to ensure that the members of the group fully understand what is to be done.

2. Arouse enthusiasm in the group for the action to be taken.

3. Organize human and physical resources to give the group the greatest potential for goal achievement.

4. Recognize individual differences in members of the group and to assign responsibilities in relation to the capacity of the individual.

5. Challenge the group with new or different ways to achieve their goals. For example, a weaving group which has produced beautiful simple weaving should be challenged to try pattern weaving.

6. Help people with superior skill in a given activity to maintain a common touch with the group. An example would be a leader who recognizes a member of the group who shows how a skill can be performed more easily and better using a method different than that taught by the leader.

7. Anticipate difficulties in a situation so that the difficulty can be prevented. An inexperienced leader might have planned a movie for his group but forgot to check to see that the projection lamp was working or to make certain that there was a replacement lamp should the lamp burn out during the movie showing.

8. Develop secondary or assistant leaders. There are several approaches to this. Secondary or assistant leaders can evolve from members of the group who have greater skill and thus can help other members of the group on an individual or small-group basis. These assistant leaders may be assigned certain tasks because they have shown a capacity for taking responsibility.

9. Work with a group by means of indirect leadership. Certain groups may be organized with indigenous leaders. The assigned leaders of such groups need to lead the group through well-established relationships with the indigenous leaders. Working through the leader of a gang would be an example of this.

Leadership styles

Leadership style depends on the personality and life style of the leader and the goals of the group. There are three basic styles:

1. Autocratic leadership is one in which the leader assumes full responsibility and dictates the actions of the group.

2. In democratic leadership the leader involves the group in the planning, the establishment of goals, the assignment of tasks that are necessary to accomplish the goals, and the evaluation of the program that was conducted.

3. Laissez faire leadership is "unrestrained doing." It is a style that grows out of the group activity.

All these styles may be used effectively depending on the situation. Autocratic leadership is frequently condemned. However, there are occasions when it is an effective leadership style. For example, a group of elderly people have come to a center for some type of activity. For most of their lives these people have been told what to do—as children by parents and teachers and as adults by their boss or some other authority. They have had little or no opportunity to express their wishes. This kind of group is not ready for a democratic approach for they would not know how to use it. An autocratic style can be effective in the beginning activities of the group with a gradual shifting of responsibility from the leader to the group as the group becomes ready for these responsibilities.

Democratic leadership style is used more frequently in leisure services, for the very essence of leisure participation is the opportunity for individuals to be involved in experiences that are meaningful to them. The leader works with the group to determine the program to be conducted. For example, a youth group may want to participate in social activities. In this situation the leader needs to draw out from the group the kinds of activities in which they are interested. Then the leader helps the group to plan and organize those activities. The leader is an enabler who helps the group to achieve their goals. The group assumes many responsibilities under the general guidance of the leader.

Laissez faire leadership grows out of the situation. For example, a group of adults in a neighborhood have informally discussed the fact that they would like to know more about their city government. Someone suggests that they have a meeting of interested people to determine how this might be achieved. One person agrees to find a place to meet. The meeting is convened. There is general discussion by all present of what they want to know about city government. As the meeting progresses, a person emerges as an individual who has certain abilities to form the group and organize it to achieve its purposes. This person may assume leadership responsibilities for a stated length of time or for certain functions. From this beginning the group may move into a democratic leadership style or even an autocratic style, or it may continue on a laissez faire basis, letting leadership emerge as the situation and needs of the group develop.

These leadership styles can be categorized in another way: leader-oriented and group-oriented leadership. Leader-oriented leadership is found in many areas of leisure services. This style is effective in conducting skill activities, organizing mass activities, and conducting information programs such as lectures or symposiums. By contrast the group-oriented style has its principle base in the group itself. The group takes the major responsibility for defining its goals and the process through which those goals will be attained. The assigned leader for a group of this kind is an enabler and a guide, and many times becomes one of the group as it plans and develops the program.

TABLE 3. Characteristics of group-oriented and content-oriented leadership styles*

Characteristic	Group-oriented (found in attitudinal type programs)	Content-oriented (found in skill type programs)
Role conceptions—the leader conceives himself as:	Flexible, permissive, interested in stimulating discussion and seeing others grow	Quite set, demanding, concerned with subject matter, and getting task done.
Leader–group relations	Close, warm, personal, informal; leader selected by group	Distant, cool, impersonal, formal; leader assigned to group
Methods and materials	Materials are incidental to the program, used primarily to present problems. Methods are informal and use social activity.	Materials are major carriers of program, used to present facts and information. Methods are formal, impersonal, few social activities.

*From *Strategies of Leadership: In Conducting Adult Education Programs* by A. A. Liveright. Copyright © 1959 by Harper & Row, Publishers, Inc. Reprinted by permission of the publisher.

A third method of defining leadership style is in terms of a content-oriented or group-oriented situation. A content-oriented situation is one in which the group is interested in content—learning to weave. By contrast, the group-oriented group is interested in the interactions within the group and the activity of the group is secondary to this major focus. Liveright has outlined these categories in *Strategies of Leadership.*[3]

Danford has outlined 16 principles of leadership that must be considered whatever the leadership style is:

1. Leadership must be based on a sound philosophy of recreation.

2. Leadership is dedicated to the principle of involvement.

3. Effective leadership depends in large measure upon the leader's insight into the nature of man and his behavior.

4. Leadership functions in harmony with the principle of individual differences.

5. Leadership is shaped and fashioned both by the group and by the situation.

6. Compatibility must exist between means and ends.

7. Leadership establishes an organizational structure for effective operation.

8. The effectiveness of leadership is measured by the degree to which it attains its goals.

9. Leadership seeks a compromise between the extremes of individualism and equalitarianism.

10. Leadership accepts responsibilities and risks.

11. Leadership operates in harmony with the principle of multiple choices.

12. Leadership seeks to expand the interests of people.

13. Extreme discrepancies between the intelligence of potential leaders and their followers militate against the exercise of leadership.

14. Leadership anticipates difficulties before they arise and acts to prevent them.

15. Leadership attempts to realize as large a return as possible on all facilities, activities, and services.

16. Leadership is based on continuous evaluation.[4]

A careful review of these principles indicates the basic premise of leisure services: to develop programs with people to help them to satisfy their

---

[3]A. A. Liveright, *Strategies of Leadership* (New York: Harper, 1959), p. 27.

[4]Howard Danford and Max Shirley, *Creative Leadership in Recreation,* 2nd ed. (Boston: Allyn and Bacon, Inc., 1970), pp. 93–103. Used with the permission of Allyn and Bacon, Inc.

leisure needs and interests. There is a clear indication that the process of leadership must be based on the demands of the situation and that, in every group, both the individual and the group needs must be given due consideration.

Leadership evaluation

The attainment of the defined production goals is the primary tool for leadership evaluation. In some situations, such as industry or the military, this may be a valid method. However, in leisure services, where the focus is on provision of meaningful leisure experiences for people, the process, or what happens to people as they participate, becomes the important consideration. For example, it should be obvious, in a boys' softball league, that, even though a team won, something was amiss if the majority of the team were hysterical as they left the field. The first question would be what happened in the process of producing a winning team that resulted in this situation? There are several methods for evaluation of leadership and the program:

1. Day-by-day evaluation of program by leader and group
2. Periodic evaluation to determine the extent of goal achievement
3. Observation and evaluation of program by outside experts
4. Self-evaluation of programs by representatives of staff and groups

Whatever method is used, the goal of every evaluation program is to improve the quality of services given to people.

Leadership functions with specified groups

Consideration must be given to the specific leadership necessary for different kinds of direct contact with groups. In all group leadership, it is necessary to consider the individual differences of members of the group and plan accordingly. Four major groups can be identified and each has a certain leadership focus.

Skill activity groups. This group represents a large segment of the leisure services program. People generally think in terms of engaging in a specific activity as leisure participation. In the skill area the leader must be able to help the individual to learn the skill, to organize the group for maximum participation by each member, and to arrange culminating experiences that will give the individual the satisfaction of performing with the attendant recognition that it brings. The culminating experience by an art group might be an exhibit. A sports group might have a tournament or league play. A leader for this type of activity needs skills in the activity and knowledge of how to teach those skills.

Club groups. The variety of club groups possible in leisure services is practically unlimited. The major function of clubs is to provide for the interaction of people in a defined situation. In these situations the leader must be able to understand the dynamics within the group, to lead the group in a definition of goals, to suggest ways to achieve those goals, and to organize and conduct the program so that the goals may be accomplished. A leader with this kind of group must understand group dynamics and have a breadth of knowledge of the experiences that will bring about satisfaction in participation with others for the purpose of achieving a goal.

Mass activity. Provision of a facility is one leadership function.

1. Provision of facilities includes everything from a neighborhood playground to a national park. The focus here is to provide an area where people can participate in unorganized activities in accordance with individual needs of the moment. Leadership for this kind of participation is based on the:

a. Ability to maintain the facility for maximum use by participants and at the same time preserve it for future use

b. Ability to analyze the needs of people for this kind of participation and locate the facility in the most advantageous place for best use

c. Provision of information on how to use the facility

d. Provision of equipment to be used at the facility on some type of rental or loan basis

e. Ability to practice sound administrative procedures so that the facility is operated efficiently, economically, and effectively

Leaders in these types of situations must recognize that the facility is maintained for people, not just for the sake of preserving the area.

2. Special events are an important part of every leisure services program. They include the many celebrations held in communities, culminating activities for periods in the yearly program, and trips of all kinds which are more and more becoming an important part of the leisure services program. In these situations a leader must be able to:

a. Organize many details into a functional structure

b. Move large groups efficiently

c. Acquire facilities and equipment to conduct the activity

d. Provide facility maintainence both before and after the event

Leadership of special events requires that a leader be able to mobilize large groups of participants to assist with the event. Planning should be done with participants and volunteers recruited to assist with the actual activity. This implies that much of professional leadership is indirect: the professional is a catalyst who motivates others into performance of the tasks to be completed. Most special events are conducted through the functioning of committees who are assigned specific tasks.

Special populations. Today it is recognized that all people should have leisure services available to them. The special populations include physically and mentally handicapped people in the community and in institutions; the elderly in the community and in institutions; and the child or adult delinquent in correctional institutions or in halfway houses in the community. Programs for these groups are not materially different than those for able-bodied groups. However, leadership of these groups requires different emphases. These include, but are not necessarily limited to the following:

1. Ability to accept the individual as a person who has the same basic needs as other people, but is limited in his capacity to satisfy them by his physical, mental, or social incapacity, or by the societal environment in which he functions

2. Ability to help the individual to accept the reality of his handicap and how to satisfy his leisure needs in spite of it. The leader must be empathetic rather than sympathetic

3. Ability to adapt activities so that the person may enjoy successful participation

4. Ability to assess the needs and interests of each person and help him to participate in those programs that have a potential for satisfying them.

5. Recognition that individuals, even though relatively severely handicapped can perform many tasks with little help if the leader has the patience to work slowly with the person until he achieves success

6. Willingness to perform certain tasks for people that are not usually associated with leisure services such as pushing a wheelchair or assisting with eating

SUPERVISION IN LEISURE SERVICES

In this section only the elementary components of supervision will be examined. Supervisory functions are performed at all levels of leisure services: by the face-to-face leader, the middle management supervisor, and by the administrator. Supervision involves the overseeing of programs in which the direct contact with participants is done by another person. The factors in the supervisory process that will be considered here are those that concern people in leader-level positions who supervise part-time and volunteer personnel and people in entry-level supervisory positions frequently called assistant supervisors. In these positions individuals carry on certain limited supervisory functions under the general direction of a middle management supervisor or administrator.

Supervision defined

Supervision is a process through which leadership of personnel is conducted so that services may be offered most effectively. In this context the supervisor is the helper of the leader.

Supervisory tasks

Anyone performing supervisory duties will perform the following tasks at certain times.

1. Lead other leaders in a subordinate position
2. Lead participants
3. Develop programs
   a. Survey the need for the program
   b. Organize the program, including securing the necessary leaders, facilities, and equipment
   c. Operate the program
   d. Evaluate the program and the leaders
4. Perform administrative tasks
   a. Requisition supplies and equipment
   b. Maintain inventories
   c. Assign facilities and equipment
   d. Conduct public relations activities such as writing news releases, promote programs through the media, and speak to groups about the program
5. Leader development and guidance
   a. Interview the prospective leader
   b. Orient new leaders
   c. Conduct regular conferences, inservice training
   d. Evaluate individual's performance on the job
6. Supervise areas of responsibility
   a. Work with those under his supervision
   b. Work with other supervisors at the same level in the department structure
   c. Work with superiors

Supervision principles

Supervisors seek to:

1. Enhance the service rendered to expand the contribution that the service makes to the participant's leisure needs and interests.

2. Work with both the strengths and weaknesses of those whom he is supervising.

3. Understand the physical, mental, and emotional and social development of people and the techniques needed to further that development.

4. Study, evaluate, and improve services. To achieve this the supervisor must keep adequate records and progress reports.

5. Use both an administrative and a scientific approach to problem solving. In the administrative approach the supervisor uses the facts presented to arrive at a decision. In the scientific approach the problem is defined, data are collected relative to the problem, the data are analyzed, solutions suggested, the solutions are tested, conclusions are drawn, and the findings are summarized with recommendations for future actions to be taken.

6. Use a democratic approach involving those supervised in the process.

7. Be creative in supervision. Supervisors in leisure services should encourage leaders to try innovative approaches.

8. Plan the supervisory process. Although leisure services are relatively informal there must be definite lines of authority, delegation of duties, and delegation of authority.

Supervision DO's and DON'Ts

1. Do's
   a. Stimulate people to seek self-development.
   b. Be supportive of a leader when necessary and uphold his policies as much as possible.
   c. Be a guide and teacher.
   d. Be an outlet for the leader's expression of hostilities, difficulties, and failures.
   e. Present the image of the best in leisure services.
2. Don'ts
   a. Oversupervise.
   b. Limit the initiative of the leader.
   c. Fail to recognize differences.
   d. Be authoritative, except in emergencies or crisis situations.
   e. Keep leaders dependent.
   f. Be critical rather than understanding.

Supervision process

The job descriptions. Supervision begins with the writing of the job description. The purpose of the job description is to list the responsibilities against which the qualifications of the applicant may be measured. It may be used also to evaluate job performance. Level of responsibility, major tasks, undefined but related duties, line of authority, method of promotion (if any), and salary and other benefits should all be included in the job description.

Application blanks. Application blanks should be used for all positions in an agency. One blank may be used for all positions with sections applicable to certain jobs, or application blanks may be developed for categories of workers such as professional leisure services personnel, clerical, or maintenance personnel. Personal data, education, experience, professional membership, honors received, community activity, hobbies, travel, references, reason for interest in job, any certificates or licenses held, and certification that the facts presented are accurate should all be included on the application blank.

The initial interview. The purpose of the interview is to give the applicant more information than was in the job description about the position to be filled, and to determine if the applicant's qualifications are compatible with the job to be done.

1. Steps in the interview
   a. Develop rapport with the applicant
   b. State the purpose of the interview which is to give the applicant information about the job, and to answer questions the applicant has about the job
2. Information derived from the interview
   a. General impressions from observation of applicant's speech, mannerisms, and dress
   b. Answers to questions which should be asked so that they *cannot* be answered by "yes" or "no"
3. Information given at an interview
   a. History, policies, and objectives of the agency
   b. Tasks to be performed
4. Role of supervisor in the interview
   a. Leads without monopolizing the conversation
5. Closing the interview
   a. Indicate that the applicant's qualifications will be reviewed in relation to other applicants.

b. Inform the applicant whether he is accepted or rejected. Only rarely is an applicant accepted or rejected at an initial interview. This is done only when the applicant is clearly best qualified or totally unqualified.

6. Followup on the interview

a. Letters of acceptance or rejection should be sent to *all* applicants.

7. References

a. Check references (Those given by former employers are usually most accurate.)

Orientation. Every new worker should have an orientation period, during which he is introduced to the agency, the community, staff, and the participants. Personnel policies need to be outlined whether the person is a paid leader or a volunteer.

Identifying leadership. From the application, the initial interview, and the preservice orientation and training, the supervisor must assess the leadership style of the person to determine the groups to which he should be assigned. In *Social Group Work Practice* Wilson and Ryland have identified leadership in terms of the experience of the group to be served and the kind of leadership that that group will require (See Fig. 1, p. 186).[5]

Another method for identifying leadership style as a means of assigning a leader to a group is that suggested by Liveright.

How to identify leadership style*

Leadership role conception—As a leader in this program, I conceive of myself as a person who is:

a. Flexible in my manner and performance _____

b. Set and determined _____

a. Interested in the group and its members _____

b. Interested in the content and subject matter _____

a. Informal and friendly _____

b. Formal and professional _____

[5]Gertrude Wilson and G. Ryland, *Social Group Work Practice* (Boston: Houghton Mifflin, 1949), p. 68.

*From *Strategies of Leadership: In Conducting Adult Education Programs* by A. A. Liveright. Copyright © 1959 by Harper & Row, Publishers, Inc. Reprinted by permission of the publisher.

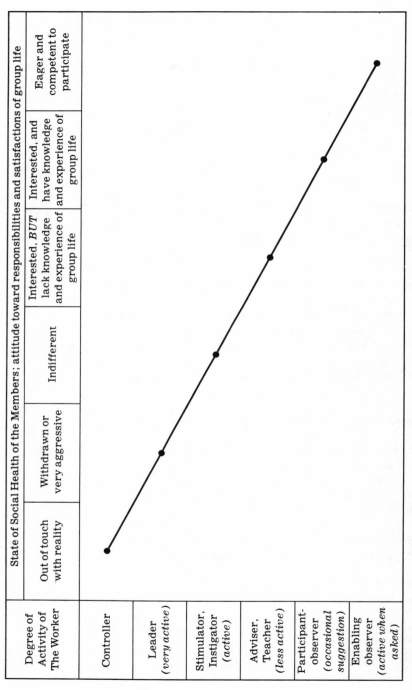

FIGURE 1. Degree of activity of worker as indicated by social health of members. From *Social Group Work Practice* by G. Wilson and G. Ryland. Copyright © 1949 (Boston: Houghton Mifflin Company). Reprinted by permission of the publisher.

a. Motivated by a desire to render "service" _____

b. Motivated by a desire to accomplish something definite _____

Total "a" items checked_____
Total "b" items checked_____

Leader-group relations—As a leader in this program, my relations with group members are (or should be):

a. Close and personal _____

b. Reserved and impersonal _____

a. Informal, with frequent use of first names and humor _____

b. Formal, with use of last names, little by-play _____

a. To include responsibility for counseling _____

b. To include no concern for personal or group problems _____

a. On a continuing basis because they want me _____

b. On a continuing basis mainly because the agency has appointed me _____

Total "a" items checked_____
Total "b" items checked_____

Use of methods and materials—As a leader in this program I feel that materials should be:

a. Flexible, subject to change _____

b. Well determined before program starts _____

a. Varied widely during sessions, and from session to session _____

b. Limited to one or two tested materials _____

a. Concerned primarily with problem solving _____

b. Concerned primarily with providing information _____

a. An incidental part of the program _____

b. The major content of the program _____

And that methods should:

a. Lead to wide and varied discussion _____

b. Hold group closely to desired facts _____

    a. Develop the wide and broad participation   _____

    b. Assure that group members will pay close attention to leader   _____

    a. Stimulate considerable outside communication   _____

    b. Concentrate communication inside the class   _____

    a. Stimulate socialization and group cohesion   _____

    b. Emphasize content rather than group development   _____

    a. Lead to continuing relationship between leader and group   _____

    b. Provide for relationship only during course of the program   _____

Total "a" items checked_____

Total "b" items checked_____

Using this approach a supervisor could identify those leaders who are more content-oriented and those who are group-oriented. It must be recognized that any of these methods give only general indications. The supervisor can use them as indicators and relate them to the impressions gained through personal contacts during the initial interview and the orientation period.

Work Distribution. Every supervisor has the responsibility for distributing work among those in the agency for whom he is responsible. This involves:

    1. Identifying the tasks to be performed

    2. Determining who is currently doing the task, and the time necessary to perform it

    3. Determining who is working above or below his capacity

    4. Identifying work loads

    5. Reorganizing the work to ensure better use of leadership and a more efficient operation

The principle tasks performed in leisure services are

    1. Program services

        a. Leadership

        b. Counseling

        c. Public relations

        d. Clerical work

        e. Budgeting

f. Maintenance of program equipment
2. Resource services
    a. Planning
    b. Maintenance of resource
    c. Resources interpretation
    d. Plan for public use of resource
    e. Budgeting
    f. Maintenance of equipment
    g. Clerical

In scheduling leaders for work, the supervisor must plan the schedule so that full-time workers work no more than three nights a week and have two consecutive days off each week.

Supervising the leader. This should be a shared experience of the supervisor and the leader for the purpose of enhancing services to participants. Supervision must never be "Snoopervision." To help the leader to develop, several procedures can be used.

Observation of the leader and the group during participation to assess interest of the group, participant activity, and management of the group is one procedure. During an observation period the supervisor should be as inconspicuous as possible and make no criticisms, either good or bad, in front of the group. A basic principle in observation is to visit frequently and stay long enough to get a full impression of the situation. Impressions from an observation should be recorded after the supervisor leaves the group.

The group process report written by the leader is another procedure. With the supervisor's observation report this can be used as a basis for a supervisory conference. The group process report includes:

1. Who was there and whether he came alone or with others
2. Where the group met
3. What was done at the group session, and what interaction occurred between group members
4. Whether the activity was successful and why, whether it was unsuccessful and why

Detailed group process reports can only be used when the group numbers no more than fifteen or twenty, for they require that the leader be able to recall the interactions of people as the group met. With larger groups a modified report might be used showing the major happenings during a group activity.

Supervisory conferences can be the backbone of the supervisory process. It is the major means of communication between the leader and the supervisor. Conferences should be held on a regular basis at a time convenient for both supervisor and leader. Conferences with full-time leaders should be held at least once a month and, preferably, weekly. Conferences with part-time leaders and volunteers should be held either before or after their session and at least once a month.

1. The setting for a conference should be a quiet room, and should be unhurried even though it may be brief.

2. The supervisory conference is a means for continuing education and for evaluation of the job performance of the leader. It provides a means of preventing problems, as well as a means for solving problems.

3. The supervisor and the leader provide items that they want to discuss at the conference.

4. The supervisor has the responsibility for leadership in the conference. At the start of the conference, the supervisor should point out positive factors in the leader's performance. The leader and the supervisor then discuss:

    a. Strengths and weaknesses

    b. Possible changes in approach

    c. Leader's suggestions for solving problems

5. Supervisory conferences may be used as a means of educating leaders in use of new methods.

6. Supervisory conferences are used to correct leadership techniques.

    a. To suggest positive changes rather than criticize

    b. To suggest ways of enhancing professional development

7. Supervisors should attempt to answer questions or say, "I'll find out."

8. There are several problems relating to supervisory conferences:

    a. Insecurity on part of either supervisor or leader

    b. The attitude of leader toward authority

    c. The use of the supervisory conference as a means of problem solving

    d. Attitude of leaders toward their mistakes

    e. Discouragement on part of leader

    f. Personal problems of leaders

Evaluating the leader. An administrative task performed by supervisors is the evaluation of leaders under their supervision. Qualities evaluated are

1. Attitudes, knowledge, and skills
2. How the leader relates to participants and staff
3. Education, leadership ability, and professional maturity

Supervisors can use any, or a combination of all, the following:

1. Self-evaluation
2. Observation
3. Critical analysis

One method that has been used effectively is to use a self-evaluation instrument which is completed by both the leader and supervisor and then discussed at a conference. In this manner the evaluation process is used as a means for helping the leader to develop his own effectiveness.

Student assignments

This part consists of 12 objectives. You will be called upon to demonstrate your mastery of each objective.

OBJECTIVE	EVIDENCE OF COMPETENCY
1. To examine concepts of leadership and their application to leisure services.	a. Discuss the power concept of leadership and the situational theory of leadership.
	b. Name three types of leadership, indicate the major characteristics of each, and which might be found more frequently in leisure services.
2. To identify the various leadership roles.	a. Identify the leadership roles and discuss their place in leisure services.
	b. Discuss the tasks performed by leaders in leisure services.
	c. Describe the challenges of leadership.

OBJECTIVE	EVIDENCE OF COMPETENCY
3. To define the characteristics of a leader.	a. Describe the basic characteristics necessary for leisure services leadership, and indicate why these are essential.
	b. Define five characteristics of an individual, any one of which specific characteristic or a combination of several that might make him a leader in a specific situation.
4. To learn the duties and responsibilities of a leader in leisure services.	Describe and discuss eight techniques that a leader in leisure services must be able to use in order to work effectively with groups.
5. To learn leadership styles and when and how they are used in leisure services.	Describe and illustrate how each of the following leadership styles could be used in leisure services: autocratic, democratic, laissez-faire, content-centered, group-centered, and leader-centered.
6. To define principles of leadership.	Discuss the 16 principles of leadership described by Danford, and apply them to leisure services.
7. To examine methods for evaluating leadership.	a. Discuss the use of attainment of a goal as a method of evaluation and show its application to leisure services.
	b. Discuss four methods that can be used to evaluate leisure services program leadership and the purpose of the evaluation process.
8. To learn the leadership needs for varying categories of program, and the leader skills needed in each category.	Identify four major categories of groups and describe the specific skills needed for each category.
9. To define the duties and responsibilities of supervisors in leisure services.	a. Define supervision and discuss its purpose in leisure services programs.

OBJECTIVE	EVIDENCE OF COMPETENCY

| | b. Describe the tasks performed by a supervisor in leisure services programs. |

10. To learn the fundamental principles of supervision and apply them to leisure services.

a. State the principles of supervision and illustrate how they apply to leisure services.

b. Discuss the Do's and Don'ts of supervision and give an illustration of each as it would be found in leisure services.

11. To learn the components of the supervisory process in leisure services.

a. Describe eight major components of the supervisory process.

b. What are the points to consider when conducting an initial interview?

c. As a leader of a craft program, how would you orient a new volunteer to the program?

d. What points should be considered in assigning a leader to a group?

e. Describe the factors that must be considered in work distribution.

f. Discuss in detail how you would supervise a leader and the kinds of records and reports that would help you in this process.

g. Describe the steps in a supervisory conference, and indicate varying goals of supervisory conferences.

12. To examine methods of evaluating leadership.

Discuss the varying methods that may be used to evaluate leadership, and indicate, with your reasons, the one that you consider most effective.

Resources

This section is divided into two parts: (1) references, and (2) other materials.

REFERENCES

CORBIN, H. DAN, and TAIT, WILLIAM. *Education for Leisure.* Englewood Cliffs, N.J.: Prentice-Hall, 1973.

DANFORD, HOWARD, and SHIRLEY, MAX. *Creative Leadership in Recreation,* 2nd ed. Boston: Allyn & Bacon, 1970.

KRAUS, RICHARD, and BATES, BARBARA J. *Recreation Leadership and Supervision: Guidelines for Professional Development.* Philadelphia: W. B. Saunders, 1975.

LIVERIGHT, A. A. *Strategies of Leadership.* New York: Harper, 1959.

Looking into Leadership. Washington, D.C.: Leadership Resources, Inc., 1966.

Personnel Criteria and Personnel Standards. Peekskill, N.Y.: New York State Recreation and Park Society, 1974.

ROSS, MURRAY, and HENDRY, CHARLES E. *New Understandings of Leadership.* NEW YORK: ASSOCIATION PRESS, 1957.

WILSON, GERTRUDE, and RYLAND, G. *Social Group Work Practice.* Boston: Houghton Mifflin, 1949.

OTHER MATERIALS

Report Forms
Sample Job Descriptions
Sample Application Blank
Miscellaneous Materials

Sample reports

OBSERVER REPORTS

1. What kind of relationship did these two people seem to have? What attitudes and feelings could you see that affected this relationship?

2. Was the real problem defined?

3. What strengths of the worker were emphasized?

4. Did the worker seem to gain self-awareness?

5. Were any solutions or decisions made? By whom?

6. Were the four basic concepts of helping people observed by the supervisor?

7. Do you think the worker received help in becoming more self-dependent? Why?

8. How do you think this worker felt after the conference?

EVALUATION SHEET*

Participation

1. To what extent did the group concentrate its efforts on the assigned discussion tasks?

_____ were at work most of the time

_____ worked, but some time spent in talking about other things

_____ spent a good deal of time on other things

2. If there were times when the group did not work well, what may have been the reason?

_____ were fighting over irrelevancies

_____ were being sociable, joking, etc.

_____ got off on irrelevant personal experiences

_____ were frustrated

3. Most of the talking done by:

_____ group as a whole _____ a few members _____ the leaders

4. As far as guiding the discussion was concerned, the leader:

_____ shared guidance with the group

_____ managed it mostly himself

_____ provided no guidance

5. Differing points of view were:

_____ acknowledged and considered impartially

_____ acknowledged, but not considered objectively

_____ neither acknowledged nor considered

6. Members participated in ways which helped make the discussion productive by:

_____ encouraging other members to contribute

_____ calling attention to points of agreement or disagreement

_____ summarizing

_____ attempting to clarify

_____ introducing new points for consideration

_____ bringing the group back to the subject

_____ trying to resolve conflicts

*From *Strategies of Leadership: In Conducting Adult Education Programs* by A. A. Liveright. Copyright © 1959 by Harper & Row, Publishers, Inc. Reprinted by permission of the publisher.

Communication and reasoning

7. Members paid attention to what others were saying
_____ always
_____ frequently
_____ sometimes
_____ rarely
_____ never

8. Members understood one another
_____ very well
_____ fairly well
_____ very little
_____ not at all

9. Members drew out one another and asked questions to clarify the c
tributions of others.
_____ always
_____ frequently
_____ sometimes
_____ rarely
_____ never

10. Attempts were made to clarify ideas and thinking by probing for reasons behind opinions.
_____ always
_____ frequently
_____ sometimes
_____ rarely
_____ never
_____ by members
_____ by leader

11. Attempts were made to examine the thinking which people used to justify their opinions.
_____ always
_____ frequently
_____ sometimes
_____ rarely
_____ never
_____ by members
_____ by leader

12. Evidence cited to support members' opinions was examined
_____ always
_____ frequently
_____ sometimes
_____ rarely
_____ never
_____ by members
_____ by leader

OBSERVATION REPORT.* Determination of Extent to Which Leadership Roles
Are Shared with Group

	FUNCTION PERFORMED BY LEADER	FUNCTION PERFORMED BY GROUP
1. Goals of discussion clarified		
2. Discussion "group-centered" so that all can participate		
3. Atmosphere developed so that all members can say what they really think		
4. Progress of group in relation to goals determined		
5. Discussion sufficiently practical so that everyone understands what is being discussed		
6. Sufficient sensitivity maintained so that participants take account of each other's wishes and keep everyone interested		
7. Concepts and ideas developed which appear to be important to group		
8. Understanding maintained between members of group		
9. Differences of opinion handled so that varying points of view accepted		
10. Individual ideas and opinions become part of total group thinking and process		

SELF-EVALUATION REPORT

Name _____**Job title**_____

Summary of job description

Instructions: In each of the following sections indicate what you consider to be your strengths and weaknesses in relation to the questions in each section. Then give yourself a rating on the eight-step scale with eight as the highest rating. Your supervisor will use the same form and rate you in the same way. Your final rating will be the outcome of a conference between you and your supervisor.

Section 1—*Professional approach to my job*

1. How have I improved my professional capacity?

2. What have I contributed to the profession?

3. To what extent have I interpreted the meaning of leisure to the groups that I lead and to the public in general?

Rating

1	2	3	4	5	6	7	8

Section 2—*Personal*

1. What are my personal leadership strengths and weaknesses?

2. What personal fulfillment am I receiving from being a leader in leisure services? Is it the right job for me?

3. Do I fully uphold the policies of the department?

4. Do I present a good image for the department through my behavior, dress, efforts?

5. Do I bring sufficient energy to the job for maximum performance, or do I permit off-the-job activities to dissipate my energies?

6. Am I professionally mature enough to be able to ask for help with problems, without creating extensive personal anxiety for myself?

Rating

1	2	3	4	5	6	7	8

Section 3—*Program*

1. In developing programs do I plan with groups rather than for them?

2. Do I determine the needs and interests of the people with whom I work?

3. Do I plan my day-to-day programs to ensure maximum involvements by participants?

4. Do I ensure that all facilities, equipment, and supplies are available and in working order for use by participants?

5. Do I prepare for each program? How effective is the preparation, and what changes should be made to make it potentially more effective?

6. Do I assess my capability for leadership of a specified group, and try to increase that capacity?

Rating

1	2	3	4	5	6	7	8

Section 4—*Relations with people*

1. To what extent am I able to accept all people for what they are, as human beings with worth and dignity?

2. Do I honestly like people, or would I prefer to work with things?

3. How much do I understand about the interaction of people in groups, and what understandings do I find most important in leading groups?

4. What do I do in my groups to help people to function together as a harmonious group? Is what I do effective? Why?

5. How do I ensure that each person in the group has maximum opportunity for participation?

Rating:

1	2	3	4	5	6	7	8

Section 5—*Administration*

1. Do I know what the policies of the department are?

2. What department policies do I always follow and which ones do I tend to overlook?

3. Am I always prompt in filing reports and records?

4. What democratic practices do I follow in my groups, and when am I authoritative? Do I regularly interpret correctly when to be democratic and when to be authoritative?

5. What practices do I follow to ensure the safety of the participants?

6. What public relations practices do I use to inform the public about the program?

7. Do leaders and others under my supervision know their duties and responsibilities and have the delegated authority to carry them out?

8. How do I supervise my subordinates?

9. Do all persons under my supervision have regular means of communication with me and other staff members?

10. How do I accept people for programs?

11. How do I evaluate the extent to which the participants are achieving their goals?

12. Is recognition given to people who make outstanding contributions to a program? How is this done?

13. How do I develop awareness in participants that all facilities are to be maintained so that everyone can use them to full capacity?

14. When vandalism occurs, what steps do I take to correct it at present and prevent it in the future?

15. How do I relate my program to other programs in the department and in the community?

Rating:

1	2	3	4	5	6	7	8

Rating Total_____ Rating score_____ (total divided by 5)

Signed_____

Summary of Evaluation Conference

Final Rating _____

Unsatisfactory score	2
Poor	4
Average	5.5–6.5
Good	6.5–7.9
Excellent	8

Sample job descriptions

RECREATION AIDE

General statement of duties
Assists in carrying out one phase of a county, town, or village recreation program; performs related work as required.

Distinguishing features of the class
Under supervision, an employee in this class is responsible for leading an assigned group in a variety of activities within a recreation program. The incumbent is required to work with all age groups in a firm and tactful manner

and must also possess the ability to rapidly acquire a knowledge of the rules and objectives of a variety of games, hobbies, and sports. Work is performed in accordance with a predetermined program under the direct supervision of the program supervisor.

Illustrative examples of work

Assists in conducting a planned activity at a recreation facility.

Instructs participants in sports, games, dancing, singing, handicrafts, plays, and other activities.

Enforces safety rules and regulations at the recreation facility; administers first aid when necessary.

Issues and cares for equipment, materials and supplies, maintains simple records, and prepares reports on activities.

Acts as a sports official.

Required knowledge, skills, and abilities

Good knowledge of sports, games, hobbies, and related recreational activities.

Ability to acquire further knowledge of the rules and objectives of a variety of games and sports.

Ability to meet the public tactfully and diplomatically.

Ability to create interest in the recreation program and give instructions in various recreational activities.

Ability to work with groups of all ages in a firm and tactful manner.

Ability to maintain records and prepare reports.

Minimum qualifications

Must be at least 16 years old.

RECREATION LEADER

General statement of duties

Conducts one phase of a county, town, or village recreation program; performs related work as required.

Distinguishing features of the class

Under supervision, an employee in this class is responsible for conducting a variety of activities at a recreation facility. The incumbent is required to work with all age groups in a firm and tactful manner and must also possess the ability to rapidly acquire a knowledge of the rules and objectives of a variety of games, hobbies, and sports. Work is performed in accordance with a predetermined recreation program. Direct supervision and review of the incumbent's work for adherence to departmental standards and program objectives is maintained.

Illustrative examples of work

Directs or assists in directing a variety of recreational activities for all age groups; encourages participation in these activities.

Instructs the participants in the various recreational activities and may supervise subordinate personnel under his responsibility.

Enforces safety rules and regulations at a recreation facility; administers first aid when necessary.

Issues and cares for equipment, materials and supplies.

Acts as sports official.

Keeps records and makes periodic reports.

Required knowledge, skills, and abilities

Good knowledge of sports, games, hobbies, and related recreational activities.

Ability to acquire rapidly further knowledge of the rules and objectives of a variety of games and sports.

Ability to meet the public tactfully and diplomatically.

Ability to create interest in the recreation program and give instructions in various recreational activities.

Ability to work with groups of all ages in a firm and tactful manner.

Ability to maintain records and prepare reports.

Minimum qualifications

Graduation from an accredited college or university with an associate's degree in recreation and/or physical education; or,

Sixty credit hours toward a bachelor's degree in recreation and/or physical education.

SENIOR RECREATION LEADER

General statement of duties

Assists in supervising a major phase of a recreation program in a county, town, or village recreation department and has direct responsibility for a specific activity area in the program; performs related work as required.

Distinguishing features of the class

Under supervision, an employee in this class is responsible for conducting and supervising a planned recreational activity within the recreation program. Work also involves operating responsibility for a particular area of recreational activity such as gym, arts and crafts, plays, playground, group and individual games. The incumbent exercises supervision over a number of subordinate personnel. Work is reviewed by the Recreation Supervisor for adherence to established departmental policies through reports, conferences, and periodic observation of the supervised activity area.

Illustrative examples of work

Conducts and supervises a planned activity at a recreational facility.

Supervises the work of a number of recreation leaders at a recreational facility in such activities as arts and crafts, group or individual games, tournaments, plays, camping, or special events.

Enforces safety rules and regulations in the recreational facility or area of his responsibility; administers first aid when necessary.

Instructs staff members in the methods of teaching and officiating at recreational activities.

Acts as a sports official.

Maintains records and prepares periodic reports on staff and recreational activities.

Issues and cares for equipment, materials and supplies.

Required knowledge, skills, and abilities

Good knowledge of sports, games, hobbies, and related recreational activities.

Some knowledge of supervisory techniques.

Some knowledge of the objectives and methods used in the field of recreation.

Ability to deal tactfully and diplomatically with the public.

Ability to create interest in and give instructions in various recreational activities.

Ability to plan and assign the work of subordinate personnel for maximum efficiency.

Ability to work with all age groups in a firm and tactful manner.

Ability to maintain records and prepare activity reports.

Minimum qualifications

Graduation from an accredited college or university with an associate's degree in recreation and/or physical education; or,

Sixty credit hours toward a bachelor's degree in recreation and/or physical education; and plus either,

1. An additional 30 credit hours in relevant professional courses; or,
2. One year of full time experience in a recreation program.

RECREATION SUPERVISOR

General statement of duties

Supervises one or more major phases of a recreation program in the county, town, or village recreation departments; performs related work as required.

Distinguishing features of the class

Under general supervision, an employee in this class is responsible for supervising the activities of one or more programs in a recreation department. Work includes responsibility for the supervision, training and leadership of subordinate personnel. The incumbent devises and conducts the recreational activities for specific phases of the recreation program. Work requires a thorough technical knowledge of the activities being supervised. Work is performed with a minimum of direct supervision and is reviewed by the department head for adherence to departmental policies.

Illustrative examples of work

Organizes and directs a variety of recreation activities in a recreation program which includes Pre-School, Youth, Adult and Senior Citizens' programs.

Enforces safety rules and regulations at the various facilities; administers first aid when necessary.

Supervises the training and conduct of the subordinate staff.

Gives instructions in one or more specialized fields of activity.

Assigns umpires and referees; acts as a sports official when needed.

Issues and repairs equipment and supplies.

Submits periodic reports on the progress and effectiveness of established programs.

Required knowledge, skills, and abilities

Good knowledge of the objectives and methods used in the field of recreation.

Good knowledge of sports, games, hobbies, and related recreational activities.

Good knowledge of supervisory techniques.

Some knowledge of administrative techniques.

Ability to work with and speak to all age groups.

Ability to meet the public tactfully and diplomatically.

Ability to supervise both group and individual activities.

Ability to plan, assign and supervise the work of others in a manner conducive to full performance and high morale.

Ability to maintain records and prepare reports.

Minimum qualifications

Graduation from an accredited college or university with a bachelor's degree in recreation and/or parks or a bachelor's degree with a minimum of 15 credit hours taken in professional recreation courses (including administration, philosophy, principles, and programs).

Sample application blank

LEISURE SERVICES DEPARTMENT
APPLICATION FOR EMPLOYMENT

1. Name _____ 2. Date of birth _____
3. Address _____
4. Number of dependents: under 12 _____
                               under 18 _____
                               18–60   _____
                               over 60   _____
5. Health status:
    General health: Good _____ Fair _____ Poor _____

Describe any health handicaps:

Height _____ Weight _____
6. Education:

SCHOOLS ATTENDED	NAME & ADDRESS	DIPLOMA OR DEGREE	YEAR RECEIVED	MAJOR	MINOR
High school					
College					
Graduate					
Special					

7. Experience: (Start with current position and list backward in order. If more space is needed attach a sheet. Include both paid and volunteer experience)

POSITION	AGENCY NAME AND ADDRESS	NAME OF SUPERVISOR	DATES OF EMPLOYMENT	REASON FOR LEAVING

8. Additional professional training (art, music, dance, life saving, etc.)

TYPE	DATES	WHERE TAKEN	INSTRUCTOR	CERTIFICATE RECEIVED

9. Honors, awards, or unusual accomplishments. List with name and dates.

10. References: List three people other than relatives.

NAME	ADDRESS	WHERE YOU WERE OR ARE ASSOCIATED WITH THIS PERSON

11. Travel: Indicate kinds of travel you have done.

12. Have you ever been convicted of a crime other than a traffic violation? Yes _____ No _____ If "yes" give details on a separate sheet.

13. Are you licensed to drive a car? Yes _____ No _____ . If you own a car could you use it on the job?

14. Indicate if you are limited in the hours of the day or days of the week when you can work.

15. Certification: I, hereby, certify that all statements contained herein are true and accurate.

Signed _____

Applicant

Notarized by:

Notary Stamp   Signature of Notary _____

Miscellaneous materials

SUPERVISORY CONFERENCES
POINTS TO EVALUATE

1. What evidence was there that the supervisor had prepared for the conference? Specify.

2. Did the leader have the opportunity to state his concerns? How was this done? Was it necessary to set priorities for topics to be discussed? Why was this important?

3. Was there any evidence of a "hidden agenda"?
4. Did the supervisor provide for an uninterrupted session?
5. Were the agenda items fully discussed?
6. Indicate how the supervisor led the leader into a solution of his problems. Was there any evidence that the supervisor dictated the solution? If so, what?

Interview rating scale

A scale of this type might be used by the observer of an interviewer. It would help to focus attention on the important aspects of the interviewer's job.

Acceptance

Supportive and accepting	Neutral—neither accepts nor rejects	Rejecting

Questioning

Unbiased—does not lead to biased information		Biased—leads to biased information

Focus

Keeps respondent speaking to objectives		Allows respondent to get lost in irrelevant material

This scale might also be used as a self-evaluation form by the person who is doing the interviewing.

A SOCIALIZED EXAMINATION FOR SUPERVISION OF RECREATION PROGRAMS

1. Discuss the principles of work distribution, and show how you would apply them in a recreation setting.
2. Discuss the principles of supervision and indicate the operating factors that may condition full adherence to these principles.
3. Describe the criteria that you would use to determine the leader who should be assigned to a specific group.
4. Describe the inservice program that you would develop for an agency.
5. Describe the functions of a supervisor in the evaluation of a worker under his supervision.

MODULE 8
Leisure counseling

What a leisure counselor needs to know

As people find that they have increased periods of free, unobligated time, they will seek ways in which to fill these periods with meaningful experiences. Many people will need information about the kinds of leisure experiences that are available in the community. Some will have to learn skills and acquire the knowledge necessary to engage in the experience with satisfying results. Others will have to assess their behavior to determine whether their experiences are bringing the full satisfaction that they are seeking. The leisure counselor in the community recreation department; in a private voluntary agency; in an institution serving the ill, the disabled, or the aged; and in a correctional institution helps the individual to make decisions about his leisure choices.

DEFINITIONS

• *Free time:* unobligated time when an individual can choose what he wants to do. It may occur either on or off the job.

• *Leisure:* a quality in living determined by the extent of involvement of an individual in an experience, and the depth of satisfaction that is derived from it.

• *Counseling:* a helping technique that seeks to assist people to define their needs and solve problems related to those needs.

• *Leisure counseling:* a process in which a leisure services specialist assists people with problems related to their free time, and their satisfactions or dissatisfactions with the quality of their living.

BEHAVIORAL OBJECTIVES

1. To define leisure counseling

2. To acquire knowledge of the scope of leisure counseling

3. To learn how beliefs, values, and attitudes influence leisure choices

4. To develop the ability to accept each person for what he is

5. To develop the competency to establish rapport with an individual who seeks help with a leisure problem

6. To learn the methods for assessing the needs and interests of people

7. To find out about agencies that provide leisure services

8. To learn various methods for individual leisure counseling

9. To learn the techniques of group- and activity-centered leisure counseling

10. To define the role of a recreator in a team approach to leisure counseling

11. To ascertain the special problems related to counseling the disadvantaged for leisure choices

12. To learn to develop a community resource file

13. To learn the techniques for developing a leisure counseling program

LEISURE COUNSELING AND ITS TECHNIQUES

I. Leisure counseling

A. Involves helping people to choose leisure pursuits that satisfy their needs and interests.

1. Choices are made by the individual who is seeking help.

2. The choice must be feasible in relation to the individual's intellectual, social, emotional, and physical capacities.

3. Counseling should lead the individual or group toward self-directed choices.

B. Involves helping the individual to establish new social ties or reestablish old ones.

C. Requires distributing information about resources that are available.

D. Requires developing resources that will permit individuals to participate in recreational experiences that will be satisfying to them.

E. Involves helping individuals make the transition from community to institution and vice versa.

F. Is not psychotherapy but a process directed toward helping the individual to make leisure choices.

G. Is not authoritative direction, but a process through which the counselor helps the individual to define his problem by indicating his leisure needs and the kinds of satisfactions the person is seeking in his free time.

II. Goals

A. To develop behaviors that are conducive to increased satisfaction in leisure experiences.

B. To give information about opportunities available.

C. To examine attitudes and values of individuals to determine leisure experiences that will suit them.

III. Approaches

A. May be individual centered and nondirective.

B. May be behavioral; choices are guided by the counselor in accordance with behavior that the individual wants to change.

C. Should be reinforcing; responses followed by a satisfying state tend to be repeated.

   1. The counselor must learn to promote a satisfying state through verbal or nonverbal reactions.

D. Is a response to a person's request for help.

E. To establish a climate that will help the person to recognize his need for help even though he may not be seeking it.

   1. The individual must be ready to accept that his free time is not satisfying.

   2. The counselor uses certain techniques to accept the reality of the situation including:

      a. Reinforcement of positive attitudes and behaviors of the individual and ignoring or downgrading of negative ones.

b. Exposure to leisure experiences that the individual might find satisfying by:

(1) Watching participants in an activity.

(2) Viewing pictures or films of participants enjoying an activity.

(3) Reading materials that explain the activity.

(4) Participating in the activity.

3. The physical setting in which counseling is done must be one which is conducive to a relaxed explanation of the individual's needs and interests.

IV. The leisure counselor

A. Enables people to make leisure choices.

B. Helps people to understand their leisure needs and interests and then is able to help them make changes in behavior that will increase their potential for making satisfying leisure choices.

C. Helps people with leisure problem solving, assisting them to better understand their leisure needs and interests and how they can make choices that will bring them self-fulfillment.

D. Is concerned with the attitudes of the person toward free time, his concepts of self-worth and how these relate to his free time choices, and the extent to which these choices are positive factors that strengthen his quality of living.

E. Can be a recreation leader, a doctor, a teacher, a clergyman, or come from some other profession.

1. Due to this wide range of people who counsel, there is need for a method to coordinate the leisure counseling services.

F. Must be aware of his own beliefs, attitudes, and values.

1. Beliefs, attitudes, and values will influence the leisure choices of an individual.

2. A leisure counselor must be able to recognize his own beliefs, attitudes, and values so that they will not influence his counseling. The Oxford Universal Dictionary defines beliefs, values and attitudes as follows:

• *Belief:* Acceptance of a proposition, statement or fact as true on the ground of authority or evidence.[1]

• *Attitude:* Habitual mode of regarding anything.[2]

• *Value:* The relative status of a thing, or the estimate in which it is

[1]Oxford Universal Dictionary, 3rd rev. ed. (London: Oxford University Press, 1955), p. 182.

[2]Ibid., pp. 120, 165, 2332.

held, according to its real or supposed worth, usefulness or importance.[3]

3. A counselor who believes that exercises are good for people and must be taken by a person every day (his value) and that anyone who does not exercise regularly is an inadequate person (his attitude), should not counsel every person to exercise.

4. The counselor must then approach each individual with:

a. An acceptance of each individual as he is.

b. Sincerity—an empathetic acceptance of the situation.

c. An understanding of growth and development of human beings.

d. An understanding of varying life styles of people and the many beliefs, attitudes, and values that are held by people. Some exercises to help a counselor develop awareness will be found in the resources section of this module (pp. 230–31).

G. Must recognize that more than one life style is accepted in society today.

1. Not only must the counselor be able to understand his own beliefs, attitudes, and values, he must also be able to assess those of the counselee.

2. Many people today are moving away from older living styles.

a. Older people are retiring earlier from jobs that require rigid scheduling. Some are seeking full retirement, but want fulfilling personal involvment in many different experiences. Others are looking for jobs in which they can work at their own pace as much or as little as they desire.

b. Many youths today are not defining success in terms of the amount of money they can earn, but how much satisfaction they can derive from the work that they do.

3. Alternative styles of working, of school hours, and of self-employment are creating new leisure patterns and require that opportunities in accord with new demands be made available.

4. People participate in leisure experiences at varying levels. Although sharp demarcations have been made, it is possible that several of these levels of participation may take place concurrently and that the lines between the levels may be blurred. A total leisure continuum contains several parts. It can be perceived most simply as perpendicular lines across a horizontal line.

[3] Ibid., pp. 174–76.

Completely outer-directed	Outer-directed but individual is motivated to participate and learn	Guided choices for a specific purpose	Participation for the sake of satisfaction in participating
Activity for the sake of activity	Leisure education	Therapeutic leisure experience	Pure leisure experience

5. Because of the many alternatives in demands of people for services, the leisure services given by public, voluntary, and private agencies must assume different styles. Until recently programs were almost entirely activity-centered. Now they must be person-centered. The individual no longer must be expected to participate in a pre-defined program or be denied service. Now these agencies must become "enablers" whose job it is not only to manage and teach activities but also to help people help themselves in finding meaningful leisure experiences.

V. The interview

   A. Establishing rapport

   1. The physical environment must be comfortable.

   a. Consider the size of the room, the type of furniture, use of colors, plants, and pictures and use of conversation pieces (an unusual sculpture, a fishing pole).

   b. Have some type of food available (cake, coffee, tea) and a place to hang wraps.

   2. Have informational material available in a browsing section or to hand to the person as you talk.

   3. As a means of establishing a relationship with the client try to find a common interest.

   B. Starting an interview

   1. The counselor must be ready for an interview.

   a. Review any information that you have about the client.

   b. Be sure that there will be no interruptions.

   2. Greet the person as he enters.

   a. Move toward him, shake hands, call him by name if you know it or state your name and ask him his name.

   3. Make the client comfortable.

   4. Start with a conversational opening (the weather or anything) that will help client to relate to you.

213

C. Introducing the problem

1. You may state the problem defined by client, if the person asked for the interview.

2. You may ask client about problem for which he wants help.

3. If person just drops in, you should ask "Can I help you?"

4. If person was referred, you can simply state "Mr. A. thought that I might help you with your problem."

VI. Assessing leisure needs and interests

A. The community

1. Interest surveys

a. An interest survey should be done on a neighborhood basis.

b. Interests common to all neighborhoods should be developed on a community-wide basis.

c. Interests that are indigenous to a neighborhood are best developed in that area.

2. Assessing needs

a. It is necessary to assess needs in a community through the people who have a depth of understanding of the people in that community and through statistical records that give basic information about people, such as census tracts.

3. When needs and interests have been assessed, a program can then be built.

a. In the community setting counseling is a secondary step rather than the primary one in individual or group counseling.

B. An institution

1. Multidisciplinary team approach

a. Varying records are used, such as medical diagnosis, social work assessment, psychological tests, and recreation interest finders.

b. Team defines goals for the individual.

c. Each discipline indicates how the program in that discipline will contribute to the achievement of the established goals.

d. The recreator then contacts the individual and counsels with him about the activities in which he is interested and which will contribute to the goals defined by the team.

2. Assessing needs in terms of normal patterns of growth and development.

   a. The literature in the field describes the normal growth and development patterns that can be expected at each age level.

   b. For each age level the range of functioning is also described.

      (1) Although norms are indicated each individual grows, develops, or deteriorates at different rates.

3. Assessing interests in institutions

   a. Talking directly with an individual will be the best method for assessing interests. This should be done as soon after admission as is feasible.

   b. Leisure counseling should then be started in relation to the needs defined by the treatment team, and the interests indicated by each individual. It is only in this way that a person-centered program can be developed.

C. Tools for assessing needs and interests

   1. Some evaluative instruments have been developed to assess the leisure needs and interests of people.

      a. An instrument of this kind has limited value.

      b. It must be followed up with some method of face-to-face contact between the counselor and the client.

   2. Survey instruments that are currently available include:

      a. National Institutes of Health—Form 744, Patient Recreation Referral.

      b. Leisure Interest Finder.[4]

      c. Personal Data Blank.[5]

      d. Avocational Activities for the Handicapped.[6]

      e. Leisure Activities Blank (LAB).[7]

      f. Self Leisure Interest Profile (SLIP).[8]

[4]Joseph Mirenda, Leisure Interest Finder (Washington, D. C.: American Association for Health, Physical Education, and Recreation, 1973).

[5]J. Gustave White, *When Your Advice Is Asked* (South Brunswick, N. J.: A. S. Barnes, 1966), pp. 172–77.

[6]Robert Overs, Elizabeth O'Connor, and Barbara DeMarco, *Avocational Activities for the Handicapped* (Springfield, Ill.: Charles C. Thomas, 1974).

[7]G. E. McKechnie, "Leisure Activities Blank Booklet" (Palo Alto, Ca.: Consulting Psychologists Press, 1974).

[8]C. P. McDowell, *Approaching Leisure Counseling with the Self-Leisure Interest Profile* (Salt Lake City: Educational Support Systems, Inc., 1973).

3. Other methods include:

a. A pictorial card sort in which the client picks out the pictures that interest him.

b. Slides or films.

4. The counselor can develop a leisure interest instrument.

a. A counselor may develop a form to be used with people in his particular situation.

b. The form should include vital statistics (name, address, age, sex, etc.), general health status, educational background, mobility (can the person get to an activity?), desired activities, and needs.

VII. Agencies that are structured to meet the leisure needs and interests of people

  A. Community

    1. Public recreation departments which provide basic services for all people

    2. Private voluntary agencies

      a. "Y's"

      b. Settlement houses

      c. Agencies for the handicapped

      d. Others that serve a defined population

    3. Public schools

      a. After-school programs

      b. Adult education programs

    4. Public and private institutions

      a. Half-way houses

      b. Residential centers

      c. Hospitals

      d. Schools for retarded or emotionally disturbed

  B. Institutional

    1. Recreational service

    2. Occupational therapy

    3. Social service and others

VIII. Methods for leisure counseling

  A. Leisure counseling as a part of leisure services

    1. In the community agency (in either the public park and recreation department or the private voluntary agencies, leisure counseling may be *one* of the services offered.)

a. Most recreation leaders and supervisors have always done a certain amount of counseling as part of activity leadership.

b. As more people seek activities for their free time, more and greater structuring of counseling services is needed.

c. Counseling may be offered as a specialized service in the department with a staff member or members who have had counseling training.

d. Every department should at least plan to develop informational materials about the resources available in the community.

2. In the institution

a. Leisure counseling is needed if programs are to be developed that are person-centered and related to individual needs. Ill, disabled, or aged people require special counseling.

3. Staff assignment

a. A person or persons, depending on the numbers to be served should be given the responsibility for leisure counseling.

b. This person should have some background in interviewing, case work, vocational, or rehabilitation counseling if he has none in leisure counseling.

c. Leisure counseling should be included as part of the activity program.

d. Every leader needs much more knowledge of the potentials in each activity than is now known.

e. A staff member who has this kind of knowledge can guide both leaders and participants so that each individual can have leisure experiences that bring him maximum satisfaction.

B. Application of general counseling methods to leisure counseling

1. Individual interviews

a. There are two major approaches to individual leisure counseling.

(1) Behavioral approach to problem solving for a specific leisure problem; the counselor helps individual to solve this problem.

(2) Client-directed approach to some problems; the counselor helps the client to define what the problem is and then to explain a means for solving the problem.

2. Group counseling

   a. This type is usually related to a specific leisure problem of a group.

3. Activity-centered counseling

   a. The problem to be solved relates to the functioning of the activity.

4. Team approach

   a. Each member of the team indicates what his discipline can contribute to the solution of the problem (a client-centered approach).

C. Individual counseling

   1. Individual interviews may be sought by the client, or the counselor may request the interview.

      a. Interviews sought by client.

      (1) The client is not satisfied.

      (2) The counselor is accepted by the client as a helper.

      (3) The client may not accept the facts about the situation that is unsatisfying.

      b. Interviews sought by counselor or as a result of a referral.

      (1) The counselor may expect hostility, failure to communicate, and resentment.

      (2) There is no recognition on the part of client that he is any way responsible for the circumstances that exist.

   2. The counselor tries to facilitate decision making by the client.

      a. The client needs help in achieving a general direction in which he wishes to go.

      b. The limits in the situation must be ascertained: age, financial status, past record, physical condition, intellectual capacity, or family status.

      c. Decisions will be affected by past leisure experiences, and these in turn will be conditioned by the client's beliefs, values, and attitudes. These will also indicate some possible expectations and what may appeal to him at the present time. The counselor must expect that the person seeking help has not been able to solve a problem, that he has not been able to assess the alternatives and come to a logical conclusion.

      d. The client must make the decision.

      (1) The client may vacillate about the choices.

         (a) This may mean that several choices have an appeal.

(b) However, it may indicate that the client has difficulty making decisions.

(c) In the latter case, the counselor must judge the extent of this difficulty, and if it seems to relate to a personal problem, refer the client to someone who can help with that problem.

(d) When the client has difficulty in making a choice the counselor should redefine the alternatives and add supplemental information, if possible.

(2) Tyler indicates that: "a counselor must consider three alternatives in helping a client to make a decision. These are a choice, a change or a doubt. In choice the client assesses the alternatives and decides on one. In change the client indicates that he finds his current situation unsatisfying and wants to make a change. The situation is considered doubtful when there is either insufficient information or the client seems confused, or the counselor feels that he is unable to help the client and needs to refer him to another person for help.[9]

e. Leisure counseling problems which inhibit decision making are:

    (1) Lack of assurance

    (2) Lack of information

    (3) Lack of skills

    (4) Dependence

    (5) Cultural conflict

    (6) Self-conflict

    (7) Lack of self-identity

    (8) Lack of feeling of self-worth

3. Preparing for the interview

    a. Review all records that are available.

    b. Observe the individual in activity settings.

4. The interview

    a. Provide for physical arrangement.

        (1) Quiet atmosphere without interruptions.

        (2) Physically comfortable.

    b. Establish rapport.

[9]Leona Tyler, *The Work of the Counselor*, 3rd ed. (New York: Appleton-Century-Crofts, 1969), pp. 68–70.

    c. First interview should be about 30 minutes long.

    d. Define the problem.

    e. Suggest various alternatives as solution to problem.

    f. Help client in decision-making process.

        (1) Choose an alternative.

        (2) Try several alternatives.

        (3) Contract with counselor to participate for a given time in one alternative.

5. Application of these methods in leisure services

    a. Behavioral adaptation in the recreation service may be more desirable.

    b. The recreation service can not devote the extensive time to counseling that is necessary for client-directed approach except in specialized situations.

6. Role play an individual interview

    a. Suggested situations

        (1) Seeking information—use resource file; verbal and nonverbal communication are the same.

        (2) Client comes to counselor with a problem. Has called for an appointment and stated problem. Set up structure for interview, including records, possible alternatives.

        (3) Counselor asks teenager in a music group to come in to talk about her participation in group; verbal and nonverbal communication are not the same.

        (4) An adult comes into recreation center and asks a supervisor for help in finding a way to have social experiences. Find out what he has done, what he likes to do and suggest possible alternatives on the basis of your findings. Indicate kinds of socialization that are possible in each.

        (5) In a psychiatric hospital, the psychiatrist has told you that a patient will be discharged in about a month. Conduct an interview with the patient to help him make the adjustment from the hospital back to his community.

D. Group counseling

  1. This type of counseling is used extensively in recreation.

    a. The group is specifically defined: a club, people interested in a special activity.

    b. The counselor is an "enabler" who helps the group with their decision making.

2. Group counseling is used for many different purposes.

    a. Group therapy

    b. Remotivation

    c. T-groups

    d. Leisure counseling

3. In leisure counseling the decision making is usually in regard to a specific problem.

    a. Sometimes goals are long-range.

    b. This type of counseling is almost entirely group-centered.

    c. The counselor is part of the group but has resource information which will assist the group in making its decision.

4. Role play group counseling.

    a. Suggested situations

        (1) Three senior citizens have asked leisure counselor for an interview to discuss their cooking group which is taught by a part-time specialist.

        (2) A group of community people walk into a recreational supervisor's office to complain that no program for teen-age girls is offered at the center. The supervisor must counsel group about what they should do to get a program started.

        (3) A community center counselor asks a group of three 14-year-old girls to come see him about their behavior towards some retarded children who come to the center.

E. Team approach

    1. This method is frequently used in institutional settings where a number of disciplines must work to help a given person.

        a. A treatment program is defined by the team after some type of evaluation has been done by each discipline.

        b. The program may encompass a wide range of participation which may be carried on concurrently or sequentially.

        c. The team may define one or all types of experiences which should be part of the person's treatment program. In leisure services the following types of participation are possible as indicated on page 213.

            (1) Exposure to an experience.

            (2) Leisure education.

            (3) Therapeutic leisure experience.

            (4) Pure leisure experiences.

d. The leisure services department is responsible for guiding the individual into each type of experience as he exhibits readiness for it.

(1) Counseling moves from the behavioral approach to the client-centered approach.

(2) Regular evaluation of the progress made by the client must be made.

(3) On the basis of this assessment, the client may be guided into different experiences.

2. Role play the team approach

a. Suggested situations

(1) A team in a residential center for handicapped children (retarded and/or emotionally disturbed) is evaluating the needs of a patient and defining the role that each discipline will have in contributing to the treatment of a 13-year-old girl who is functioning on about a six-year-old's level. Present are the psychologist, psychiatrist, education counselor, medical doctor, recreation counselor, and social worker.

(2) In a community center, a supervisor has been assigned counseling duties for the teenagers in the center. The counselor has found that there is a gang of 14-year-old boys who are taking money from the younger children. The counselor brings the problem to the center staff meeting.

F. Activity-centered counseling

1. Counseling sessions may be interviews or they may be a group discussion of a problem in the activity.

2. Counseling is concerned with a problem that relates to an activity or the choice between two activities.

3. The counselor must understand not only the needs of the individual or group but also the potentials for the activity to bring satisfying experiences to the people concerned.

4. Role play activity-centered counseling.

a. Suggested situations

(1) A craft group

(2) A sports group

(3) A group of senior citizens in a community center

(4) A patient's council in a nursing home

(5) An adult discussion group

IX. Counseling the disadvantaged

A. Disadvantaged people may be any whose leisure experience programs are less than what satisfies their leisure needs and interests, but more specifically it is those who are:

1. Physically and/or mentally disabled

2. The elderly

3. The socially disadvantaged

   a. Poor

   b. Minority groups—women, blacks, ethnic groups.

   c. Middle class people who are above poverty level, but for whom no services are provided and who can not provide services for themselves

   d. The affluent who use free time destructively

   e. Prisoners and exprisoners

B. Powerlessness and apathy frequently are characteristics of the disadvantaged.

1. They need to develop feelings of self-worth.

2. The counselor needs to carefully examine his feelings and attitudes toward disadvantaged groups.

   a. He must be able to accept different life styles. Can the counselor accept the concept that there is no one life style that is better, but that there is one life style in a given community that is pre-dominant?

   b. In many cases he must help the individual to preserve his identity with his cultural past.

   c. He must respect the disadvantaged, foster self-directed choices, and make sure the client understands that some of the choices may not be accepted by the predominant group.

      (1) He must understand the problems of being different.

         (a) There is need for continuous education.

         (b) There is need for regular exposure to those who are different—not tokenism, but exposure to situations in which groups of people learn to appreciate each other for what they are, not what they are not.

      (2) He must learn to use nonverbal techniques.

C. Counselors/leaders working with disadvantaged groups must broaden their basic understanding of social problems such as housing, sanitation, transportation, and others.

D. Counselors must learn to work with dissatisfaction and alienation.

       1. They can help to alleviate some of the problems by helping people participate in satisfying leisure experiences.

       2. They should gain a rapport with one or two individuals and then recruit those individuals to help with the group.

    E. Situation analysis[10] (pp. 232–35)

       1. Analyze the following situations and suggest solutions.

          a. Recreation in the Seminole nursing home.

          b. Can the recreation program help George?

          c. José's rehabilitation.

X. New concepts in leisure counseling

    A. Use of community-based centers

       1. Intermediate care

          a. Halfway houses

          b. Group homes

       2. Community placements

          a. Mentally retarded—cooperative residences and supportive care residences.

          b. Mentally ill and aged—apartments or foster homes

          c. Day centers for the chronically ill

          d. Day–night hospitals

       3. In each of the above leisure counseling is needed to:

          a. Assess the needs and interests of the people

          b. Give information about community resources

          c. Provide leisure services when not otherwise provided

    B. Leisure counseling as a private enterprise

       1. Individuals counsel as a business

       2. Qualifications can be a problem.

    C. Counseling the individual from the community to the institution and vice versa

       1. In the institution

          a. Counseling should begin as soon after the person is admitted as is feasible.

          b. Counselor must relate the leisure program to the total treatment plan for the individual.

          c. The treatment program should be a continuous process in relation to patient progress and evaluation.

---

[10] Joseph Bannon, *Problem Solving in Recreation and Parks* (Englewood Cliffs, N. J.: Prentice-Hall, 1972), pp. 174–76, 182, 329–30.

d. Leisure counseling in relation to discharge should be done as soon as the date of discharge is known.

2. Community contacts

a. The counselor should have a list of who to contact.

b. The counselor can make referrals to community agencies in the counseling interview.

(1) He should use the patient's knowledge of his community to help with this.

(2) He should ascertain the patient's preferences for participation.

3. Follow-up

a. If the client is in the same community, follow-up can be by personal contact.

b. If the client is out of the community, follow-up must be by mail.

D. New concepts in counseling

1. Mental health centers for after care including counseling and provision of leisure services.

2. The catchment area in the mental hospitals by which patients from a given area are grouped.

3. Communes

a. Team members and clients or patients are members of the commune with similar rights and privileges.

b. In this type of setting the leisure counselor is much more of an enabler, or resource person.

Student assignments

This part consists of 11 objectives. You will be called upon to demonstrate your mastery of each objective.

OBJECTIVE	ACHIEVEMENT OF COMPETENCY
1. To define leisure counseling.	Write your definition.
2. To gain knowledge of the scope of leisure counseling.	Show how you would counsel a high school girl who indicates that she wants to meet boys and girls in socializing experiences: Include the physical setting in which you would do counseling and the kinds of experiences that you would suggest to meet her needs and interests.

OBJECTIVE	ACHIEVEMENT OF COMPETENCY
3. To learn how beliefs, values, and attitudes influence leisure choices.	Describe how a belief, value, and an attitude that you hold might influence your counseling.
4. To develop the ability to accept each person for what he is.	Discuss and demonstrate the difference between tolerance and acceptance.
5. To develop competency in establishing rapport with a person who seeks help with a leisure problem.	a. Describe three methods that you would use to establish rapport with a preschool child, a teenager, a handicapped person in a wheelchair. b. Design a room that you would consider desirable as a counseling room.
6. To learn the methods to assess needs and interests of people.	a. Describe records that you would use to determine needs of people in a community or in a school for retarded children. b. Design an interest finder for people in a leisure setting with which you are familiar (for example, a boys' club, a hospital).
7. To learn about agencies that provide leisure services.	Survey a community and define the leisure services provided in that community by types of agencies.
8. To learn various methods for individual leisure counseling.	a. Describe a situation in which you would use a behavorial approach to a problem. b. Describe a situation in which the counseling should be client-centered.
9. To learn the techniques of group- and activity- centered leisure counseling.	Describe the principal elements in each.
10. To define the role of the recreator in the team approach to leisure counseling.	Describe a situation in which a team approach to a problem is used and indicate what contribution the recreator would make to the solution of the problem.

OBJECTIVE	ACHIEVEMENT OF COMPETENCY
11. To ascertain the special problems related to counseling disadvantaged people.	Discuss five problems encountered in counseling the disadvantaged for leisure experiences and indicate how you would approach the problem.

Resources

READING MATERIALS

The resources section is divided into four sections: (1) reading materials, (2) a pre-test, (3) exercises for situation analysis, and (4) problems for situation analysis.

Supplemental texts

EDWARDS, PATSY. *Leisure Counseling Techniques, Individual and Group Counseling Step-by-Step.* Los Angeles: University Publishing, 1975.

McDOWELL, CHESTER, JR. *Leisure Counseling, Selected Lifestyle Processes.* Eugene, Ore.: University of Oregon, Center of Leisure Studies, 1976.

These two very recent texts present two approaches to counseling. Edwards approaches counseling from the point of view of private enterprise but also includes a leisure education model for schools. McDowell presents counseling more as a guidance and education process. Both are excellent resources.

General bibliography

BERNE, ERIC. *Games People Play.* New York: Grove Press, 1964.

CORBIN, H. DAN, and TAIT, WILLIAM. *Education for Leisure.* Englewood Cliffs, N.J.: Prentice-Hall, 1973.

DANFORD, HOWARD, and SHIRLEY, MAX. *Creative Leadership in Recreation*, 2nd ed. Boston: Allyn & Bacon, 1970.

KAPLAN, MAX. *Leisure: Theory and Policy.* New York: Wiley, 1975.

NEULINGER, J., and BREIT, M. "Attitude Dimensions of Leisure." *Journal of Leisure Research*, vol. 4, no. 3 (1972): 108–15. Arlington, Va.: National Recreation and Park Assoc.

NIRENBERG, JESSE S. *Getting Through to People.* Englewood Cliffs, N.J.: Prentice-Hall, 1963.

SIMMONS, CARL, and PEDERSEN, FRANCINE. *Leisure in Our Changing Society.* New York: Hofstra University and New York State Recreation and Park Society, 1974.

Books related to counseling in leisure services

BANNON, JOSEPH. *Problem Solving in Recreation and Parks*. Englewood Cliffs, N.J.: Prentice-Hall, 1972.

BENJAMIN, ALFRED. *The Helping Interview*. Boston: Houghton Mifflin, 1969.

OVERS, R. P. *Avocational Activities for the Handicapped*. Springfield, Ill.: Charles C Thomas, 1974.

SIMON, SIDNEY; HOWE, L.; and KIRSCHENBAUM, H. *Values Clarification*. New York: Hart, 1972.

TYLER, LEONA. *The Work of the Counselor*, 3rd ed. New York: Appleton-Century-Crofts, 1969.

WHITE, J. GUSTAV. *When Your Advice Is Asked*. New York: Barnes, 1966.

WITT, PETER, et al. *Leisure Counseling and Leisure Education Resources Kit*. Ottawa, Ontario, Canada: University of Ottawa, 1973.

Articles

AMERICAN ASSOCIATION OF HEALTH, PHYSICAL EDUCATION, AND RECREATION. "The Concepts of Lifestyles." *Leisure Today, Journal of Health, Physical Education and Recreation*. Washington, D.C.: AAHPER, December, 1974.

AMERICAN ASSOCIATION OF HEALTH, PHYSICAL EDUCATION, AND RECREATION. "Recreation for Special Populations." *Leisure Today, Journal of Health, Physical Education, and Recreation*. Washington, D.C.: AAHPER, May, 1975.

Survey instruments

CURATIVE WORKSHOP. Avocation Activities Inventory. Milwaukee, Wis.: Curative Workshop, 1973.

HUBERT, EDWINA. "The Development of an Inventory of Leisure Interests." Ph.D. dissertation, University of Michigan, 1969.

McDOWELL, C. P. *Approaching Leisure Counseling with the Self-Leisure Interest Profile*. Salt Lake City, Utah: Educational Support Systems, Inc., 1973.

McKECHNIE, G. E. *Leisure Activities Blank Booklet*. Palo Alto, Ca.: Consulting Psychologists Press, 1974.

MIRENDA, JOSEPH J. *Leisure Interest Finder*. Washington, D.C.: American Association of Health, Physical Education, and Recreation, 1973.

NATIONAL INSTITUTE OF HEALTH. Patient Referral Form 744. Washington, D.C.: NIH.

Suggested pre-test

Circle the letter of the statement that completes the sentence most adequately. Students should complete this test before reading the text.

1. Leisure counseling is needed today because:
   a. of increased free time for most people.
   b. people have no skills in activities.
   c. people are seeking ways in which to make their free time more satisfying.

2. Free time or leisure time is that period when a person:
   a. has nothing to do.
   b. can choose what he wants to do.
   c. is not at paid work.

3. Leisure counseling is:
   a. a method of telling people how to use their free time.
   b. a process through which a counselor helps a person to choose what he wants to do when he has free time.
   c. giving people information about facilities in the community.

4. Leisure counseling is a process of:
   a. developing a recreation program for a community.
   b. building a program for individuals or groups based on other needs and interests.
   c. helping individuals to fit into the community recreation program.

5. The leisure counselor is a person who has:
   a. developed an awareness of his own beliefs, values, and attitudes and how they influence his actions.
   b. learned how to direct people to find good recreation experiences.
   c. completed a course in counseling.

6. A person or group who comes to a counselor is:
   a. asking for information.
   b. seeking help in solving a problem.
   c. unhappy.

7. A leisure counselor helps the individual to find satisfying leisure experiences through:
   a. presenting a variety of alternatives to him and helping him to make a choice.
   b. showing him what activities he can do.
   c. giving him brochures that he can read and decide what he likes.

229

8. A leisure counselor is:

a. a recreation specialist in a leisure services department.

b. a teacher.

c. any person with a desire to help an individual to make a satisfying choice of a leisure experience.

9. A leisure counselor must be able:

a. to recognize when people have a problem.

b. to accept all people for what they are.

c. to work with disadvantaged people.

10. A leisure counselor can best assess the needs and interests of people:

a. by talking with them.

b. by showing them the kinds of activities that are available and in which ones they are interested.

c. by using a needs and interest finder and then discussing with them what the test shows and experiences that might be satisfying.

Exercises for situation analysis*

VALUES GRID

State three issues. Next to each issue, the student writes a few key words that summarize his position on the issue.

Issue	1	2	3	4	5	6	7
1.							
2.							
3.							

If you can answer "yes" to the seven questions listed below put a check under the number representing the question.

1. Are you *proud* of (do you cherish) your position?

2. Have you *publicly affirmed* your position?

3. Have you chosen your position from *alternatives*?

4. Have you chosen your position after *thoughtful* consideration of pros, cons, consequences?

5. Have you chosen your position *freely*?

*Reprinted by permission of Hart Publishing Company, Inc., from its copyrighted volume *Values Clarification: A Handbook of Practical Strategies for Teachers and Students* by Sidney B. Simon, Leland W. Howe, and Howard Kirschenbaum.

6. Have you *acted on* your beliefs?

7. Have you acted with *repetition, pattern,* or *consistency* on this issue?

TWENTY THINGS YOU LOVE TO DO

Write the numbers 1–20 as shown

1
2
3
4
5
6
7
8
9
10
11
12
13
14
15
16
17
18
19
20

Now list 20 things you love to do in life.
Now do the following:

On left side of numbers:

1. Place a $ sign next to any item that costs more than $3 each time it is done.

2. Place an A for those items you like to do alone.

3. Place an AP for items you like to do alone or with people.

4. Place a P next to items requiring planning.

5. Place an N5 next to those items that would not have been listed five years ago.

On right hand side of numbers:

1. List from 1–5 those items you like best.

2. Indicate when you last participated in the activity.

Situation Analysis

How do you react to these situations?

1. You are a recreation leader of a Co-ed teen Club. At a meeting the group tells you that you do not plan activities that they like.

   a. What is your first reaction?

   b. How would you handle this?

2. In a senior citizens group two women tell you (the leader) that the group should be for women only.

   a. What is your first reaction?

   b. What would you do?

Recreation at the Seminole Nursing Home*

SITUATION

Seminole Hospital is a 75-bed private nonprofit general hospital serving Seminole County and adjacent communities. Attached to the hospital is a 55-bed extended-care facility (nursing home) called Seminole Resident Home.

The hospital is a three-story building; the patients are housed on the second and third floors and the administrative offices and service areas on the first floor. The resident home is a one-story building with direct access to the hospital.

Patients in the resident home are usually over the age of 55. Their diagnoses include terminal cancer, stroke, coronary difficulties, and other diseases that accompany old age. Individuals are grouped to some degree by the amount of nursing care required, with those patients needing the most care assigned to rooms in the wing immediately adjacent to the hospital. Otherwise, an attempt is made to group them by mutual social interests and personality.

The resident home is made up of four-bed, two-bed, and single rooms. There is a large dining room—lounge combination, which is a pleasant gathering place for the patients. It is equipped with a fireplace, two pianos, comfortable lounge chairs and sofas, and attractive small dining room tables and chairs. There is another lounge area in the cross wing to the hospital equipped with sofas, chairs, tables, and TV. Equipment in this area also includes two pianos, a hi-fi, and a handicraft area. There is no game equipment, indoor or outdoor, provided by the home. The grounds around the resident home consist of a grass area of approximately two and a half acres. There are a few flower beds, but no equipment such as outdoor furniture, game equipment, and cooking equipment.

*Joseph J. Bannon, *Problem Solving in Recreation and Parks,* © 1972, pp. 329–330. Reprinted by permission of Prentice-Hall, Inc., Englewood Cliffs, New Jersey.

Recreation staff at the resident home includes a large and active women's auxiliary, with a paid director of volunteers. The local ministerial association provides somebody each week to conduct activities.

The surrounding community is largely agricultural, although there is one small industry—a shoe factory. Most of the people are farmers and small businessmen and professional persons supporting the farm community. The population of the community has not changed significantly in the last few years, but the average age of the residents has increased, due to the fact that the young people are leaving the county to seek their fortune elsewhere. There are no municipal recreation and/or park departments in the county, though two of the communities operate swimming pools during the summer months. There is one county golf course and three commercially operated bowling alleys. Sports events in the public schools play a large part in the recreation life of the community, as do church events and activities. There are no private community agencies similar to the Y.M.C.A.

Health agencies such as the TB Association, the Board of Health, the County Association for Retarded Children have active leadership.

Visiting hours at the residence home are from 1:00 P.M. to 8:00 P.M. each day.

PROBLEM

What kind of recreation program could be offered at the resident home? What facilities and equipment would be needed for such a program? What kind of recreation program could be offered using the existing facilities and equipment? How can the volunteers be used most effectively?

Can the recreation program help George?*

SITUATION

Your present position is recreation center director on the East Side of New York. Your primary function is to provide wholesome activities for those who attend the recreation center. The neighborhood is 95 percent black with a few Puerto Ricans. You have been requested to assist the New York City Welfare Board in helping to rehabilitate George Worthington, a member of the Solid Rock Rangers, a street gang in the 120th Street area. George is a 19-year-old black youth who dropped out of school last year and states he has no intention of returning. He is a fairly heavy drinker and is reported by the welfare counselor to smoke marijuana frequently. While attending school, he had difficulty in getting along with his schoolmates and with female teachers. He was often truant prior to dropping out. George is very interested in sports and is active in the recreation department's softball and basketball leagues. At present,

*Joseph J. Bannon, *Problem Solving in Recreation and Parks*, © 1972, p. 182. Reprinted by permission of Prentice-Hall, Inc., Englewood Cliffs, New Jersey.

George is going steady with Mary Dennis, a white girl, who recently graduated from high school, and is presently working in a dress shop in the garment district. In discussion with George, he states that "Mary is the first person he ever really cared for." He would like to get married but feels it is impossible because he is not able to get a well-paying job.

At present, George lives with his mother and two younger brothers (ages 10 and 13) in a five-room apartment in a run-down tenement, in which the hallways and steps are littered with garbage. The neighborhood is described by the police department as an area of high delinquency. The area appears to be congested with drug addicts, peddlers, and people drinking in the street.

George has a rather negative attitude toward the establishment and the social agencies in the neighborhood. He has indicated to the welfare counselor that most of the agencies "never really come through with what they promise." However, he has agreed to meet with you a week from today to discuss how you might help him.

PROBLEM

How do you feel you can help George? What other information do you need to have in order to properly analyze the situation? Would you discuss George's situation with his mother or Mary Dennis? What other agencies could help with this problem? Is this the proper function of the recreation department? What reasons would you give that would encourage George to return to school? Would you report George's marijuana smoking to the police? Why? How would you help him with his drinking problem.

José's rehabilitation*

SITUATION

In a large metropolitan area of the United States, one of the programs sponsored by the department of parks and recreation is the "outreach" program. This program is partially funded by the Department of Housing and Urban Development through the model-cities program. The primary purpose of the outreach program is to stimulate participation of hard-to-reach youth by engaging them in wholesome recreation programs and assisting them in using community resources in educational, health, employment, and related social services. As an outreach worker in this program, you have been requested by the director to assist the juvenile division of the police department in the rehabilitation of José Mantiz. In order that you may become familiar with the background of José, the chief juvenile officer sends you the following summary:

*Joseph J. Bannon, *Problem Solving in Recreation and Parks*, © 1972, pp. 174–76. Reprinted by permission of Prentice-Hall, Inc., Englewood Cliffs, New Jersey.

José Mantiz is a 17-year old Puerto Rican youth who lives with his mother, two brothers, and one sister. At present, José is having difficulty in school; his grades are failing in all courses; he has little desire to stay in school; and he is thinking of dropping out. He is a member of the Black Nights, a street gang that has been allegedly involved in street fights, thefts, drug use, and a number of neighborhood disturbances. The gang members seldom participate in recreation activity but occasionally play stickball in the street. Gang members do participate in dances sponsored by the Catholic Youth Organization and attend movies in the neighborhood movie theaters. José has been arrested once for smoking marijuana. The family lives in a one-family dwelling that has been converted into two apartments. The house is located in a dilapidated tenement area. The area is littered with debris and uncollected garbage. The neighborhood has a high degree of delinquency and has been described by the police who patrol the area as being congested with drug addicts and peddlers. The neighborhood is primarily made up of a black and Puerto Rican population.

José's mother is in her late forties and was born and raised in Puerto Rico. She is unemployed and receives Aid to Dependent Children assistance from the public welfare department. She provides "good" physical care for her children but admits she has a great deal of difficulty in disciplining them. Mrs. Mantiz cannot read or write and has had no formal education. She takes little interest in José's school situation. However, she has participated in some volunteer work with the church, and with the community action group.

Mr. Mantiz is a Puerto Rican, also in his late forties, and has been employed by the Coast Guard for the last 15 years. He is seldom at home and when he is, he takes little interest in the activities of the children. It is reported that his financial support of the family is less than $50.00 per month. Mr. Mantiz is a very heavy drinker and it has been said that he "plays around with other women." It is apparent that he does not assume the father leadership role in the family. José has a rather "detached" relationship with his two brothers (ages 13 and 15) and with his one sister (age 19).

PROBLEM

What would your immediate approach be in this situation? How would you make contact with José? How would you involve the family in José's rehabilitation? Would you attempt to discourage José from participating in gang activities? What kind of reporting system would be best in keeping the police department informed? How would you utilize the recreation staff, school staff, and other social services? What other information would be helpful to you in dealing with this situation? As an outreach worker, what part of your training and expertise would be most helpful in solving this problem?

MODULE 9

Survey of the administration of leisure services

Principles and practices

This module is designed to give the entry-level practitioner an understanding of basic principles of administration and their application to the delivery of leisure services. Certain administrative duties are necessary at all levels of service.

The provision of leisure services for people, today, is considered a necessary part of community life. How these services will be provided will depend on factors inherent in the total management of that specific community. As people acquire greater amounts of unobligated time, there will be demands for many kinds of services. As demands increase, the means for meeting these demands will bring many problems, and new methods for solving them will be necessary. These increased demands will also necessitate the coordination of services so that duplication will be avoided.

Leisure services administration is concerned with planning, organizing, conducting, controlling, coordinating, and evaluating the program provided in a community to satisfy the leisure needs and

236

interests of the people in that community. Administrative procedures relating to these various functions are carried on by leaders, supervisors, top executives, and board or commission members.

At the leader level, planning, organizing, and conducting programs are the major functions. Examples of administrative duties at this level are control of the program area, provision of activity supplies, and inventory of supplies, scheduling of team play, and maintaining good public relations with activity members and groups.

Supervisors are responsible for groups of personnel and for program areas for a center with many activities or for a city-wide program, such as art. Administrative duties that might be performed by supervisors include fiscal responsibility for a specific part of the program, scheduling and control of personnel, assignment of groups to facilities, or assessment of community needs and interests.

Top executives have major administrative duties including fiscal management, planning, resource development, public relations, and carrying out policies set by boards or commissions.

Boards and commissions are concerned with policy making, entrusting the carrying-out of policy to the top executive and his staff.

Generally recreation/leisure services is considered a grass-roots activity. This implies that local government must assume a major role in the organization, management, and coordination of services.

COORDINATION OF SERVICES

There are four major categories of operating agencies: public departments (federal, state, and local), private voluntary agencies (Y's, settlement houses), private groups (golf clubs, bridge clubs), and commercial enterprises (bowling alleys, theaters). If the needs and interests of all people are to be met, all services given by these various agencies should be available. Since the needs and interests of people are highly individualized, the local agencies have the major responsibility for interpreting needs and interests, making available all the resources needed to satisfy them, and operating, coordinating, and evaluating the services rendered.

The local public agency today is the most logical choice for the role of assessing needs and interests, organizing, managing, coordinating and evaluating services. This includes the municipal, town, or village department and, in some cases, a county department. The public department can coordinate services as well as provide a liaison with other public departments such as health, welfare, transportation, public works, and others. In its role as a coordinator, the public department works with all agencies that have a potential for providing a leisure service. It helps to channel resources, including financial, human, and physical resources, to the agency considered best able to provide the service to satisfy specific needs and/or interests. This is a relatively recent concept and is only in the beginning stages of implementation. There have been a few instances in the past when this has been done. An example is the funneling of federal monies for summer employment of youth through the public recreation department to a private voluntary agency which has the physical facility to carry on a given program such as a swim program. A much wider use of this practice is needed if the basic principle of providing services for all people on an unduplicated basis is to be carried out.

An interdisciplinary approach to problem solving is needed if the complex problems of providing services are to be solved. No one agency can feasibly provide all of the services independently. An agency might have fine facilities for swimming for a large number of people in the community. However, it is possible that not all the people can reach the facility because of inavailability of transportation, which problem might be solved through the public transportation system or through coordination with the schools using buses on some type of cooperative basis. The public department because it is part of local government has the potential for an easy liaison with these other departments and can work out a method for organization and operation.

The public department becomes the catalyst and coordinator making the necessary arrangements for the agency best equipped to render a service to provide that service. In this way the many needs and interests of people may be satisfied in a way that makes it possible to provide service to the greatest number of people. For example educational programs might be most effectively conducted in a museum, a library, or theater rather than in a school building. A bowling alley could be used under contract to provide space to teach bowling to school-age boys and girls under a physical education program or to adults under the community education program. The potentials in this type of approach are limited only by the creativeness of the department administering the program.

Another role that may be assumed by the public department is dissemination of information about leisure services available in the community. This has been developed in some communities through the use of the local newspaper in which activities of the day and coming events are listed. Much greater expansion of this is needed. All of the media should be used because many people never read a newspaper. Furthermore, some attempt should be made to set up a community-wide calendar of events so that major events will not be scheduled on the same day. The horizons of people need expansion not curtailment. In developing a community calendar the public department should assume a coordinating role.

Another area where coordination is needed is in the scheduling of services. As greater flexibility in work hours occurs in industry and business and school programs become year-round, many changes will be necessary in leisure services scheduling.

DEFINITIONS

• *Administration:* To direct, manage, and control the affairs of an agency or department.

• *Leisure services:* Those services provided in a community to meet the free time needs and interests of the people in a specific governmental unit, geographic area, or defined population.

OBJECTIVES

1. To identify the auspices under which leisure services are conducted

2. To learn the methods for coordinating these services to satisfy the leisure needs and interests of all people in the community

3. To survey the types of laws that govern the operation of leisure services programs

4. To learn the principles of administration and apply them to leisure services management in public, private voluntary, private, and commercial agencies

5. To analyze personnel management problems and the techniques for solving them

6. To learn to use office management personnel to support leisure services programs

7. To learn the methods of financing leisure services and how to budget for these services

8. To acquire knowledge of the basis on which facilities, supplies, and equipment are provided and of the techniques necessary for purchase, control, and maintenance of them

9. To learn the methods for organizing a leisure services program

10. To understand the importance of public relations and how to develop an effective public relations program

I. Provision of leisure services

    A. Basic principles of coordination

        1. The delivery of leisure services should be made by the agency best suited to give the service.

2. Public funds should be provided to agencies as needed.

3. The public recreation/leisure service has a major role in assessing needs and interests in the community; disseminating information; defining the need for new human, physical, or financial resources; and evaluating the leisure services provided in the community.

4. The public agency has a basic responsibility for stimulating community interest in leisure programs and interpreting those programs to the public.

5. Effective delivery of services is dependent upon unduplicated services to the greatest number of people.

B. Categories of agencies

1. Public agencies, whether at the local, state or federal level, have the responsibility for providing basic services for all people for whom they are responsible. Public agencies are tax supported.

a. Federal agencies are responsible for services which cannot be provided on a local basis. These include services through the following federal departments:

(1) Agriculture—Forestry Service, Extension Services (4-H clubs, adult rural groups), soil conservation

(2) Interior—Bureau of Outdoor Recreation, National Park Service, Bureau of Indian Affairs, Land Management, Land Reclamation, Fish and Wildlife Service

(3) Health, Education and Welfare—Child Development Bureau, Public Health Service, maternal and child health

(4) Department of Defense—military services and Army Corps of Engineers

(5) Commerce—Bureau of Census

(6) Various other federal agencies—Aging, Environmental Protection Agency, Tennessee Valley Authority, Veterans Administration, National Council on the Arts

b. State agencies are responsible for providing basic services for all people in the state which can not be provided on a local level. As an arm of state government, the county provides for services that local towns, villages, and cities are not able to provide. Such services are usually those that require more extensive financing or are needed by special groups of people of which there are too few in any given town to warrant the provision of that service. The types of state agencies that provide leisure services are:

(1) Department of Agriculture (4-H clubs)
(2) State Parks and Recreation Department
(3) Fish and Wildlife Service
(4) Youth Commission
(5) Art Commission
(6) Education Department
(7) State hospitals and schools
(8) State interagency committees
(9) Welfare department—services to poverty areas

c. Local agencies whose prime responsibility is the provision of basic leisure services are the local recreation and parks departments. In some communities these are separate departments but more and more they are combined into one department. Their role is to provide basic services for all people in the community based on the needs and interests of the people in that community.

2. Private voluntary agencies generally *operate* programs at the local level even though the agency may be national or international. Some of these agencies are:

a. The Y.M.C.A.–Y.W.H.A.
b. The Y.M.C.A.
c. The Y.W.C.A.
d. Settlement houses
e. Boy Scouts
f. Camp-Fire Girls
g. Girl Scouts
h. Junior Achievement
i. Boys Clubs of America
j. Girls Clubs of America
k. 4-H Club
  (1) Although operated under the Extension Service of the Department of Agriculture, the clubs operate on the local level similarly to other private voluntary organizations.
l. Health agencies
m. Churches
n. Hospitals and nursing homes
  (1) Many hospitals today operate leisure services either as part of the treatment program or as a diversional activity.

(2) Nursing homes *must* operate a leisure services program in order to meet the standards of the federal and/or state laws to be eligible for Medicare and/or Medicaid funds.

o. Private voluntary agencies are supported by the donated dollars. In some instances they may be eligible for tax money for conduct of special programs.

3. Private agencies are membership organizations supported by the dues of the members. There are many kinds, including:

  a. Rotary
  b. Golf clubs
  c. American Legion

4. Commercial agencies operate specified activities for profit. They include:

  a. Camps
  b. Bowling alleys
  c. Theaters
  d. Sports arenas
  e. Concert halls

The public is urged to participate for the fee that is imposed. Through this myriad of agencies the public can pursue the leisure experience of their choice. Today it is estimated that, overall, including the sale of all types of equipment including clothing and through provision of transportation to resources, leisure services are over a forty billion dollar industry in the United States.

C. Factors that must be considered in order to meet the leisure demands in a community

1. Today leisure services are being operated in relation to needs and interests of people rather than providing activities which people must accept or go unserved.

2. As movement toward individualized programs increases, computerized systems will be necessary. Figure 2 shows the basic principle.

D. Organization of public leisure services departments

1. Public departments at the local level can be organized in several ways. Figures 3–7 show some of the most common organizational patterns.

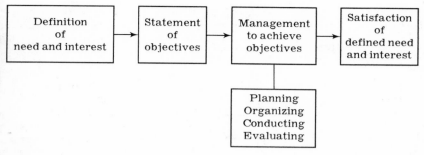

FIGURE 2.

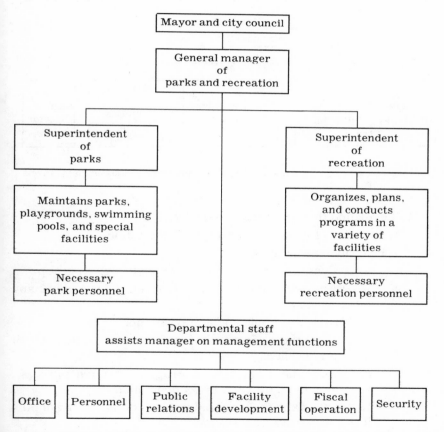

FIGURE 3. This organization shows integration of park and recreation services through the office of a general manager. This pattern is frequently found in larger cities.

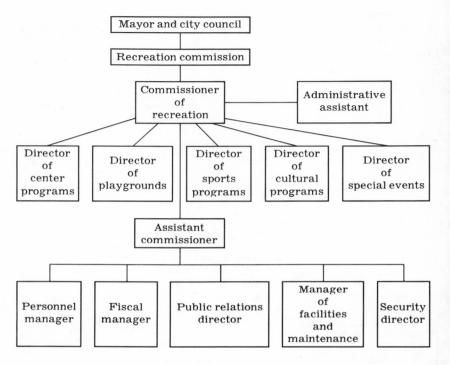

FIGURE 4. This type of organization is found in many smaller cities and large towns.

II. Legislation that affects leisure services

    A. State laws for tax-supported public recreation

        1. Enabling legislation

            a. Assigns responsibility for operation to a given group

            b. Defines joint and cooperative action among public and other agencies in the community

            c. Permits the employment of personnel

            d. Permits the equipment, operation, and maintenance of areas and facilities

            e. Permits the acquisition of property through purchase, lease, donation, transfer, or condemnation

            f. Enables expenditure of public funds or the levying of public funds for leisure services

            g. Enables collective action between two or more communities

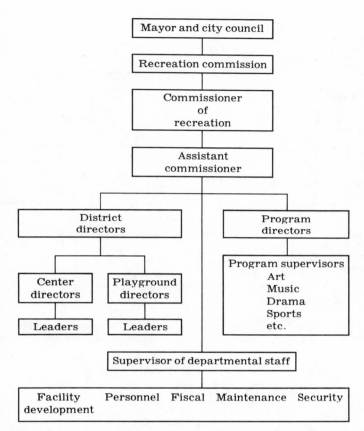

FIGURE 5. This type of organization shows decentralization of services. This brings management closer to the people to be served. The community is divided into districts each of which has a director with a complete staff to serve the district.

h. Defines methods for appointment of officers, number, type of representation and terms of officers

i. Defines rights of counties and home-rule cities to operate leisure services

   (1) A charter is given by the state to home-rule cities to conduct specific governmental services including the levying of taxes for that purpose.

2. Service laws

   a. Permit a state agency to provide service and sometimes to operate programs—state recreation commissions

245

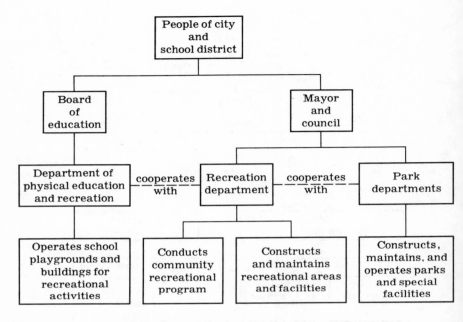

FIGURE 6. This type of organization shows three separate programs; cooperation depends largely on the interpersonal relationships of personnel in the departments.

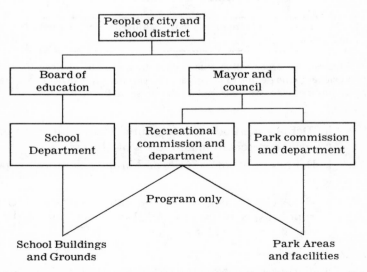

FIGURE 7. This type of organization shows the recreational departments which use the facilities of park and school departments.

b. Permit agencies that have other than recreation as a main function to conduct recreation programs—boards of education, conservation departments, welfare departments, youth boards

3. Regulatory laws

a. Regulate and control services in the interest of the public welfare and safety—film boards, fish and game, sanitary laws for swimming pools, speed of motor boats

4. Special project laws

a. Authorize expenditure of funds or action for a specified locality—use of watershed property for a day camp or use of an airport for recreation.

5. District legislation

a. Establishes an area that crosses usual boundaries and centers on locations of population

b. Is enacted by the state and includes:

(1) Minimum number of residents required and population limitation in a district

(2) Method of annexing additional territory

(3) Method of petitioning for a district

(4) How managing authority will be established

(5) Financing possibilities, methods, and limitations including the minimum and maximum tax levy

(6) Powers in acquiring, developing, and operating areas and facilities, providing services, employing personnel and accountability

B. Private voluntary agencies

1. Chartered by the state in accordance with the defined purposes of the agency

C. Private membership organizations

1. Incorporated under state laws of incorporation

2. Incorporation relieves individual liability

D. Commercial enterprises

1. Licensing laws for different types of operation such as theaters, taverns, bowling alleys

2. Local as well as state licensing

E. Federal legislation

1. Affects nationwide programs, includes regulations concerning such programs as:

a. Flood control

b. Highway and parkway acts

c. Forest Service Act of 1897 authorized recreation in national forests

d. Housing acts

e. Bureau of Outdoor Recreation (1962)

f. Housing and Urban Development and Legacy of Parks

g. Small Business Administration and Soil Conservation in the Department of Agriculture

h. Fish and Wildlife Division of the Department of Agriculture

i. Wild rivers legislation

F. Governmental and proprietary functions of public agencies

1. A governmental function is an action of a municipality that is a public duty performed on the part of the state for the benefit of the public welfare.

2. A proprietary function is a function of a government normally considered a private duty, performed primarily for the benefit of its own residents although the public generally may be benefited.

a. The Supreme Court has not established a rule regarding proprietary functions.

b. The function is defined by the courts in each case in accordance with common law and damages are awarded for injuries.

3. In many states, schools, although defined as a governmental function, are held liable for a tort, (a wrong to a person or property) for actions by their officers or personnel, while conducting services legally authorized by their governing legislation.

This determination has also been applied to parks and recreation.

4. Governmental immunity is given in some cases but not in others.

G. Types of liability

1. Criminal involves acts such as murder, robbery, rape.

2. Contractual involves failure of a party to keep a promise to provide goods or services.

3. Tort involves interference with the rights of others and compensation is given for injury to the person, his property, or reputation. Cases are decided on the basis of precedence.

H. Insurance for both public and private agencies

  1. Protection of agencies from many claims and extensive awards take a large portion of the agency's resources.

    a. Individual and agency lawsuits are possible.

    b. No one may sign away legal rights of an individual.

    c. If negligence is proven there is liability.

    d. In transportation of participants in a private vehicle the owner of the vehicle is liable.

    e. Liability can be charged in relation to maintainance of an "attractive nuisance," such as an unfenced swimming pool.

    f. In the operation of all services there must be evidence of operation with "due care."

  2. There is need to keep up with new laws or acts of government at the federal, state, and local levels.

III. Principles of administration and application to leisure services

  A. Administration as a process for goal achievement

    1. The chief administrator is an integral member of the department.

    2. The administrator provides the services specified in the establishment of the department.

      a. Through interpersonal relationships with those who set policy

      b. Through his staff who must carry out policy

    3. Administration involves:

      a. Planning—including situation assessment which means assessment of the needs and interests of people and the resources of the community, definition of alternatives to solve the problems in the situation, and establishment of the methods for program development.

      b. Organizing—on the basis of the assessment of the situation, to structure human, physical, and social resources to develop the program.

      c. Motivating—stimulating the public to a desire to participate and generating in the staff an enthusiasm to conduct the program.

      d. Directing—the systematic procedures that will permit a smooth operation of programs.

  e. Coordinating—to develop a method for cooperative effort that will make it possible for the greatest number of services to be made available to the greatest number of people.

  f. Controlling—to operate the program in accordance with established policies and with checks to determine that all resources are used effectively and efficiently.

  g. Evaluating—to determine the extent to which objectives have been achieved and suggest alternatives in cases where objectives have not been attained.

B. Tools of administration
 1. Leadership
 2. Decision making
 3. Communication
 4. Planning
 5. Conducting
 6. Research

C. Administrative organization
 1. A basic principle of administration is that any function defined as a separate entity of government should be operated as a separate unit with specifically defined goals. For example: The defined goal of a department of education is educating people. Any other goal is secondary to this purpose. Should it become necessary to define priorities, anything not considered education would need to be eliminated.

D. Administrative skill a defined skill
 1. A star performer or a good leader does not necessarily make a good administrator.
 2. Administrative skills include:
  a. Ability to define a problem
  b. Ability to divide the problem into workable parts
  c. Assignment of tasks in accordance with personnel skills that are needed to solve the problem
  d. Establishment of a system of operation and necessary rules to complete the task efficiently
  e. Evaluation of the results
  f. Redefinition of problem if the results achieved are not satisfactory
 3. Other administrative duties include but are not limited to:
  a. Meetings with influential people in the community

b. Meetings with union officials

c. Appearances at local, state, and federal hearings the outcome of which may affect the operation of leisure services

d. Attendance at various civic activities

E. Methods of organization

1. Grouping by age

2. Grouping by geographic area

a. Services are decentralized.

b. The area director is responsible not only for all program services but also for all support services such as personnel, fiscal, maintenance and others.

3. Grouping by time of day

a. One person directs all day services another all evening services.

b. This plan is usually only applicable to a single center and not to a whole department unless the department is part of a larger organization such as a hospital.

4. Grouping by activities

a. In this pattern a person on a central staff is responsible for a given activity area and directs it on a department-wide basis.

5. Grouping by operating functions (financing, public relations, etc.)

a. This applies generally to the support services in a central office with a person directing each function for the department.

b. These people are the staff of the top administrator who help him to carry out his duties.

c. This same kind of organization may be used in situations where the department is decentralized on a geographic area basis.

d. Each area then may have a person who directs a given function for that area and reports to the area director.

6. Many combinations of these organizational patterns may be found.

F. Administrative responsibilities

1. Advantage must be taken of specialized skills of personnel.

2. There must be adequate control of all functions and facilities.

3. The organizational pattern must aid in coordination of functions.

4. It must facilitate adequate attention to each function.

5. There must be recognition and careful attention paid to local conditions.

6. The organizational patterns must result in the most economical operation.

G. Organization of leisure services departments

    1. Line and staff organization (see Fig. 8)

        a. There are two forms for authority.

        b. The line organization shows the flow of direct authority that moves from the lowest to the highest echelon.

        c. Staff are designated to assist the administrator in carrying out certain functions common to all branches of the service.

    2. Team organization

        a. More than one person is assigned to accomplish a defined task.

        (1) A team of three might be assigned the task of managing the top executive duties of the agency.

        (2) One top executive could be assigned to facility development and maintenance, one to program services, and one to special facilities (a baseball stadium) and special events (a bicentennial celebration).

        (3) Although each is assigned a task to achieve overall objectives, the three work as a team to carry out the objectives and policies of the agency.

        b. A group of specialists (a psychiatrist, a physician, a physical therapist, a social worker, a therapeutic recreation specialist, or a variety of others) function as a team to define the treatment objectives for a patient and then assign to each discipline certain objectives that will contribute to the overall treatment objective for the patient.

        c. Program teams can be formed to carry out certain objectives.

        (1) Specialists in music, drama, and dance could make up a team to determine the objectives for a program, assign tasks, and define how the programs were to be conducted to make achievement of the objectives possible.

    3. Management by objectives

        a. Organization by objectives applies more to programs than to overall agency administration.

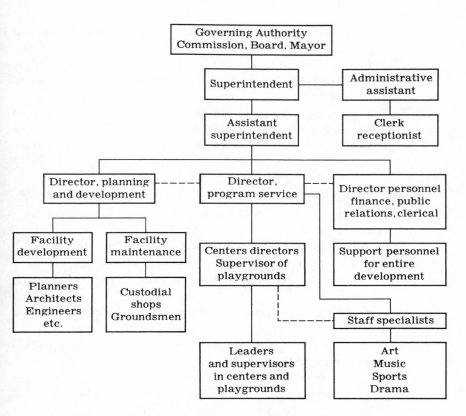

FIGURE 8. The solid lines represent a direct flow of authority. The broken lines show cooperative relationships without direct flow of authority. Line personnel have direct responsibility for carrying out specified objectives. Staff personnel give specialized services that assist line personnel to achieve their objectives.

b. A specific task is outlined and a task force assigned to complete that task.

(1) A special Olympics program is an example.

(2) This task involves many different problems that must be solved to bring about a successful program.

(3) A task may be only a once-a-year event.

c. Many people with a variety of skills are needed.

d. Program people, facility arrangement personnel, overall organizers and perhaps many more would be needed.

e. A central committee would be organized representing the variety of tasks to be performed. Each member of the central group would have a specific assignment.

f. The central group would define the objectives, assign the tasks, and evaluate the program to ascertain whether the objectives had been achieved.

g. This kind of organizational pattern might be applied to any kind of situation in which there is a defined problem to be solved, and in which the problem does not involve a continuously operating program, or in which a program operates within a defined time.

H. Motivating personnel

1. Leisure services is people-oriented rather than product-oriented.

2. All personnel must be concerned with the effect that their job performance has on the people they are serving.

a. This idea needs to be internalized by *every* worker in the agency.

b. This is not something that a supervisor or executive *tells* a worker.

3. The worker should contribute to a regular analysis of the job to be performed.

4. Competencies of individuals should be assessed, and persons should be placed in positions in which their skills will be used most effectively to promote the goals of the agency.

5. Continuous communication with all personnel is essential.

a. Face-to-face interpersonal communication is most important.

b. Communication by memoranda is of secondary importance.

c. Personnel need day-to-day recognition by others that their job contributes to the goals of the agency.

d. Nonverbal as well as verbal communication can show appreciation.

6. Adequate tools to permit top job performance must be provided.

a. Adequate tools include appropriate and adequate help for the individual.

7. Motivation of personnel is a continuous process which permeates all facets of job performance.

I. Methods of control

1. Defined checks and balances must be established to ensure that the procedures developed are producing the desired product.

a. This includes facilities and programs that satisfy the leisure needs and interests of the public.

b. Every facet of the department operation must be geared to achieve this.

2. Procedures, rules, and regulations must be established for planning and research, facility development, business operation, program operation and evaluation, and public relations.

a. Procedures must be developed in relation to legal authorization given to the agency and the policies developed to carry out that authorization.

b. These then must be put into a manual that is available as a reference for every person in the department.

3. Personnel must be designated to carry out those procedures and a method devised for checking that the procedure has been followed.

a. This is usually achieved through a variety of reports.

b. Reports may be forms to be completed, or they may be narrative.

(1) A form to be completed might be an inventory of supplies.

(2) A narrative report might be a group process report detailing the progress of a specific group.

J. Operating procedures

1. Decision-making processes must be established.

a. At every level of operation specific decision-making processes must be developed.

b. The basic principle to be followed is that every person or representatives of the people who are to be affected by the decision should be involved in the process.

2. A system of planning and budgeting must be defined.

a. A system called PPBS—planning, programming, and budgeting system—has been developed in recent years by the federal government.

b. This system includes an apportionment of all costs to a specific operation, including administration and supervision, program operation, supplies, maintenance, equipment, personnel office and office utilities, financing, and insurance.

c. For each operation, such as an art program or a baseball league, the total cost can be outlined.

d. The number served can then be defined and the per capita cost of the operation indicated.

e. This system becomes an important tool to be used in establishing priorities for programs to be conducted.

IV. Agency operation

  A. Policy making

    1. Policy making is the responsibility of the body legally authorized to operate the service.

      a. The chief executive of the service has the responsibility for carrying out policy.

      b. The chief executive frequently must inform the policy-making body of the need for certain policy.

    2. Boards, commissions, and advisory councils have different roles in different agencies.

      a. Boards and Commissions in public agencies are independent or semi-independent.

        (1) An independent board is elected or appointed.

          (a) It has full responsibility for policy making and implementation.

          (b) It is completely autonomous.

          (c) It is responsible for the allocation of funds.

        (2) A semiindependent board functions under the mayor and city council, board of supervisors, or other governing body.

          (a) The allocation of funds comes from mayor and city council.

        (3) Advisory boards have no final authority or responsibility for policy making or administration.

      b. Board in private voluntary agencies

        (1) Have complete autonomy for policy making

        (2) Where recreation is just one function of the agency, the board sets overall policy for the agency. There is a board committee responsible for recreation, e.g. hospitals or residential schools.

c. The roles of all boards are:

(1) To employ the chief executive.

(2) To establish by-laws to govern the organization within the legal framework.

(3) To work with executive to carry out policies.

(4) To develop a financial plan

(5) To define the program and develop resources.

(6) To interpret the program to the community.

(7) To participate in public relations program.

(8) To stimulate citizen support.

d. The role of advisory councils is to advise, recommend, and interpret

e. If board members are to function effectively, they must be oriented to the duties they are to perform and understand:

(1) The purposes of agency

(2) How the agency is supported

(3) The physical and human resources needed to operate the agency and how these are acquired

(4) The qualifications needed by various personnel

(5) The relationships between board and committees of board

(6) The relationship of the board and committees to the chief executive and other departmental staff

(7) The day-to-day operation of the agency

(8) Personnel policies of agency

B. Planning and acquisition of physical resources

1. An orderly procedure should be developed to plan for current and future needs for physical resources.

2. Planning involves a detailed inventory of existing resources.

3. An analysis of the physical, intellectual, and social characteristics of the people in the community and the economic status of the community, population density, and projected population growth is helpful.

C. Fiscal operation

1. Two types of fiscal operation are needed in every leisure services agency.

a. One relates to program operation and the other to capital development.

b. Budgets must be developed for each of these and the means for obtaining the funds for each defined.

2. In public agencies capital improvements are frequently financed through bond issues.

a. The operational funds come from taxes and fees.

3. In private voluntary agencies capital improvements are financed through a special fund-raising effort and the operational funds come from the donated dollars and fees.

4. Procedures for acquiring these funds must be established in accordance with the legal authority given to the agency.

5. Profit making and membership organizations are financed by investments by the owners or members and by fees and charges.

D. Personnel management

1. Procedures relating to the functioning of personnel are some of the most sensitive in the agency.

2. Necessary procedures include:

a. Position classification and a job analysis must be made to determine the functions performed.

(1) The competencies needed to perform the task must be compiled.

(2) The ways in which these competencies may be acquired are outlined.

b. The steps necessary for recruitment and placement of personnel.

c. Orientation and on-the-job training.

d. Methods for evaluation and promotion.

e. Steps to be taken to transfer personnel from one situation to another.

f. Definition of wages, benefits, and increments for each type of position.

g. Personnel development through supervisory conferences, inservice education, and other kinds of educational programs.

h. Evaluation, grievance procedures, and dismissals.

i. Union activities.

j. Maintenance of personnel records.

2. A personnel handbook containing the procedures for each of these areas should be given to *every* employee at the time of the initial employment and at regular intervals thereafter supplemented as need arises.

3. The rules and regulations should be discussed by small groups of employees and the personnel manager.

E. Fiscal management

1. Procedures for fiscal management represent the methods by which the agency indicates its accountability for the funds given to it for its operation.

2. Some of the kinds of reports that it is necessary to establish are budget, income and expenditure ledgers, inventories of supplies and equipment, status of physical resources, insurance, contractual agreements, wages and various withholding for taxes and others depending on the particular situation.

3. All of these help the department to show cost relationships to program operation and the extent to which program operation has been in line with the budget projected for it.

4. These reports also permit the department to indicate areas of operation that need additional funds to operate effectively.

F. Program operation

1. Policies, rules, regulations, and types of programs to be conducted need to be definitively outlined.

2. These include procedures related to populations to be served, kinds of facilities needed, fees related to the service, personnel needed, special services or events to be conducted, transportation, supplies and equipment, and others to be found in a given situation.

G. Maintenance of facilities

1. No program can be conducted effectively unless the facilities needed are maintained in an operating condition.

2. Whether indoors or outdoors, standards for the facility must be established and adequate controls set up to ascertain that these standards are met constantly.

H. Evaluation and research

1. Whether under public, private or commercial auspices programs need to be evaluated regularly to determine whether they are continuing to meet the needs and interests of the populations they purport to serve.

2. Simple procedures can be developed to evaluate day-to-day operations and more involved measures can be used on a six-month or yearly basis.

3. These latter may be staff-participant evaluations or evaluation by an outside expert.

4. When an evaluation shows certain inadequacies in the program it may be necessary to conduct a research study to determine why the inadequacies exist and how they may be remedied.

 a. This requires the establishment of a research team either from the agency or from another source such as a university.

 b. When the research findings are reported, the agency then has the responsibility for establishing procedures for changing the program in accordance with the research recommendation.

V. Personnel management

 A. Personnel required for leisure services agencies

  1. There are six broad categories of personnel needed in a leisure services agency.

  2. These categories include:

   a. Administration

   b. Finance

   c. Program (both paid and volunteer)

   d. Business (clerical, personnel, public relations)

   e. Maintenance

   f. Planning and facility development

  3. There are a variety of qualifications needed by personnel in these six categories.

   a. Personnel in administration must have:

    (1) An indepth understanding of the leisure/recreation field

    (2) An ability to:

     (a) Make judgements based on facts

     (b) Time decisions so that they are presented in the most favorable climate

     (c) Stimulate the highest effort on part of all staff

     (d) Be consistent in all management affairs

    (3) An ability to act as a catalyst to stimulate other agencies or departments to render certain services to meet recreation/leisure needs

(4) An ability to coordinate a variety of services in the community and in the department

b. Personnel in finance must be able to understand and manage the fiscal affairs of the department, including:

(1) Budgeting

(2) Cost analysis

(3) Computer technology

(4) Accounting and auditing

(5) Bookkeeping

(6) The department and its policies of operation

c. There are three levels of program personnel, and they must have an indepth understanding of the recreation/ leisure field. At each level of program management there is need for knowledge of administration, supervision, and direct leadership of programs; the depth of knowledge varies at each level.

(1) Administrators must have knowledge of administration, an understanding of supervisory techniques, an ability to lead personnel, and some competency in program leadership.

(2) Supervisors must have an ability to work with people to mobilize their greatest efforts, an ability to administer programs establishing controls for effective program operation, and ability to evaluate personnel performance and conduct programs, and an ability to manage facilities.

(3) Leaders and specialists are responsible for the conduct of specified programs.

(a) They must be able to teach skills, organize groups, assist individuals in choices of activities, conduct activities, plan and conduct special events, and evaluate programs conducted.

(b) They must be able to work with all types of supportive personnel.

(4) Volunteers may function in all areas of program services, and they need qualifications for the type of service they are to give and an orientation to the agency.

d. Business personnel services include:

(1) Clerical maintenance of all kinds of program records and reports, maintenance of schedules for personnel and

programs, personnel records and reports, and maintenance of public relations records and reports.

(2) Telephone operation.

(3) Secretarial services.

(4) Maintenance of financial records and reports.

(5) Maintenance of facility records, schedules and reports.

(6) Records of supplies and equipment.

(7) Legal records.

(8) Scheduling of transportation and reports on transportation.

e. Business management personnel need basic qualifications
necessary for efficient operation and maintenance of files,
including:

(1) An ability to produce necessary written records and
reports by typing, mimeographing, and other means.

(2) An ability to provide secretarial services to all personnel as needed.

f. All business management should be under the supervision
of an office manager who has all of the needed skills and can
organize, and conduct a business office efficiently and effectively.

g. Maintenance personnel needed will vary with the type of
facilities and equipment used in the program and include, but
are not limited to:

(1) Grounds keeper.

(2) Shops for electrical, plumbing, painting, etc.

(3) Horticultural nurseries.

(4) Supplies warehouse.

(5) Maintenance of pools or other special facilities.

(6) Construction workers for minor work such as laying a
walkway or building a fireplace.

h. Planning and facility design personnel have special qualifications; they include:

(1) Engineers.

(2) Architects.

(3) Draftsmen.

(4) Computer technologists.

(5) Research specialists.

i. Specialists must have an understanding of the purpose of the agency and how their specialty contributes to that purpose.

B. Factors involved in personnel management

1. The major problem in personnel management is lack of communications.

2. Methods for overcoming this include:

a. Establishing regular means of communication by direct face-to-face contact with each employee and by lines of authority.

b. Publishing personnel policies and making sure that every employee has a copy and has an opportunity to discuss each policy.

3. Decision making in relation to personnel must be based on:

a. Facts and their accuracy.

b. Facts in the light of past experiences.

c. Written records.

d. Policies

e. Labor agreements.

f. Identification of key obstacles.

g. Determination of the limit of authority.

h. The effect of the decision.

4. Personnel management must be designed to bring about achievement of goals and potential for personal achievement by individual staff members.

5. Supervisory personnel should evaluate the quality of their leadership.

a. What kind of leader of leaders are you?

b. Do you support your staff? What should you do if there is a conflict of interests?

c. How do you persuade staff members to change their position?

6. Unions play a role in leisure services departments.

a. The union security agreement is an agreement between the union and employer to require union membership.

b. Any such agreement must be in accordance with state laws.

c. Strikes occur for economic reasons and because of unfair labor practices.

d. Unlawful strikes occur if there is no union security agreement.

(1) An employer cannot dismiss an employee for failure to join a union.

(2) A strike to compel this is illegal.

e. Unlawful strikes also occur if there is a no-strike clause in the contract.

f. There should be bargaining in good faith relative to wages, working conditions, new contracts.

g. The bargaining unit:

(1) Consists of two or more persons in similar jobs.

(2) Excludes from belonging agricultural laborers, independent contractors, supervisors, executives, and employees acting in confidential capacity to an employer's labor relations official.

(3) Elects the bargaining agent.

h. Personnel:

(1) Take part in elections

(2) Take part in election of representatives

i. The bargaining process must answer question of who determines major questions, rights and obligations. People in the bargaining process include:

(1) The mediator—a counselor.

(2) The arbiter—a judge.

(3) The fact-finder—defines the issue and collects evidence on both sides, defines the position of each party and makes recommendations.

(4) The arbiter makes a decision that is binding.

VI. Office management

  A. Office purpose and location

    1. The recreation office performs a service function.

a. The office is a filing, preparing, coordinating, and communicating center.

b. The office performs a multitude of tasks that help keep the flow of work moving and increases the overall efficiency of the organization.

c. The office will reflect the philosophy of the people who work there.

d. It is the directing headquarters for the leisure services department.

e. It also plays a major role in determining the public's image of the service.

(1) To create and maintain a desirable image, each person must realize what his work contributes to the success or failure of the department's objectives.

(2) Many people will have their first contact with the department through the central office, and it is important that the office operate in a professional manner.

f. The central office usually houses the chief executive of the department and sets the tone for the whole department.

(1) The executive carries on duties involving research, correspondence, public relations, information, staff relations, purchasing and financial management and others.

(2) The manner in which people are received, the accessibility of the executive and all the functions of the office largely determine the effectiveness of the department.

2. The office should be centrally located in relation to the people to be served.

a. It is desirable to have the general offices in a single building so that there is ease of communication, and no time lost in moving from one unit of the department to another.

b. Criteria for office location:

(1) Does it serve the purpose of the organization?

(2) Is it accessible to the people to be served?

(3) Is the space adequate?

B. Office functions

1. The overall function of the office is the administration of the leisure services department.

2. These functions are part of the day-to-day operation of the department, and the manner in which they are conducted are a reflection of the chief executive.

3. Much of the work in the administrative office is routine.

4. Office hours should be regular and posted.

5. All communications should be handled in a quick and courteous manner (within 24 to 48 hours of receipt).

a. Letters should be given to the person best able to answer it.

b. Not all letters need to be answered by the chief executive personally.

c. Form letters can be used for certain correspondence that is routine.

d. Copies of all letters should be filed.

e. All outgoing mail should be proofread to correct any errors.

6. Filing is the system of storing information so that it may be readily available when needed.

a. Two types of information filed are correspondence and informational materials.

b. Types of filing systems are:

(1) Alphabetical

(2) Numerical coding

(3) Subject matter

7. In addition to the active files, there should be an inactive file.

a. It is often recommended that files be cleared every six months.

b. Materials are then put into the inactive file for six months and then those materials that must be kept indefinitely are put into an inactive archive file.

8. Each office should establish a policy in relation to confidential files that may only be used by designated personnel.

9. If possible a library should be established containing leisure/recreation books, magazines, pamphlets that are needed by both personnel in the department and participants.

10. Telephones are an essential part of office operation, and definite policies in regard to their use must be established.

a. A system for answering all telephones must be established.

b. Personnel must learn hʋw to answer the phone. The telephone company will train personnel for this task.

c. A system for taking messages for personnel away from the office should be set up.

d. A policy must be established in relation to periods when staff are not be be disturbed to take telephone calls.

e. A positive or negative image of the department can be formed by the way in which telephones are answered.

11. A method for making and recording appointments must be arranged.

12. Every visitor to the office should be given prompt and courteous attention.

13. Time should be allocated for preparation and research in regard to programs.

    a. A conference room or small office should be provided for this program.

14. Methods must be used to record data in regard to participation in programs, participants, personnel, supplies and facilities, finances, and maintenance of areas and facilities.

    a. These records provide data for evaluation, the scope of the program, statistical information, and objectives of the program and the degree to which objectives have been achieved.

15. Types of records and their purpose include:

    a. Administrative—relate to policy making, contracts, boards.

    b. Program records—include classification of participants in a variety of categories, attendance, schedules, special events, program activities, and others.

    c. Personnel—include materials related to board member, paid and volunteer staff and advisory councils

    d. Property—include all data related to supplies and equipment. Forms are needed to show requisitions, purchase order, inventories, etc.

    e. Finance records—budget data, income and expenditure records, payroll information are a few of the records that must be kept.

    f. Miscellaneous—include materials relating to conferences, institutes and inservice training, research, library materials, and various directories.

16. The annual report of the department is dependent on the records and reports submitted by the personnel of the department throughout the year.

    a. Accurate filing of these materials is essential if a complete annual report of stewardship by the department is to be developed.

C. Office personnel and problems

1. The importance of efficient secretarial personnel cannot be overemphasized.

2. Well-trained office personnel provide invaluable supportive services for the professional staff of the agency.

3. Office personnel often fail to understand that the role of the office is service.

4. An office manager or supervisor should be assigned if an efficient office is to be operated.

    a. This person defines tasks to be done, assigns tasks, and evaluates work performed.

5. In an organized office:

    a. Every person should be assigned specific tasks.

    b. Each person must know to whom he is accountable.

    c. Office duties of similar nature should be grouped.

    d. Specific authority should be delegated to each person.

    e. The limits of that authority should also be defined.

D. Physical environment

1. Physical layout of the office must be carefully planned to achieve the greatest efficiency with the least expenditure of time and effort.

2. Objectives in office planning should include:

    a. Providing a functionally efficient environment.

    b. Flexibility in layout within the limits of the standards established for private and general offices.

    c. Providing equipment that will enhance the working conditions of personnel such as adequate lighting, ventilation, air conditioning, and heating.

    d. Establishing a policy for space allocation of personnel and equipment.

3. To achieve a pleasing atmosphere, furniture, carpets, drapes, and other furnishings should harmonize.

    a. When possible, personnel should be permitted to choose the colors and furniture to be used in their offices.

4. An analysis of the functions to be performed in the office must be made and equipment purchased that will permit the most efficient operation by personnel.

    a. In setting up offices today, consideration must be given to the use of computers in office management.

VII. Financing leisure services

  A. Methods for financing leisure services

1. Public agencies are financed by:
   a. General fund
   b. Taxes
   c. Mill levies
   d. Bond issues
   e. Fees and charges
   f. Concessions
   g. Leases
   h. Gifts and endowments
   i. Grants
2. Private voluntary agencies are financed by:
   a. Donations
   b. Foundation, federal, state, and local governmental grants
   c. Fees and charges
   d. Concessions
   e. Leases
3. Private and commercial agencies are financed chiefly by membership fees and/or user fees and investments by owners.
B. Problems in fiscal management
   1. The agency must be accountable to its financial source.
   2. There are several methods for keeping accurate accounts, including:
      a. Simple bookkeeping
      b. Computer records
   3. Feasibility studies are based on:
      a. Objectives
      b. Demand
      c. Economics
      d. Policy of the department relative to cost distribution
      e. Funds available
      f. Income projection
      g. Effect on similar facilities in the community
C. Budgets
   1. There are two types of budgets: operating and capital.
   2. The entire staff should be involved in developing the budgets.
   3. There are two sets of materials that must be prepared for an operating budget.

a. The summary sheet to be presented to the mayor and citizens.

b. The detailed analysis sheets including cost analysis of previous years and the breakdown of items with documentation for each expenditure.

4. The line item budget is organized in accordance with object classifications:

Code number	Service
1000	Personnel services
2000	Contractual services
3000	Commodities
4000	Current charges
5000	Current obligation (Interest, pensions, taxes)
6000	Properties
7000	Debt payment

5. The Planning, Performance Budget System is another method of budgeting. It gives exact costs for each part of the program (see p. 282).

a. It is a quantitative analysis, and does not in any way indicate the quality benefit derived by the participant.

b. It is still necessary to justify why a program that serves a few participants is a viable and valuable part of the program.

c. Included in a performance budget are:

(1) Criteria of service, number of staff for efficient operation, program justification, number of days of operation of a facility.

(2) Standard of efficiency, job analysis, task distribution, service units (number of hours of classes, etc.), and production units (grass sown, building cleaned, etc.).

6. The capital budget is a completely separate budget defining expenditures for major investments such as buildings, parks, or any equipment having a life of more than five years.

VIII. Areas and facilities

A. Types of facilities

1. Indoor facilities required include:

a. Neighborhood community center.

(1) Large, multipurpose room with kitchen

(2) Craft room

(3) Small meeting room

(4) Outdoor facilities including a playground for children, a ball field, and game courts

b. A community-wide center

(1) All of the above plus a gymnasium, and auditorium, swimming pool, and tennis courts

2. Outdoor facilities include:

a. Neighborhood facilities such as vest-pocket parks, tot lots, center strips on streets, circles

b. Community parks

c. Regional or county parks

d. State parks

e. Federal parks or facilities

3. Special centers include:

a. Teen centers

b. Little theaters

c. Senior centers

B. Standards for facilities

1. At present there are no universally accepted standards for the provision of recreation facilities.

2. The number and types of facilities should be related to density of population, ages of population, and culture of population.

3. Function determines structure

4. Maintenance costs for the facility must be considered.

5. Safety factors are important.

6. Control of the facility is essential.

7. Traffic patterns within the building and outside must be considered.

8. Attractiveness and environmental quality are important.

9. Landscaping is frequently not only for beauty but also for noise control.

C. Maintenance of facilities

1. Five factors govern the maintenance program

a. Functional level of the facility or equipment

b. Safety

c. Sanitation and cleanliness

d. Attractiveness

e. Convenience

2. Procedures for maintaining facilities include:

a. Analysis of tasks to be performed

b. Design of a systematic maintenance program

(1) Assignment of definite tasks to each worker

(2) Definition of the range of time necessary for the efficient completion of each task

(3) Establishment of a maintenance calendar

(4) Development of a maintenance manual

3. Goals and objectives, standards of performance (time, level of efficiency), staff, necessary tools, necessary material, location of tools and equipment, and job description for each maintenance worker must be defined for each task.

D. Methods for purchase control and delivery of maintenance services

1. Centralized services for purchase of supplies and equipment provides a means to evaluate new equipment and supplies but may bring problems regarding their distribution.

a. If centralized purchasing is done, a procedure must be developed so that supplies and equipment are available to the field when they are needed.

b. Factors that must be considered in such a procedure include:

(1) Time necessary for requisition and delivery

(2) Regularity of inventories to determine shortages

(3) Method for transporting supplies

(4) Method for delivery of large equipment

(a) Is it necessary to deliver it to a central warehouse for acceptance?

(b) If delivered to a central warehouse, how will it be delivered to location where it is to be installed?

(c) How is equipment to be installed?

IX. Program development

A. Organization of the leisure services program

1. Feasibility studies and community surveys are used to assess the total resources of the community and to determine the need for, and location of, facilities.

2. Before developing a program it is necessary to:
   a. Assess the needs and interests of people to be served.
   b. Assess all human and physical resources that are available.
B. Steps in organizing the program
   1. The people to be served should be involved
   2. Human and physical resources must be surveyed.
   3. Programs must be coordinated.
   4. Basic services must be included.
      a. Resources that may be used by all.
      b. Services that may be used by large groups of individuals or organized groups.
   5. Special services are required for special facilities, special equipment, and special populations such as the handicapped.
   6. Special services for handicapped include integrated services and segregated services.
   7. Staffing of services includes generalists, specialists, full-time and part-time.
   8. Programs can be started by a special event or by gradual introduction—group by group.
C. Program evaluation
   1. Reasons for evaluation include:
      a. To determine the extent to which objectives are reached.
      b. To determine the effectiveness of current programs.
      c. To ascertain new needs or changing needs.
      d. As means of interpreting to the community the validity of the agency.
      e. To extend knowledge in the field.
   2. Techniques for evaluation are:
      a. Statistical measurement
         (1) Index of opportunity
         (2) Distribution of participation
      b. Behavior changes
         (1) Sociometric testing of group behavior
         (2) Interviews
         (3) Diaries
         (4) Observation rating scales
         (5) Behavior rating scales

        c. Self-survey by agency

        d. Survey by outside investigator

        e. Annual reports

X. Public Relations

    A. Creating an image

        1. Public Relations = Performance/Reaction of Public or PR = P + R.

        2. Public relations involves every staff member in the organization.

        3. The public is every citizen.

    B. Elements of public relations.

        1. There are many elements in public relations:

           a. Face to face contacts

           b. Telephone contacts

           c. Correspondence

           d. Program services

           e. Mass media

    C. Developing public relations

        1. Inventory of public attitudes is essential.

        2. Techniques include:

           a. Informal discussions

           b. Formal questionnaires, citizen forums, and neighborhood meetings

           c. Block surveys

        3. The agency should have staff development programs for public relations.

        4. To promote good public relations, staff must:

           a. Enjoy contacts with people.

           b. Be able to communicate verbally and nonverbally.

           c. Be courteous.

           d. Continuously evaluate the program.

           e. Know department policy, objectives, and plans.

           f. Know their jobs.

           g. Understand the work of others on the team.

           h. Be able to interpret the recreational value of each program.

           i. Know the rules and regulations of the department.

D. Staff public relations duties
 1. Speaking to people
 2. A smile
 3. Calling people by name
 4. Friendliness
 5. Genuine interest in each person and *his* concerns
 6. Liking people
 7. Being generous with praise
 8. Respect for the opinions of others
 9. Cautiousness with criticism
 10. Alertness to the opportunity to give service
 11. Graciousness and giving people the impression that he finds pleasure in doing his job

E. Correspondence
 1. First class, individual letters should be used if possible.
 2. The tone of letters is crucial.
 3. Letters should be short, simple, specific, and sincere.
 4. Stationery should give a good image of department.

F. Handling complaints
 1. Supervisor should receive the complaint.
 2. The supervisor should assign the responsibility for the investigation of the complaint and the means for correcting complaint.
 3. There should be followup on the correction.
 4. Complainant should be notified of the correction.

G. Use of personalities, such as outstanding artists and awards to people who have made contributions.

Student assignments

This part consists of ten objectives. You will be called upon to demonstrate your mastery of each objective.

OBJECTIVE	EVIDENCE OF COMPETENCY
1. To identify the auspices under which leisure services are conducted.	a. Define the four major categories of agencies and indicate the types of agencies that are found in each category at the local state and national level.

OBJECTIVE	EVIDENCE OF COMPETENCY

b. Indicate how each category is financed and the special characteristics of each type of agency.

2. To learn the methods for coordinating these services to satisfy the leisure needs and interests of all people in the community.

Discuss coordination of local leisure services and the role of the public leisure services agency in coordinating services.

3. To survey the types of laws that govern the operation of leisure services programs.

a. Define five types of laws that govern operation of public leisure services agencies at the local level and indicate the purpose of each.

b. Show laws by which private voluntary, private, and commercial agencies operate.

c. Indicate five nationwide programs that are governed by federal legislation.

d. State the difference between governmental and proprietary functions of public agencies.

e. Discuss tort liability indicating persons who may be liable for damages and the legal rights of individuals in liability suits.

4. To learn the principles of administration and apply them to leisure services management in public, private voluntary, private, and commercial agencies.

a. Define *administration*.

b. Discuss the seven factors included in the administrative process.

c. Discuss the basic skills of administration.

d. Discuss the methods of organizing leisure services *programs*.

e. Discuss methods of organizing a leisure services department.

OBJECTIVE	EVIDENCE OF COMPETENCY

f. Discuss methods of motivating leisure services personnel.

g. Why must control of operations be established and how can personnel be informed about them?

h. Define the operational management procedures needed in a leisure services agency and discuss each.

5. To analyze personnel management problems and techniques for solving them.

a. Define the categories of personnel needed in a leisure service agency, indicate the principal duties of each and the kinds of competencies needed to carry out these duties.

b. Discuss the factors involved in personnel management.

c. Discuss the place of unions in leisure service agencies.

6. To use office management personnel to support the leisure services program

a. What is the purpose of a central office and where should it be located?

b. What are the functions of the central office and what procedures are needed for each?

c. What types of records and reports must be kept?

d. Discuss three problems related to office personnel.

e. What must be considered in designing and furnishing an office?

7. To learn the methods of financing leisure services and how to budget for them.

a. Discuss the method for financing leisure services under the auspices of a public, a private voluntary, a private membership club, and a commercial agency.

277

b. Discuss the various accounting procedures necessay to provide the public with the necessary figures to show how monies provided for the service were used.

c. What is a feasibility study and on what is it based?

d. What is the purpose of an operating budget and a capital budget?

e. Discuss a line-item budget and a performance budget.

8. To acquire knowledge of the basis on which facilities, supplies, and equipment are provided and of the techniques necessary to purchase, control and, maintain them.

a. Discuss the major types of facilities needed to provide leisure programs.

b. What are the factors that must be considered in providing facilities?

c. Discuss the five factors to be considered for the maintenance of facilities and the procedures necessary to adequately maintain them.

d. Discuss the advantages of centralized purchase of supplies and equipment and indicate kinds of problems that may be involved.

9. To learn the methods for organizing a leisure services program.

a. Discuss the steps that needed to be taken in developing a program.

b. Discuss the several methods for starting a program.

c. Discuss program evaluation, the importance of it, and the methods of evaluation.

OBJECTIVE	EVIDENCE OF COMPETENCY
10. To understand the importance of public relations and how to develop an effective public relations program.	a. What is the purpose of a public relations program?
	b. How would you develop a public relations program?
	c. What is the role of the total staff in a public relations program?
	d. What methods should be used in a public relations program?

Resources

There are two parts to the resources section. The first part includes supplementary reading materials and the second includes forms and additional content materials.

READING MATERIAL

Suggested source book
MEYER, HAROLD D.; BRIGHTBILL, CHARLES K.; and SESSOMS, H. DOUGLAS. *Community Recreation: A Guide to Its Organization*, 4th ed. Englewood Cliffs, N.J.: Prentice-Hall, 1969.

References
BANNON, JOSEPH. *Problem Solving in Recreation and Parks*. Englewood Cliffs, N.J.: Prentice-Hall, 1972.

DRUCKER, PETER F. *The Practice of Management*. New York: Harper, 1954.

HJELTE, GEORGE, and SHIVERS, JAY S. *Public Administration of Recreational Services*. Philadelphia: Lea and Febiger, 1972.

LUTZIN, S., and STOREY, E. *Managing Municipal Leisure Services*. Washington, D.C., International City Management Association, 1975.

NATIONAL RECREATION AND PARK ASSOCIATION, Management Aids, Arlington, Va.

No. 1: *Manual for Park and Recreation Boards and Commission*

No. 3: *Park Equipment for Cities of 150,000 Population or Less*

No. 7: *Vandalism—How to Stop it*

No. 13: *A Safety Guide for Park and Recreation Employees*

No. 17: *Audio Visual Aids Manual*
No. 21: *Mass Communications*
No. 26: *A Manual on Concession Contracts*
No. 31: *User Fees*
No. 40: *Creative Playground Equipment*
No. 41: *Trends in Consolidation of Parks and Recreation*
No. 45: *Financing—Sources of Income for Parks and Recreation*
No. 46: *Budgeting for Parks and Recreation*
No. 48: *Annual Reports*
No. 57: *Filing Systems*
No. 59: *Fees and Charges*
No. 61: *Administrative Policy Manual*
No. 63: *Personnel Policies*
No. 65: *In-Service Training Manual*
No. 66: *Management of Professional Cultural Performances*
No. 67: *Office Administration—Management and Procedures*
No. 68: *Current Management Concepts on Personnel Policies and Practices*
No. 76: *Sample Leases, Licenses, Permits*
No. 78: *Staff Public Relations Manual*
No. 79: *Publicity Handbook*
No. 80: *Visual Tools Handbook*
No. 81: *Public Employee Unions Organizations*
No. 82: *School Community Park and Recreation Operations*
No. 83: *Effective Use of Consultants*
No. 91: *Administrative Development Series Part 1*
No. 92: *Administrative Development Series Part 2*

SUPPLEMENTARY MATERIALS

A. Materials to be included in a community survey
B. Steps in preparing PPBS budget
C. Expenditure budget
D. Income analysis
E. Expenditure ledger
F. Staff policy handbook
G. Staff information book
H. PPBS in recreation management

Recreation study

PURPOSE

Determine the need for a full-time, year-round recreation department; the pattern of administrative organization most appropriate for the needs of the community; and the financial obligations involved in such an undertaking. Examine and appraise present land holdings, facilities, and programs in light of present and future needs. Examine and appraise present recreational policies, procedures, and practices as they relate to administration, programs, and finances.

I. Examination and report on community
   1. Community tradition and recreation history
   2. Population trends
   3. Master plan
   4. Existing surveys
   5. Land use—park and recreation
   6. Capital programs
   7. Tax rates and assessed valuations
   8. Annual reports
   9. Legislation
   10. Others

II. Public recreation—examination and appraisal
   1. Organization and administration
   2. Policies and procedures
   3. Properties—park and recreation
   4. Recreational facilities
   5. Programs
   6. Records, reports, participation, others
   7. Personnel
   8. Expenditures
   9. Capital developments
   10. Relationships
   11. Others

III. Schools (public, private, parochial)—examination and appraisal
   1. Policies and procedures
   2. Records and reports
   3. Areas and facilities
   4. Programs

281

     5. Personnel

     6. Expenditures

     7. Relationships

     8. Capital developments

     9. Long range development plans

    10. Others

IV. Semiprivate and voluntary agencies (churches, scouts, civic associations, others)—examination and appraisal

     1. Areas and facilities

     2. Programs

     3. Leadership

     4. Finance

     5. Relationships

     6. Others

V. Recreation programs and facility needs—spot checks

     1. Schools

     2. Neighborhood associations

     3. Civic associations

     4. Scouts

     5. Church groups

     6. Voluntary agencies

     7. Others

VI. County and state agencies—examination and report

     1. Relationships

     2. Available areas and facilities

     3. Available programs

     4. Available leadership

     5. Available services

     6. Available funds

     7. Others

VII. Recommendations

Preparing a PPBS budget for a unit

    1. Title of activity

    2. Number of personnel used in activity. Indicate proportion of individual's time spent in activity and that the salary is for that portion of time.

    3. Number of times per week and number of weeks it is operated to arrive at total number of sessions

4. Number of participants in activity

5. Cost of supplies

6. Cost of equipment

7. Prorate cost of heat, light, space

8. Add all costs

9. Divide total cost by total number of participants to get per-capita cost

10. Divide total cost by total sessions to get per-session cost.

11. Objectives of the activity—describe the benefit to the participant.

Staff policy handbook

Buck Hill Camp Club
Bob Cipriano, Director

TEN CAUSES OF MAJOR PROBLEMS AT BUCK HILL CAMP CLUB

Ninety percent of Director's headaches in counselor relationships have come from these 10 areas; the Director hastens to add that problems in counselor relationships have been virtually nonexistent.

1. Every boy and girl is to be under director, counselor, or assistant counselor supervision at all times. Supervision cannot be given out the window, while reading, chatting, knitting, or when a counselor is visiting with another group. That is, every counselor is responsible for every member of his group at all times.

2. Counselors are to be at their duty stations promptly at 8:45 every morning and at 1:45 every afternoon. Director should be notified immediately when this is not possible.

3. Every counselor is to check his mail box before 8:45 each morning; after this check, the mailbox should be emptied. Storage boxes are to be cleaned out at frequent intervals.

4. The hours of 11:00 P.M. to 7:30 A.M. are quiet hours at every staff cottage. Talking except as absolutely necessary, bathing, interroom visiting, phonograph or radio playing are normally not appropriate.

5. All staff members are on official duty from 8:15 A.M. to noon and from 2:00 to 4:30 P.M. Exceptions to this are to be made only by the Director. Attendance reports are due promptly every morning.

6. Camp Club is on inspection every second, particularly at the swimming pool. Counselors should be alert at all times and games for the play period should be carefully chosen, always excluding rough-type games such as British Bulldog and Red Rover.

7. The appearance of the grounds and building is the responsibility of every counselor. Playgrounds, the back porch after supervised lunch and midmorning lunch, crafts lodge, senior lodge, and all other activity areas are to be cleared by the group after leaving each time. All sports game equipment is always to be returned to storage after use.

8. Any group leaving Camp Club should notify the Secretary BEFORE leaving and upon returning.

9. Counselors do not smoke when in supervision of Camp Club children.

10. The Crafts Lodge is never to be used for personal projects during Camp Club hours. Counselors are expected to assist the Crafts counselor in working with the boys and girls on their projects.

CARS

1. A camper is not allowed in a car driven by a staff member under the age of 21 or in a car not sufficiently insured for any emergency.

2. Staff members are allowed 8¢ per mile for the use of their cars for official Camp Club travel, as approved in advance by the Director. No travel allowance is permitted for the staff member travel in getting to Camp Club for the opening of season or returning at the close of season.

CONDUCT

1. The staff member shall, while in the employment of the Buck Hill Falls Company, adjust his personal habits and actions to the customs, policies, and ideals of the Company and Camp Club as outlined in these policies and explained to the staff member while at Buck Hill. He shall so conduct himself at all times so that he will be a credit to himself and to the Camp, keeping hours and habits which will enable him to remain in excellent physical condition.

2. Cursing and the use of questionable or profane language by Counselor, Assistant Counselor, CIT or Assistant CIT while with campers in any official capacity will not be tolerated. Smoking by a counselor when with campers is considered not appropriate. Use of alcoholic beverages by a counselor while at Buck Hill is discouraged; at no time will alcohol beverages be permitted in or around Camp Club activities. Any use of alcoholic beverages which in any way affects the staff member's efficiency in his work will be cause for immediate dismissal. (See Dismissal Policy.)

3. If these policies of conduct create problems for a prospective staff member, it is probable that the Buck Hill Camp Club is not the place the applicant would wish to seek employment.

COTTAGE LIVING QUARTERS

1. Staff members will live in the cottages of Buck Hill. Maid service, towels, soap, linens, and blankets are all furnished. (See Staff Housing in Staff Handbook for further information.)

2. There is no curfew and no reveille for Camp Club staffers living in Company cottages. However, personal habits considered detrimental to the Camp Club program or morale or the counselor's health are to be considered within the responsibility framework of the Camp Club Director.

3. The hours between 11:00 P.M. and 7:30 A.M. are quiet hours in these cottages:

    a. There should be no unnecessary talking or interroom visitation.

    b. Phonographs, musical instruments, or radios should not be played.

    c. During these hours all cottages are reserved for those who wish to sleep. Staff members who wish to visit, play cards, or participate in other activities from 11:00 P.M. to 7:30 A.M. are asked to do it elsewhere.

    d. Due consideration should be given to those who wish to rest or sleep at the cottages during other hours.

4. Horseplay is always forbidden in the Camp Club cottages. Loud talking or other undue noise which might be offensive to cottagers or other Buck Hillers is also out of place.

5. By directive of the company management, no sleeping on balconies or roofs is permitted at any time.

6. Extreme caution is requested in the use of irons and other electrical appliances and also by anyone who smokes in the cottages. Irons have been forbidden in our cottages until just recently because of a carelessly caused fire a few years ago.

7. Staff members are reminded to borrow only by asking in advance. Many misunderstandings in Camp Club cottages have come through "borrowing" without the permission of the person who owned the article.

8. The refrigerator and stove at Cottage 102 and the living room and games room may be used by any Camp Counselor or Assistant at any time from 7:30 A.M. to 11:00 P.M. The person is responsible to clean up any dishes, records, books, cards, tables and chairs, etc. immediately after use.

9. No male resident, other than the director, and no nonresident female should ever be in Cottage 16 between the hours of 11:00 P.M. and 7:30 A.M. No one is allowed to walk Cottage 16 residents to the door after 11:00 P.M. Strictly enforced company rules require that Cottage 16 residents returning after 11:00 P.M. be let out of the car and that the car should then go on.

10. If any resident of 102, 16, or 103 ever feels these guidelines could be improved or that one or more is unfair to him in any way, he should talk to the Camp Club Director concerning this; it will be assumed that he has accepted the responsibilities implied by these guidelines.

COUNSELOR DUTIES

1. All Camp Clubbers shall be under the immediate and direct supervision of a staff member at *all* times during Camp Club hours. This is the major reason there is a Camp Club. This means that staff members cannot be inside and children outside or vice versa. This means that staff members of younger children are responsible to see that the child gets with his parents at lunch and after swim. This means that ALL staff members must be at Camp Club at *8:45 or before* in the morning at Camp Club or the pool at *1:45 or before* in the afternoon. This means that Supervised lunch must be that (THE ITALICS ARE THE DIRECTOR'S TO EMPHASIZE THAT THIS IS A MOST IMPORTANT DUTY AND THE ONE THAT IF NEGLECTED FOR A MOMENT CAN HURT CAMP CLUB A GREAT DEAL).

2. Counselors are expected to check their notice box and staff bulletin board in the Director's office between 8:30 and 8:45 each morning and leave box empty after this check.

3. In the three lower age groups, Assistant Counselors and Counselors are expected to be on duty throughout the regular Camp Club no matter how many children are present. Any exceptions to this must be made in advance with the Director.

4. It will be the responsibility of the Counselors to see that the children are on time for the specific scheduled periods, that the Nature, Arts and Crafts, and Music Specialist meets with their groups, and that under usual circumstances they stay for the full Crafts, Nature, and Music period as scheduled.

5. During regular Camp Club duty hours, Nature, Music, and Crafts Specialists are expected to use any hours when Camp Clubbers are not scheduled for official planning and cleanup, or with permission of Director, to assist with the Camp Club swim program.

CRAFTS

1. Children must always be accompanied and attended by their counselor when entering or using Crafts Lodge, unless otherwise requested by Crafts Specialist. They will never be in the Crafts Lodge except at their scheduled group time unless arranged in advance by the Crafts Specialist.

2. Each counselor is expected to assist the Crafts Specialist in helping the campers to get a fuller crafts experience. No staff member or CIT is ever permitted to work in individual projects during Camp Club hours except by prior arrangement with the Camp Club Director.

3. Counselors may work on personal crafts projects after Camp Club hours by prior arrangement and under the supervision of the Crafts Counselor. All staff members will pay the wholesale cost of the materials they use *prior to this use.* Materials are priced by and bought from the Crafts Specialist.

4. Materials and equipment borrowed from the Crafts Lodge must be signed out through the Crafts Specialist and should be returned just as quickly as possible and immediately after use.

5. Each group using the Crafts Lodge is responsible for cleanup before leaving and immediately after use.

DINING ROOM AND GUESTS FOR ROOM AND MEAL AT THE BUCK HILL

1. Camp Club staff eats in Side Hall, the staff dining hall. Staff may eat in the Main Dining Room with guests, only by paying the full price for meals. Guests of staff may eat in Side Hall (at a rate lower than Main Dining Room rate) by buying a meal ticket at the Main Desk after getting approval from Side Hall Captain. The prices for meals for guests of staff members are as follows: Monday through Saturday—Breakfast, 89¢; Lunch, $1.46; Dinner, $1.78. Sunday—Breakfast, 89¢; Dinner, $1.78; Supper, $1.46.

2. With at least 24 hours prior approval by Camp Club Director, staff may normally have a guest at the Inn (25% discount) or a single guest in a staff cottage ($2.50 per night). It is of vital importance that advance clearance is received from Director and that guest and staff member fully understand the Company policy and procedures on this.

3. Horseplay and undue noise are out of place in Side Hall.

4. T-shirts without collars, tight slacks, short shorts, shirt tails hanging out are not permitted in Side Hall. Other casual clothing of a reasonable sort is always permitted for meals there.

5. Staff is urged to come for meals at least 15 minutes before the end of the serving hours to permit waitresses to clean up and finish their duties during their working hours. Otherwise staff can report for meals any time during the flexible, preannounced meal schedule.

DISMISSAL

1. In the case of gross misconduct, inability to fit into the Buck Hill traditions, and Camp Club policy, incompetency or other reasons which the Director deems sufficiently serious as to damage the efficiency of the Camp Club operations, a staff member may be dismissed by the Camp Club Director.

2. All dismissal notices are to be in writing, with reasons for dismissal clearly stated, and with the staff member always having the right of appeal to the General Manager of the Buck Hill Falls Company.

3. The notice period will be a minimum of seven days with pay. However, the Camp Club reserves the right to relieve the employee at once in case of gross misconduct.

EXTRA DUTIES

The following are the normal extra duties required of all staff members outside the regular Camp Club Day (8:45–12:00 Monday through Saturday; 1:45–4:30 Monday through Friday):

1. Each staff member will assist with a square dance or similar Camp-wide entertainment on an alternating basis (which would usually put the staffer on duty one evening every other week).

2. Three or four evening entertainment programs are usually given for parents and/or the community during the year, starting with that on the Fourth of July. Staff members are responsible for costumes for their children and decorations, usually improvised on a small budget provided by Camp Club. Also all staff are on duty for these occasions.

3. Each counselor (with a helper) is in charge at various times during the summer of supervised lunch from 12:00–2:00 P.M. when two to eight children bring their lunches and eat them on the back porch of Headquarters Building. The counselors supervise a lunch, rest period, and play period and normally eat box lunches from the Inn.

4. Intermediate, Junior, and Senior counselors are responsible for camping trips which range from two a season for Intermediate Boys to four or more a year for Seniors.

5. Twice a year, a horse show is held, and staff members are encouraged to attend. However, attendance is not mandatory.

THE INN

1. Camp Club staff is permitted to use the game rooms as long as they do not monopolize them, watch TV in either TV room, attend movies at staff rate, attend all free programs, musicals and lectures at the Inn, use the putting green without charge, buy anything in the Bluestone Room (grill—with variety of candy and drug needs) or Gift Shop.

2. Female staff members should not wear shorts or slacks in the Inn after 6:00 P.M. Male staff members should wear jacket and tie.

EMERGENCY LEAVE AND SICK LEAVE

1. In unusual circumstances, such as a death in the close family or other major emergency, emergency leave not to exceed three days with pay could be granted by the Director.

2. In harmony with the Standards of the American Camping Association, a staff member would be permitted a day's sick leave with pay for each two-week period during the Camp Club season, sick leave to be taken only in case of inability to fulfill Camp Club responsibilities and not to be carried over from season to season. Before Sick leave is granted and meals served without charge, the Director must be notified at the earliest possible moment and the Buck Hill nurse or doctor consulted.

LAUNDRY AND CLEANING

1. Laundry may be done free in community machines in the employee building at Buck Hill during the hours it is open. A 24-hour laundromat is located in Canadensis, 1 mile away. Commercial laundry is available, but even with staff discounts probably runs somewhat higher than you would have been accustomed to paying in nonresort areas.

2. A commercial cleaner is located less than a mile away from Buck Hill; rates are somewhat higher than in nonresort areas.

PAYMENT OF SALARY

1. Pay day is twice a month. However, Staff is reminded that the first pay day will not come until July 7 and thereafter on the 7th and 22nd of each month. Therefore, each staff member needs to bring along enough extra money to get him to this first pay period.

2. Income tax and social security are deducted from your gross salary.

MAIL

1. Camp Club has a mail box in the Post Office located in the Inn. All incoming mail is placed here. Mail comes in about twice a day and staffers may pick up their mail at the Post Office box or in their Camp Club notice box after it has been brought down by Camp Club Staff. The box number is 312.

SPORTS CLOSET

1. Games and equipment for Camp Club will be checked out by a group from the Sports Closet and returned when group is finished using the equipment. A Counselor will be placed in general charge of sports closet; only staff members will be permitted in the Sports Closet except under unusual circumstances approved by the Director.

SENIOR LODGE

1. Senior Lodge will be kept locked at all times except when a Counselor or Assistant Counselor is using it for Camp Club activity. Each Head Counselor who wishes to have one will be given a key to the building. Campers are never to be left in the Senior Lodge alone.

2. Each Counselor using Senior Lodge is responsible to see that all games, equipment and materials are thriftfully used whenever he is in the Lodge and that the Lodge is cleaned up by his group before they leave.

3. No campers are allowed to jump at any time from the platform to the floor just inside the side door of Senior Lodge, or to play in and around closets.

4. Counselors are permitted to use Senior Lodge at any time other events are not scheduled after Camp Club hours. Senior Lodge may be used for group parties with prior permission of the Director.

5. Any abuse of Senior Lodge or Camp Club equipment should be reported immediately to the Director.

6. When Senior Lodge is in use by two or more groups, every precaution must be taken to see that noise and confusion by one or more of the groups does not interfere with activities of another group. Patience and courtesy will pay great dividends in this situation.

SOCIAL SECURITY NUMBER

1. Any staff member under 18 (except CITs) is required to have Pennsylvania working papers. These are to be requested of Camp Club Director before May 15, signed by parent and sent along with birth certificate to Camp Club Director before June 1. Birth certificate will be returned later.

SWIMMING

1. All Counselors and Assistant Counselors, with the exception of Crafts Counselors, are expected to be at the pool on swim days by or before 1:45 P.M. and at their instruction positions by or before 1:55 P.M.

2. Children at the pool for the first time should be directed by their Morning Counselor to report to the Camp Club Swimming Head, who will be designated by a colored patch.

3. The Camp Club Swimming Head is in charge of supervision and efficiency of the swimming program and is delegated full responsibility by the Camp Club Director toward this end.

4. Every Counselor is assigned an instructional group. He is fully responsible for conduct and participation of this group from 2:00–3:00 P.M. Each preschool group will be designated by a colored patch also worn by the Counselor.

5. Each Counselor is responsible to get his entire group together at 3:00 P.M. for supervised play. He is solely responsible for his children. Should two or more groups combine, all Counselors of the combined groups combine, all Counselors of the combined groups would share in the planning and carrying out of supervised play. Supervised play games should be chosen with careful consideration of the fact that Camp Club is never more on display; games involving horseplay or roughness are strictly taboo.

Every care should be exercised to see that children do not run into or around sunbathers.

6. Every Counselor and Assistant Counselor will be on attentive and active duty during the Free Swim period as during the rest of the afternoon. Reading, knitting, writing, and any other activity which might seem to make the Counselor appear not on active duty will not be in the best interest of the Camp Club program.

7. Assignments for the Instructional Period and the Free Swim Period are made by the Camp Club Swimming Head with the overall program in mind; persons may be switched at the discretion of the Swimming Head. During the Free Swim period, swim breaks may be taken by the baby pool and shallow pool guards but should not last more than 15 minutes for any one person at one time. Either the Head Counselor or the Assistant should remain with his group at all times. Other counselors, whether watching from shore or pool, should be attentive at all times.

8. It is the responsibility of all counselors to see that children in their respective dressing rooms are aided when necessary and get out of the dressing room without undue delay both when coming for swim and leaving afterward.

9. Counselors are expected to deliver their own children to parents or leave them in the proper place. The Counselor's afternoon is not completed until dressing rooms are emptied of children under their responsibility and these children have been taken as expected by parents.

10. It is the responsibility of each Counselor to know the swimming ability of each child in his group and to see that he swims in an area of the pool in accord with his ability. The Counselor should see that the pool regulations are obeyed by his children, that all of his children are in sight at all times, and that none leave the immediate pool area without his permission.

11. No food is allowed in the swimming area. No running in the pool area. No swimming in the diving well except to swim away after dive. No horseplay in the pool or the pool area. Pushing in is prohibited.

12. Each Camp Club Counselor has free towel service and free use of the Camp Club lockers at the pool.

13. On every day when swimming is questionable for the younger children, a sign such as this will be posted at Camp Club: PRESCHOOL (SWIMMING OR CAMP CLUB); INT, JR, SR (SWIMMING). Two preschool Counselors will then take care of children at Camp Club who decide to go there, four at swimming. Counselors will rotate this responsibility always leaving either a Counselor or Assistant Counselor of each group at the pool.

14. Every Primary, Kindergarten, and Nursery child is to be given a red ribbon on the first day he reports to Camp Club. He will be told to report to Counselor with red ribbon (Swimming Head) that afternoon at the pool just after he dresses for swim. The Swimming Head will classify the child and give him the ribbon of his swimming group (ALL Camp Club guards will have the same color ribbon if in his area). He will continue to wear this ribbon until the close of swim or until he leaves pool area permanently, at which time he will give ribbon to Camp Club guard in his swimming area or his counselor. He will pick up ribbon each day when he reports dressed to swimming area. Each Intermediate, Junior, and Senior should be contacted by the Swimming Head during flag raising on his first day in Camp Club and given instructions about the use of the swimming area.

TEENAGE CLUB

1. On payment of $5, any teenage Camp Club staffer may become a member of the Guest's Teenage Club with full privileges to take part in the weekly open houses, trips, picnics, and many other planned activities.

TERMINATION OF AGREEMENT

1. Agreements (contracts) will be mailed out by the Director on or about February 1 to staff members already verbally contracted. Agreement, if returned within 10 days is binding on the Buck Hill Falls Company within the limits of company policy. However, with reasonable explanation, the staff member has the right to request release from contract without prejudice if requested before April 1.

2. The employment is for the full term of camp unless mutually agreed upon by camp director and staff member. Under unusual circumstances, staff member may terminate agreement during Camp Club season, giving a minimum of one week's notice and being paid for the number of days worked. However, this contract shall continue only as long as the employee complies with its terms. In case of resignation, worker is expected to do all in his power to protect the interests of Camp Club by leaving his work in good shape and by assisting in paving the way for his successor.

TRIPS AND CAMPING

1. Field trips and trips outside the Camp Club property are permitted with advance permission of Director. Group should also leave word with secretary when they are leaving and when returning, and notify secretary on return. Otherwise group should always be in Camp Club property area. Anytime a group leaves the Camp Club grounds, counselor should fill out an "Out-of-Camp Information Sheet".

2. Juniors may not take a camping trip of more than one night. Intermediates may not take a camping trip of more than one night and this must be on Camp Club property.

3. All campers are expected to do their share of the camping trip duties and chores. Violations of this should be reported to the Director, and campers will most likely be barred from the next camping trip.

4. At least two staff members will be on every camping trip. All boat trips will require life jackets to be worn by every camper while on the water in a canoe or rowboat, except by prior written permission of the parent.

5. The Counselor of the group is in full charge of a camping trip. Assistant Counselor orders and packs the food and equipment and is on the trip to assist the Group Counselor in any way that the Group Counselor requests.

6. Taps and reveille are to be strictly enforced as announced on camping trips. Violations are to be reported to the Director. Boys and girls are expected to be under the direct supervision of the Counselors at all times and are never to be allowed to leave the camp grounds except in unusual emergencies and then only when accompanied by a staff member.

7. Acts to frighten children or pranks such as snipe hunts, trips for keys to car locks, etc. are not permitted at any time. Ghost stories are not permitted at any time except with Senior Boys and with permission of the Director. All counselors should warn campers about rules on snipe hunts and similar tomfoolery.

8. Other than the regular installation of the Tribes, Camp Club does not permit initiation of any kind. This should be made clear to all campers and any disobedience of this rule should be reported immediately to the Director.

TUTORING AND BABYSITTING

1. There are often tutoring and baby sitting opportunities (at $4 per hour and $1.50 per hour respectively). All these positions go through the Camp Club secretary and this staff member keeps a record of all staff members interested in tutoring and babysitting and their specialties.

OTHER REMINDERS

1. *Weather*—It has a habit of getting cold in the evening at Buck Hill and occasionally for three or four days straight. Staff members in the past have asked that this be stressed in advance so that each new staff member can be forewarned. For comfort, warm clothes are a must for these rare days and common nights.

2. *Opening camp and closing camp*—A routine responsibility of all staff members who report before the Monday camp officially opens for children, is to join together to carry chairs, tables, clean windows, floors, and other odds and ends of getting camp set up.

A routine responsibility of all staff members who stay through closing day is to work until about 2:00 P.M. that day repacking chairs, tables, etc. and completely clearing out several of the Camp Club quarters.

It is most necessary that, except in emergency, any person unable to take part in this setup and cleanup operation see for certain that the Director understands this far in advance. Both operations are small jobs for a group, almost impossible jobs for one or two.

3. *Plays and games*—At no time are children allowed on roofs, up trees, in other potentially dangerous places during Camp Club activities.

It is the responsibility of the Nursery, Kindergarten, and Primary Counselors to keep all toys out of the playground areas after regular Camp Club mornings (or afternoons when children are at Camp Club). Children should consider it their responsibility to leave their playground in reasonable neat order after use.

All games are meant to entertain children, not Counselors. Counselors need to beware of games getting counselor- and CIT-centered rather than camper-centered. Counselors play in games only insofar as their participation encourages more campers to participate also. Counselors are never to dominate games.

Children are not allowed to stand in swings or merry-go-round or to go down backward on the slide.

4. *Early arrivals*—Many employees' children arrive before Camp Club time each morning. They are expected to stay outside the building until their counselor arrives.

5. *Other odds and ends*—As in any camp or school situation, other duties and unforeseeable problems come up which are not covered in any policy booklet. It will be the attempt of the Director to keep these to a minimum. It is the responsibility of anyone signing a contract with Camp Club to bring anything which might affect the morale or smooth operation of Camp Club to the attention of the Director.

GRIEVANCE PROCEDURE

We at Camp Club believe in an "open door" policy in regard to complaints that any staff member may deem essential to the overall efficiency of Camp Club. Consequently, any staff member may feel free to come in and informally present his views to the Director.

Buck Hill Camp Club, Buck Hill Falls, Pennsylvania: An informational booklet for all staff members

Bob Cipriano, Director

WHAT IS THE CAMP CLUB?

The Camp Club of Buck Hill Falls, Pa., is a day camp for approximately 150 children from 2½ to 13 years of age. The camp is located about a three hour drive from both Philadelphia and New York City on an imaginary triangle connecting the two cities with Buck Hill.

As part of the Buck Hill Falls Company, the Camp Club is a day camp operated for the children of guests of the Inn at Buck Hill Falls, the cottagers who live in the complex surrounding the Inn, and children of Company employees. The Inn at Buck Hill Falls is the largest resort hotel in Pennsylvania (10,000 acres).

A trained staff of approximately 25 Counselors will supervise a widely diversified, highly individualistic and meaningful day-camp program for children in the above mentioned age groups. The day camp is open daily from 9:00 A.M. to noon and 2:00 P.M. to 4:30 P.M. Mondays through Fridays, and Saturdays from 9:00 A.M. to noon. The children will be divided in the following groups:

AGE	GROUP
2½–4½	Nursery
5	Kindergarten
6	Primary
7–8	Intermediate*
9–10	Junior*
11–13	Senior*

WHAT ARE THE STAFF POSITIONS AT CAMP CLUB?

Head Counselors	(Usually female) for the following groups: Nursery, Kindergarten, Primary, Intermediate Girls, Junior Girls, Senior Girls.

*Separate groups for boys and girls at these levels. An attempt will be made to maintain a ratio of 10 campers to one Counselor in all groups.

Head Counselors	(male) for the following groups: Intermediate Boys, Junior Boys, Senior Boys.
Asst. Counselors	(Usually female) for the following groups: Nursery, Kindergarten, Primary.
Crafts Specialist	(male or female)
Camping and Grounds Specialist	(usually male)
Nature Specialist	(usually male)
Music Specialist	(male or female)
Secretary	(female)
Counselors-in-Training	(male and female)
Asst. Counselors-in-Training	(male and female)
Roving Counselor	(male and female)
Super Activity Specialist	(usually male)

WHAT ARE SOME OF THE PRIVILEGES INCLUDED IN EACH CONTRACT?

• Room @ $10 per week	$100.00
• Board @ $80 per week	800.00
• Golf privileges @ $160 per season	160.00
• Tennis privileges @ $5 per season	5.00
• Swimming privileges @ $15 per season	15.00
• Maid and linen service @ $7 per week	70.00
• Reduced rate at movies, app. 50¢ per week	5.00
• Free laundry, app. $2.00 per week	20.00

• Free leisure time use of shufflleboard, croquet, TV, pool table, ping pong, games room, lawn bowling.

• Free admission to many lyceums and lectures held regularly at the Inn.

• Access to famous summer stock theater 1 mile from the Inn—famous stars and plays at summer stock rates.

• Fellowship and friendship with some of the finest staff members you'll ever meet anywhere.

• Total approximate market value—more than	$1,185.00

When is Camp Club season?

Begins about 15 each summer for all Counselors

Closes about September 1 for all Counselors

WHAT IS THE USUAL STAFF DAY AT THE BUCK HILL CAMP CLUB?

8:30– 8:45	Prepare for campers
9:00– 9:10	Flag raising and opening ceremonies
9:10–10:00	Activities planned by counselors for each age group

10:00–10:30	Midmorning lunch (light snack provided by Camp Club; given to Nursery, Kind., Pri. and Intermediate groups)
10:30–12:00	Activities planned by counselors for age group

During these morning periods, some of the children will leave for private golf, swimming, tennis, and horseback lessons. Groups will often go under Head Counselor supervision to receive instruction in Nature, Music, and Crafts Counselor. All of these extras are scheduled in advance on a regular basis.

12:00– 2:00	Break for all Counselors except two on supervised lunch duty.
2:00– 3:00	Swimming instruction period at pool, with supervision by Counselors.
3:00– 3:30	Quiet activity period planned by Counselors
3:30– 4:30	Free swimming at pool with supervision by Counselors.
4:30– 8:30 next morning	Normally free time for Counselors
Saturday noon to Monday 8:30 A.M.	Normally free time for Counselors.

WHAT ARE OTHER STAFF DUTIES?

- Square Dance once every other week
- Occasional campfires and Indian ceremonies
- Supervised lunch (12 noon–2:00 including supervised quiet play period; Counselors assigned on a rotating basis).
- Weekly staff meetings
- Special activities (Staff parties, talent show, Camp Club operetta, etc.)
- Twice-a-summer Sunday afternoon horse shows (optional)
- Camping trips (Usually Junior and Senior boys and girls are the only groups which plan periodic camps outside of grounds. Intermediate boys and girls have two camping trips each summer on Camp Club grounds).
- Special events include golf, tennis and swimming tournaments, a Fourth of July parade and pageant, track and field days, and all outside attractions that the Director and counselors feel will be meaningful.

WHAT ARE THE GENERAL REQUIREMENTS FOR ALL STAFF MEMBERS?

If you cannot answer all these questions with an unqualified YES, you would probably not be happy or a satisfactory Counselor on the Camp Club staff.

1. Do I sincerely enjoy working with and for children?

2. Can I emotionally accept the disappointments and problems of working with children, parents, and fellow staff members without having these disappointments adversely affect my overall efficiency as a counselor?

3. As I plan and carry out the program of activities with my children can I place foremost the traditions and rules of Camp Club, the necessity of safety first, and the importance of the very best public relations?

4. Am I willing to accept extra responsibilities and duties when deemed necessary and advisable by the Camp Club director?

5. Am I prepared, while under contract to Camp Club, to give full loyalty and cooperation to camp-wide policy and decisions, accepting them as my own after they are finally made?

6. Am I sincerely interested in what I can do for Camp Club as a staff member rather than what Camp Club can do for me?

7. Can I take suggestions and criticisms with understanding rather than resentment?

Our staff philosophy is that most probably a staff member who does not accept the above responsibilities in print and fully put them in practice would not fit into the Camp Club staff as it is now organized. Please consider this carefully before you complete an application or sign a contract with Camp Club.

WHERE IS THE INN AT BUCK HILL FALLS?

Martz buses from Philadelphia to Swiftwater, planes to the Wilkes-Barre-Scranton and Allentown-Bethlehem-Easton airports are met on request.

Delaware Valley Transportation Company buses go directly from Philadelphia to the Inn.

Private autos are allowed.

WHAT ABOUT STAFF HOUSING?

Women live at a cottage near the Inn, which has a living room, dining room, and kitchen. Men live at a cottage near the Inn. Linens, towels, and maid service are provided.

The Camp Club and the Inn are within short walking distance of all staff residence facilities.

WHAT ABOUT MEALS?

The Camp Club Staff eats in the Staff Dining Room just off the Main Dining Room of the Inn. Food is the same as that served Inn guests (at $15 a day). In the opinion of many Inn guests and past Camp Club staff members, there is no better food in any large resort hotel in the USA.

WHAT ARE THE DUTIES AND REQUIREMENTS FOR STAFF POSITIONS?

Head Counselors

GENERAL RESPONSIBILITIES

1. Plan and supervise morning Camp Club activity program for counselor's group of children.

2. Help supervise swimming program in the afternoon (2:00–4:30) or be ready with alternate activities in case swimming program is cancelled because of weather.

3. Take turns serving with supervised lunch period.

4. Help plan and carry out special Camp Club events, such as Junior Olympics, Christmas in July, etc.

5. Help with periodic Camp Club square dances.

6. Such other responsibilities as may be assigned by Camp Club Director.

REQUIREMENTS FOR CAMP CLUB HEAD COUNSELORS:

1. Four years of college or the equivalent in experience significant for day camping.

2. Emotional maturity and integrity.

3. Enjoyment of out-of-door living.

4. Liking for children and deep satisfaction in working with and for them.

Music Specialist

GENERAL RESPONSIBILITIES

1. Overall direction of music program for Camp Club, including Staff talent show, leading of group singing, and periodic camp-wide music shows.

2. Cooperation with and leadership of other camp activities as requested by the Director.

REQUIREMENTS: SAME AS HEAD COUNSELOR.

Nature Specialist

1. The overall operation of nature program for Camp Club.

2. Supervision, in cooperation with Director, of the purchase of all nature supplies.

3. Cooperation with, and leadership of, other camp activities as requested by Camp Club Director.

REQUIREMENTS: SAME AS HEAD COUNSELOR.

Arts and Crafts Specialist

GENERAL RESPONSIBILITIES

1. Development and operation of a well-planned program of arts and crafts for all Camp Club age groups.

2. Supervision, in cooperation with Director, of the purchase of all crafts supplies.

3. Cooperation with, and leadership of, other camp activities as requested by Camp Club director.

4. Supervision of crafts program and crafts training program for Camp Club staff.

REQUIREMENTS: SAME AS HEAD COUNSELOR

Assistant Counselors

GENERAL RESPONSIBILITIES

1. Assist Head Counselors in all their general responsibilities as listed above.

2. Other responsibilities as may be assigned by the Camp Club Director.

REQUIREMENTS FOR ASSISTANT COUNSELORS

1. At least 19 years of age or unusual maturity in working with children.

2. Two years of college education or equivalent in experience significant for day camping.

3. Emotional maturity and integrity.

4. Enjoyment of out-of-doors living.

Counselors-in-Training

GENERAL RESPONSIBILITIES

1. Assistance in many areas of Camp Club activities and plans.

2. Responsible leadership and dependability in many training activities.

REQUIREMENTS:

1. At least 14 years of age.

2. Mature and capable of taking an active role in the responsibilities of the CIT program.

Assistant Counselors-in-Training

REQUIREMENTS:

1. 13 years of age.

2. Same as Counselors-In-Training.

Sample Expenditure Budget
January 1–December 31

OBJECT CLASSIFICATION	ADMINIS-TRATION	ATHLETICS	BUILDINGS AND CENTERS	SWIMMING POOLS	PLAY-GROUNDS	SPECIAL ACTIVITIES	TOTAL
1000 Personal services							
1100 Regular salaries	$18,258	$ 5,700	$21,800	—	$ 7,400	$ 4,800	$ 57,958
1200 Temporary salaries	480	3,400	9,400	12,514	43,600	5,590	74,984
1300 Other (consultants etc.)	—	—	—	—			
2000 Contractical services	3,546	255	7,451	3,387	2,541	906	18,086
2100 Communication and transportation							
2200 Heat, light, power							
2300 Printing, etc.							
2400 Subsistence, care, and support (animals, vehicles, persons)							
3000 Commodities							
3110 Office	3,225	1,460	5,139	3,478	6,148	1,560	21,010
3120 Fuel							

Account							
3130 Food							
3140 Supplies (pro-grams)							
3150 Materials							
3160 Repairs							
4000 Current charges	350	134	320	475	195	75	1,549
4100 Rents							
4200 Insurance							
4300 Memberships (e.g., NRPA)							
5000 Current Obligations	5,000	—	16,750	—	—	—	21,750
5100 Interest							
5200 Pensions and retirement							
5300 Grants and subisidies							
6000 Properties	380	1,635	6,200	—	3,056	760	12,031
6100 Equipment							
6200 Buildings and improvements							
7000 Debt payments	—	—	—	—			
7100 Bonds							
Totals	$31,239	$12,584	$67,060	$19,854	$62,940	$13,691	$207,368

Income analysis book

ACCOUNT TITLE: GOLF COURSES

SUBTITLE:

NUMBER: 4B   Year Ending _____ 19 ___

DATE	DESCRIPTION	RECEIVED FROM	TOTAL	TAXES	RIGHTS AND PRIVILEGES	FEES AND CHARGES	SALES OF SERVICES	SALES OF COMMODITIES	BORROWINGS
7/12	Players permits		$54.00			$54.00			
7/12	Season tickets		45.00			45.00			
7/13	Refreshment sales		21.00					$21.00	
7/13	Golf lessons		12.50				$12.50		
7/13	Club rental		11.00		$11.00				
7/13	Players permit		68.00			68.00			

Expenditure ledger

ACCOUNT TITLE: PERSONAL SERVICES
SUBTITLE: SAL. AND WAGS.-REG.
NUMBER: 1110

(LEADERSHIP) YEAR ENDING _____ 19 _____

					FACILITIES					SPECIAL SERVICES		
DATE	VOUCHER OR CHECK NUMBER	PAYEE	TOTAL EXP.	ADMINISTRATION	PLAY-GDS.	INDOOR CENTERS	BEACHES	ATHLETIC FIELDS	GOLF COURSES	COMMUNITY ATHLETICS	ARTS AND CRAFTS	COMMUNITY MUSIC
7/15	10659	J. M. Jones	$52.00	$52.00								
7/15	10660	R. T. Smith	28.00		$12.00	$10.00		$6.00				
7/22	10841	T. N. Clark	34.00								$34.00	
7/22	10842	W. R. Wilson	45.00		25.00	20.00						

Expenditure ledger

ACCOUNT TITLE: PLAYGROUNDS
SUBTITLE: TB

YEAR ENDING _____ 19 _____

				SERVICES-PERSONAL								
				SALARIES-WAGES REGULAR		SALARIES-WAGES TEMPORARY						
DATE	VOUCHER OR CHECK NUMBER	PAYEE	TOTAL EXP.	LEADERSHIP	OTHER	LEADERSHIP	OTHER	OTHER COMPS.	SERVICES CONTRACTUAL	COMMODITIES	CURRENT CHARGES	CURRENT OBLIGATIONS
7/15	10670	D. O. Smith	$38.00	$38.00								
7/16	10661	Horton Co.	82.00						$20.00	$62.00		
7/16	10683	Gas Co.	11.00						11.00			
7/17	10691	R. A. Jones	29.00		$29.00							
7/17	10695	Hendrix Realty Co.	62.00						18.00		$62.00	
7	99	J. T. Wilson	18.00						18.00			

PPBS in recreation management*

As part of Planning Associates' continuing recreation management research, the Consultants have been recommending careful study of the Planning, Program, Budgeting System (PPBS) adopted by the federal government. The PPBS is of particular interest to us as recreation planners because our clients are constantly under pressure to evaluate their programs, examine the budget allocations, and ensure that recreation indeed serves all residents.

PPBS gives local government a very effective system for evaluating its program and resultant financial resource allocations. PPBS is ideally suited to managing government and organization operations where the normal profit measurement is not available for guidance and decision making. PPBS fully accounts for all costs and expenses of operation and allocates them to the consuming activity or program. Thus, a proper share of overall administration costs, building maintenance, service expenses and the like are determined and prorated to each activity. In contrast, a conventional line-item budget fails to distinguish costs for individual activities but rather lumps all costs in general budget categories. Under PPBS, an activity such as baseball would include program supervision, area (ball field), operations (maintenance), and administration, supplies, debt service, awards and trophies, and a share of other overhead administrative expense—in short, any cost properly related to the overall operation of the baseball activity. Under conventional budgeting, ball-field maintenance would be buried in a category for facilities' maintenance and would be impossible to individually identify or describe.

When it is properly implemented, PPBS quickly and clearly identifies the actual overall costs of *each program element* as a portion of the total recreation budget. This allows and encourages comparisons of program "benefits" simultaneously with its full costs and enables full and meaningful program evaluation. If, for example, the baseball program was consuming 43% of the recreation department budget but had somewhat less than commensurate interest or attendance, the Recreation Director would know that a reevaluation of the program and community interests was necessary. With conventional budget categories such objective analysis are all but impossible because the total program costs are not clearly known.

Use of PPBS can help ensure the municipality or agency the greatest amount of recreation effectiveness for its budget dollars. The following example should illustrate the advantages of PPBS.

BUDGET

Baseball league   PPBS **Year 19xx**
Direct (consumer-oriented) expenses
Supervision costs (line) $15,000

*Mimeographed publication provided by Arthur H. Mittelstaedt, Jr., Recreation Planner, and Allen Wurzbach, Recreation Research. Also published in *Communique* (Arlington, Va.: Copyright © National Recreation and Park Association, 1972).

Operation costs (line)
   Programs $ 5,000
   Supplies   4,000
   Maintenance   10,000
   Equipment   2,000   21,000

	$	
Operation costs (line)		
Programs	5,000	
Supplies	4,000	
Maintenance	10,000	
Equipment	2,000	21,000
Total direct costs		$36,000
Indirect (nonconsumer-oriented) expenses		
Operation costs (staff)		
Personnel	$ 2,000	
Program support (office, telephone, utilities prorated)	1,000	$ 3,000
Administration costs (agency charges prorated		
Financing	$ 3,000	
Insuring	500	3,500
Total indirect costs		$ 7,000
Total direct and indirect costs		43,000

Ice skating (hockey) team
Direct (consumer-oriented) expenses

	$	
Supervision costs (line)		$ 9,500
Operation costs (line)		
Programs	$ 6,000	
Supplies	2,500	
Maintenance	5,500	14,000
Total direct costs		$23,500

Indirect (nonconsumer-oriented expenses

	$	
Supervision costs (staff)		
Personnel	$ 2,000	
Program support (offices, telephone, utilities prorated)	1,000	
		$ 3,000
Administration costs (agency charges prorated)		
Financing	$ 4,000	
Insuring	500	4,500
Total indirect costs		$ 7,500

Senior Citizens' Club
Direct (consumer-oriented expenses

	$	
Supervision costs (line)		$10,000
Operation costs (line)		
Programs	$ 4,000	
Supplies	1,500	
Maintenance	2,400	

Equipment		1,000	8,900
Total direct costs				$18,900

Indirect (nonconsumer-oriented) expenses

Operation costs

Personnel (staff prorated)	$ 2,000	
Program support (offices, telephone, utilities prorated)	1,600	$ 3,600

Administration costs (agency charges prorated)

Financing	$ 1,100	
Insuring	400	3,500
Total indirect costs			$ 7,100
Total direct and indirect costs			$26,000

Recapitulation

Baseball league	$ 43,000
Ice skating (hockey) team	31,000
Senior citizens' club	26,000
Total costs	$100,000

In conclusion, the contrast with the traditional line-item budget is apparent. PPBS gives users a superlative management tool. It is ideally suited to analyzing actual costs and then relating costs to program outcome. In this way, the benefits of the program expenditure can be simultaneously compared with costs. This comparison also relates the expenditures to the program objectives, thus giving a measure of recreation effectiveness. All of these "benefits" are unavailable in the line item budget, yet it would seem that this information is invaluable in recreation management decisionmaking. PPBS is one of the many useful modern management techniques to be derived from systems analysis.

MODULE 10

Supervised
field work

Interpretations

The National Recreation Education Accreditation Project on standards and evaluative criteria, sponsored by the National Recreation and Park Association Board on Professional Education, indicates that professional laboratory experiences should enable students to obtain competencies to relate theory to practice. Logically, this objective can best be obtained through a *progression* of laboratory experiences. Upon interpretation of this objective, members of the project wrote that:

a. Guided observations of recreation and park programs in operation under professional leadership. At least two different settings such as municipal, state, institution, voluntary agency, should be included.

b. Practical professional experiences in conjunction with course work, for example, preparing a layout for a recreation area; conducting an activity program for the physically handicapped; working with a group of senior citizens; assistance with a resident outdoor education program.

307

c. Written analysis of the program and facilities of a recreation and park department or agency in conjunction with course work.[1]

Sessoms, Meyer, and Brightbill wrote that professional preparation in recreation at the undergraduate level should provide students with "practical experience through internships and supervised field practice."[2] In addition, a Field Work Information Manual developed by the Department of Human Kinetics and Leisure Studies at George Washington University depicts the practicum program as constituting three distinct levels of experience: (1) observation, (2) participation, and (3) fieldwork.[3] Each level of experience should be presented to students in a logical and sequential manner in degrees of continuity. Ideally, each level should build upon experiences learned in previous levels:

> Each level allows the student a different type of personal and academic involvement in learning, and each supplements and complements didactic activities, including textbooks, class assignments, formal papers and research activities.[4]

Kraus and Bates quoted from the Field Work Manual of the Western Illinois University at Macomb:

> One of the most difficult and yet one of the most important adjustments for the graduating senior from a curriculum in recreation and park administration is the application of what he has studied at the college or university to the "live" situation in the "real world." The recreation and park laboratory field experience is designed to provide an opportunity for practical application of classroom theory in professional field work before graduation. The student should acquire experience in recreation and park planning, leadership, supervision, and program evaluation by working in a private or public recreation and/or park agency under highly trained personnel in the local department and university faculty supervision.[5]

A written guide, with its materials updated and reevaluated regularly, is of importance in the operational efficiency of the laboratory experi-

---

[1]National Recreation Education Accreditation Project, rev. (Washington, D.C.: NRPA Board on Professional Education, Standards and Evaluative Criteria, September, 1971), p. 17.

[2]H. Douglas Sessoms, Harold D. Meyer, and Charles K. Brightbill, *Leisure Services: The Organized Recreation and Park System* (Englewood Cliffs, N.J.: Prentice-Hall, 1975), p. 325.

[3]*Field Work Information Manual.* (George Washington University, Department of Human Kinetics and Leisure Studies), p. 1.

[4]Ibid.

[5]Richard G. Kraus and Barbara J. Bates, *Recreation Leadership and Supervision: Guidelines for Professional Development* (Philadelphia: W. B. Saunders, 1975), p. 101.

ences. This written guide is usually in the form of a manual. Students, faculty, and agency supervisors should thoroughly familiarize themselves with this manual. Written materials included in the manual should encompass the following:

1. Philosophy of laboratory experiences
2. Goals of laboratory experiences
3. Objectives of laboratory experiences
4. Forms, records, and reports to be submitted
5. Delineation of responsibilities of the student, the academic institution, and the field experience agency
6. Evaluation criteria
7. General policies and procedures aimed at familiarizing all parties with the laboratory experiences
8. Field work site and placement criteria/procedures
9. Specific requirements for students to complete in addition to working at field site

A supervised field experience is considered the third phase of the continuum comprising laboratory experiences. It is a partnership between the student, academic institution, and recreation and park agency. A supervised work experience should enable students to synthesize, transfer, and apply academic experiences in a setting similar to that associated with professional employment. It affords a student preprofessional training in an area of specialization that will become a career situation. The field work experience in leisure services is analogous to "Student Teaching Experience" in the teaching profession.

An essential competency for students, as outlined by members of the National Recreation Education Accreditation Project, is the "ability to function as a student practitioner in a recreation and park system assuming assigned responsibility, showing appropriate initiative, and contributing to the staff effort effectively."[6] Weiskopf indicates that "Field work offers the student-leader laboratory situations in which he is confronted with practical situations. Field work should be a cooperative effort between the student, the institution, and the agency or department he is working for."[7]

Students have recounted on numerous occasions, both in formal seminar sessions and in informal advisement, the significance of super-

[6]National Recreation Education Accreditation Project, p. 18.

[7]Donald D. Weiskopf, *A Guide to Recreation and Leisure* (Boston: Allyn & Bacon, 1975), p. 311.

vised field work. Most students are in accord that field work is the single most important component of their education. Kraus and Bates further substantiate this concept:

> At a national professional preparation conference sponsored by the American Association for Health, Physical Education and Recreation, it was emphasized that professional competencies in recreation can best be developed through meaningful laboratory experiences.[8]

The National Recreation and Park Association sponsored a forum on "Educating for Tomorrow's Leaders" in which it was recommended that field work become an integral part of the professional preparation of recreation personnel. Verhoven indicates that:

> Prerequisite to adequate preparation for a professional career is a proportionate amount of on-the-job experience under the supervision of competent and qualified personnel. The effectiveness of blending classroom course work with practical experience has been proved time and again.[9]

A supervised field work experience affords each student an opportunity to gain knowledge and attitudes necessary for successful job performance. It exposes the student to the real world of work in a variety of leisure agencies. The student learns to assume responsibility, gain good work habits, and develop personality, poise, and confidence in a job. In addition, the student will acquire skill in getting along with fellow workers, employers, and people he is serving. Although earning money is not the primary objective of a supervised field work experience, it is recommended that the student receive wages commensurate with the agency's hiring policies. However, the failure of a leisure agency to pay students should not be the sole criterion for placing or not placing students. Each student will discover the relationship between educational preparation and job success. Students will have a chance to explore and broaden their knowledge of many different job possibilities in the leisure fields. Therefore, they will gain a wide range of experiences in a variety of leisure agencies. Students will also be able to accurately and objectively ascertain specific areas of strengths and weaknesses, determine operational efficiency of a vast array of leisure agencies, and bridge the gap between the didactic and the practical.

---

[8]Kraus and Bates, *Recreation Leadership and Supervision,* p. 97.

[9]Peter Verhoven, ed., *Educating Tomorrow's Leaders* (Washington, D.C.: National Recreation and Park Association, 1968), p. 35.

DEFINITIONS

• *Observation:* may take place in class during a demonstration of a particular programming technique, type of equipment or testing procedure, or it may occur on-site, when students visit an agency to learn about the operation and service delivery system. Observation is a learning experience of low-level involvement.[10]

• *Participation:* students may take part in role playing activities, problem solving exercises, sensitivity encounters, or in similar training and learning techniques. They may present a paper or project in the manner in which they would address a professional body or citizens group. They may conduct programs at leisure facilities or may demonstrate techniques and methods for recreators and/or parents. This on-site approach, along with the classroom experience previously articulated, brings students closer to the realities of a professional environment. This is a higher level of involvement than observation.[11]

• *Field Work:* brings the student into the professional world in a supervised situation through which he or she has an opportunity to achieve a synthesis, transfer, and application of the academic experience in a setting similar to that associated with professional employment.[12]

Mundy indicates that field work is:

> That phase of professional education in recreation and parks in which the student is placed in an off-campus field setting for an extended period of time under the supervision of both a practicing professional employed by a cooperating agency and a college representative. This experience serves as part of the student's formal academic preparation, and comprises a substantial part, or the entire course load, of the student for the academic semester during which the experience is scheduled.[13]

Student assignments

This part consists of eight objectives. You will be called upon to demonstrate your mastery of each objective. Some answers will require a written response. Some responses are of a demonstrable nature;

[10]Field Work Information Manual, p. 1.

[11]Ibid.

[12]Ibid., p. 2.

[13]Clair Jean Mundy, "A Descriptive Study of Selected Practices in the Administration and Supervision of Field Work Programs in Selected Four-Year Recreation and Park Curricula." (Ed.D. diss., Columbia University, 1972), pp. 9–12; cited in Kraus and Bates, *Recreation Leadership and Supervision*, p. 98.

that is, you will demonstrate use of specific forms applicable for field work. Success in field work is highly reliant upon each student's ability to transfer academic experiences to an employment (job) setting.

OBJECTIVE	ACHIEVEMENT OF COMPETENCY
1. To describe or demonstrate use of forms needed to initiate supervised field work.	Correctly fill out, describe, and/or demonstrate use of the following six forms needed to initiate supervised field work experience: Community Survey Form, Student Interest and Application Form, Cooperative Station Job Order Form, Field Work Placement Supervisor Confirming Initial Interview, Agency Acceptance of Supervised Field Work Student, and Agency Assignment Sheet.
2. To describe or demonstrate use of field work/site evaluation forms.	Identify, describe and/or demonstrate use of the following six field work site/evaluation forms: Time Reports, Program Coordinator Visitation Records, Agency Supervisor Evaluation Form, Field Work Student Weekly Field Report, Field Work Student Daily Activity Report, and Program Coordinator Evaluation Form.
3. To write an evaluation of the supervised field work experience.	Write an evaluation of the supervised field work experience in terms of the group, the agency, and the total personal experience and/or knowledge acquired.
4. To identify your own strengths and weaknesses in recreation settings.	Identify a minimum of three strengths and weaknesses in a variety of recreation settings.
5. To indicate differences between observation, participation, and field work.	Differentiate between observation, participation, and field work.
6. To write a definition of field work.	Write a definition of field work.
7. To describe a progression of laboratory experiences.	Write a minimum of 100 words describing a progression of laboratory experiences.

OBJECTIVE	ACHIEVEMENT OF COMPETENCY
8. To describe advantages of field work.	Verbally describe advantages and benefits of field work.

Resources

This part is divided into two sections: (1) a list of reference materials and (2) a problem-solving activity.

TEXTBOOKS

BANNON, JOSEPH J. *Problem Solving in Recreation and Parks*. Englewood Cliffs, N.J.: Prentice-Hall, 1972.

BUTLER, GEORGE D. *Introduction to Community Recreation*. New York: McGraw-Hill, 1967.

CORBIN, H. DAN and TAIT, WILLIAM J. *Education for Leisure*. Englewood Cliffs, N.J.: Prentice-Hall, 1973.

HEITMANN, HELEN M., and KNEER, MARIAN E. *Physical Education Instructional Techniques: An Individualized Humanistic Approach*. Englewood Cliffs, N.J.: Prentice-Hall, 1976.

HJELTE, GEORGE, and SHIVERS, JAY S. *Public Administration of Recreational Services*. Philadelphia: Lea and Febiger, 1972.

KIMBRELL, GRADY, and VINEYARD, BEN S. *Strategies for Implementing Work Experience Programs*. Bloomington, Ill.: McKnight and McKnight, 1972.

KRAUS, RICHARD. *Recreation Today: Program Planning and Leadership*. New York: Appleton-Century-Crofts, 1966.

————. *Recreation and Leisure in Modern Society*. New York: Appleton-Century-Crofts, 1971.

————. *Therapeutic Recreation Service Principles and Practices*. Philadelphia: W. B. Saunders, 1973.

KRAUS, RICHARD G., and BATES, BARBARA J. *Recreation Leadership and Supervision: Guidelines for Professional Development*. Philadelphia: W. B. Saunders, 1975.

SESSOMS, H. DOUGLAS; MEYER, HAROLD D.; and BRIGHTBILL, CHARLES K. *Leisure Services*. Englewood Cliffs, N.J.: Prentice-Hall, 1975.

TILLMAN, ALBERT. *The Program Book for Recreation Professionals*. Los Angeles: National Press Books, 1973.

WEISKOPF, DONALD C. *A Guide to Recreation and Leisure*. Boston: Allyn & Bacon, 1975.

FILMS

Careers in Recreation. Chicago: The Athletic Institute.

Cast No Shadow. Universal City, Ca.: Professional Arts, Inc.

Of Time, Work and Leisure. Bloomington, Ind.: Indiana University, Audio-Visual Center.

UNPUBLISHED MANUSCRIPTS

BERRYMAN, DORIS. "Development of Educational Programs for New Careers in Recreation Services for the Disabled." Washington, D.C.: US Department of Health, Education and Welfare, Office of Education, Bureau of Research, 1971.

————. "Training Paraprofessionals for New Careers in Recreation Services to the Disabled." Washington, D.C.: US Department of Health, Education and Welfare, Office of Education, Bureau of Research, September, 1971.

"Careers in Parks and Recreation." Washington, D.C.: US Department of Health, Education and Welfare, Office of Education, 1971.

CIPRIANO, ROBERT E. "A Career Education Program With Competency Based Mini-Courses for Entry Level Positions in Therapeutic Recreation." Ed.D. dissertation, New York University, 1974.

"Fieldwork Information Manual." Therapeutic Recreation and Adapted Physical Education, Department of Human Kinetics and Leisure Studies, The George Washington University, 1975.

"Guidelines for Professional Preparation Programs for Personnel Involved in Physical Education and Recreation for the Handicapped." Washington, D. C.: American Association for Health, Physical Education, and Recreation, February, 1973.

MUNDY, CLAIR JEAN. "A Descriptive Study of Selected Practices in the Administration and Supervision of Field Work Programs in Selected Four-Year Recreation and Park Curricula." Ed.D. dissertation, Teachers College, Columbia University, 1972.

National Recreation Education Accreditation Project. Sponsored by the National Recreation and Park Association Board on Professional Education, Standards and Evaluative Criteria, Revision, September, 1971.

Recreation Program Leadership: A Suggested Two-Year Post High School Curriculum. Washington, D. C.: US Department of Health, Education and Welfare, Office of Education, 1969.

VERHOVEN, PETER, ed. *Educating Tomorrow's Leaders*. Washington, D.C.: National Recreation and Park Association, 1968.

VERHOVEN, PETER J., and VINTON, DENNIS A. *Career Education for Leisure Occupations.* Washington, D.C.: US Department of Health, Education and Welfare, Office of Education, December, 1972.

Vocational Education: The Bridge Between Man and His Work. Washington, D.C.: US Department of Health, Education and Welfare, General Report of the Advisory Council on Vocational Education, 1968.

ARTICLES

BALL, EDITH L. "Academic Preparation for Therapeutic Recreation Personnel," *Therapeutic Recreation Journal,* vol. 2 (fourth quarter, 1968), pp. 13–19.

BERRYMAN, DORIS. "Manpower for Therapeutic Recreation Services," *Recreation in Treatment Centers,* vol. 3 (September 1964), p. 24.

FRYE, VIRGINIA. "Crisis-Challenge-Change in Personnel Recruitment for Therapeutic Recreation," *Therapeutic Recreation Journal,* vol. 2 (fourth quarter, 1968), pp. 4–8.

"Jobs for this Year's College Grads," *Changing Times,* vol. 26 (June 1972), p. 9.

RATHFELDER, R. R. "Industry Looks at Motivation," *Therapeutic Recreation Journal,* vol. 2 (fourth quarter, 1968), pp. 3–4.

TIMMONS, LOIS. "There Isn't Any Wine!," *Therapeutic Recreation Journal,* vol. 2 (fourth quarter, 1968), pp. 8–12.

Case No. 9: Volunteers in trouble*

The West Greenville Y.W.C.A. conducted an after-school sports and physical fitness program in the gymnasium of the Crawford Elementary School located in a nearby community. It was held once a week at the school, on Wednesday afternoons from 3 o'clock to 5 o'clock, and involved approximately 80 fifth- and sixth-grade girls. The program was free, since the Y.W.C.A. relied for leadership on three recreation majors from nearby Edgemont College who participated in the program as part of a required field work assignment. These three young women were assigned by the Y's program director, Alice P., to the Crawford School, to organize an intramural sports program.

The program was held for the first time on February 3. Girls were organized into groups according to age, and they took part in volleyball, badminton, gymnastics, and group games. A mother, who represented the Crawford Parent-Teachers Association, helped in the organization. Things seemed to

*Richard G. Kraus and Barbara J. Bates, *Recreation Leadership and Supervision: Guidelines for Professional Development* (Philadelphia: W. B. Saunders, 1975), pp. 70–72. Reprinted by permission.

be going fairly well that afternoon when Alice P. dropped by to see how the program was faring.

Two weeks later, however, a complaint report was submitted by the building custodian to the school principal. Entitled *Report of After-School Program*, and dated February 18, the complaint stated:

> On February 17, the Y.W.C.A. was in our building. When they left the gym was in a mess. These people leave the gym in a mess every time they are here. The girls are always running in the hallways. They spit water at each other in the halls. They also leave the gym mats thrown about. Mr. La Vena (physical education teacher) reported that two mats were ripped. On the same day, someone opened the gate that is across the hallway, left through the side door, and kicked a barrel of trash down the stairs into the basement. There is very poor supervision at this activity. The three people in charge cannot control the activity.

Immediately, Alice drove to the school and met with the principal and custodian to discuss the matter. She later met with the three volunteer leaders and the mother who assisted them. She concluded on the basis of these talks that the young women involved had never had experience with large groups of children before and lacked the ability to carry on the program in an orderly manner. They did not exercise disciplinary control successfully and spent a good deal of time chasing the less cooperative children through the hallways. When they did this, the sports activities began to fall apart, and all the children started to act up. The mother had been helpful in keeping the girls in line during the first two sessions. However, she had been late in arriving on February 17, and by the time she did arrive, things were well out of hand.

When Alice reviewed the situation with the Executive Director of the Y.W.C.A., the major causes of the problem appeared to be the following: first, there had been inadequate training or screening of the three field work students from Edgemont College. It had been assumed that, because they were recreation majors, they would be able to handle the situation. The students had received only a brief orientation session before beginning the Wednesday program, and the mother had no preparation or training at all. Finally, the children had been recruited in a completely haphazard fashion, and no attempt had been made to determine their previously learned skills or interests. When they saw how informal and permissive the sports program was — compared with their carefully structured and supervised daytime physical education program — they began to challenge the leaders and misbehave whenever possible.

Because of the damage that had been done and a lack of confidence in the ability of the three field-work students to carry on the program successfully, the program was terminated without meeting again.

Alice developed the following set of recommendations following this experience:

1. All volunteers for such programs should be carefully screened. Care should be taken to select individuals who have had experience in the appropriate activities, and in working with children.

2. Volunteers should be given a detailed orientation before beginning the activity. They should be given a written job description and a list of objectives to be accomplished. They should be informed that this is an important job, and that tardiness or absenteeism is not acceptable.

3. Appropriate disciplinary measures must be taken against those hindering the operation of the program or seeking to destroy school property.

QUESTIONS FOR DISCUSSION

Do you feel that blame for this unsuccessful program should be assigned primarily to the volunteer field-work students from Edgemont College, or should it rest primarily with the Y.W.C.A.?

How adequate were the recommendations developed by Alice P. to improve the use of volunteers in future programs?

Could you suggest other procedures that would assist volunteer programs of this type, which are situated in decentralized operations that are not in the Y.W.C.A. building itself, and that therefore are not easy to supervise regularly?

Index